I0151679

EVERYTHING MAKES PERFECT SENSE

A MEMOIR

A Young Woman's Journey
to Healing and Forgiveness

BRINN LANGDALE, LMFT

Trigger Warning: *While this book covers a variety of topics that could be triggering to many people, please note the chapter, My First Memories, describes sexual abuse that took place over twelve years. If it feels appropriate to skip this chapter, please do, and know that the integrity of the story will not be lost.*

Copyright © 2025 by Brinn Langdale

All rights reserved. This book may not be reproduced or stored in whole or in part by any means without the written permission of the author except for brief quotations for the purpose of review.

Some names, locations, and other identifying details have been changed, and certain events may be compressed, consolidated, or reordered.

ISBN: 978-1-966343-68-4 (hard cover)
      978-1-966343-69-1 (soft cover)

Langdale. Brinn
Edited by: Amy Klein

Warren publishing

Warren Publishing
Charlotte, NC
www.warrenpublishing.net
Printed in the United States

For Scout.
We did it.

PRAISE FOR *EVERYTHING MAKES PERFECT SENSE*

"I have to say I couldn't put this book down. ... I found [Brinn's] story of abuse, awareness, and healing to be remarkably honest and truly generous. The way she grapples with the complex issues ... that arise with abuse truly shows us a path forward as we work to confront this painful reality."

– JIM KEDDY, EXECUTIVE DIRECTOR, YOUTH FORWARD

"... a brave and beautiful story of post-traumatic growth and recovery. Brinn gives us hope that the wounds of childhood can be met with resilience, insight, and profound self-discovery. ... I will be sharing this book with clients who are seeking their own unique paths towards healing."

– VICTORIA HOLLIS, LCSW, EMDR CERTIFIED & IFSI LEVEL 1

"... Brinn's empowering account ... provides valuable strategies to help anyone going through challenging life circumstances, especially survivors of intrafamily abuse. The courage she has to ... forgive her abuser is an inspiration. It gives us all hope that we, too, can use our voices to find true healing and the freedom that comes with forgiveness."

– LOGAN KINGSTON, LCSW, MS ED. PSYCHOTHERAPIST I AUTHOR

"... an honest and spiritually reflective memoir of recovery from sibling sexual trauma. This memoir will resonate with survivors, therapists, and families who seek to understand and support the healing journey following trauma. ... As a survivor myself, I see how Brinn beautifully weaves together memories and adult insights as she navigates a difficult yet achievable path toward recovery."

–JANE EPSTEIN, ADVOCATE I AUTHOR I SPEAKER I COFOUNDER OF 5WAVES.ORG

"Brinn ... highlights the tools and methods she has employed to transcend the harm she experienced and transform the shattered parts of herself into a whole, loving, and integrated individual. A must-read for anyone dealing with a traumatic background."

— CHRISTOPHER L. MATHE, PHD/ OWNER AND
CLINICAL DIRECTOR/ AUTHENTIC COUNSELING ASSOCIATES

"... This book is not only for those who have experienced chronic abuse. It is for all of us. It's a reminder that no matter the wounds we carry, we can rise, reclaim our lives, and move forward with strength and grace."

— WHITNEY NATIELLO, LICENSED ACUPUNCTURIST, CREATOR OF B.R.A.I.N.S. TECHNIQUE™

"... I applaud Ms. Langdale for her strength and vulnerability in sharing this story of navigating childhood sexual abuse, substance use, and mental health challenges as an adolescent and young adult. This book will provide much needed insight, psychoeducation, and hope to all those who ask themselves if there is a way out of trauma."

— ELIZABETH NGUYEN, MD, CHILD, ADOLESCENT, AND ADULT PSYCHIATRIST

"I was completely riveted by this courageous memoir ... It not only was raw and honest, but also deeply healing. ... While the subject matter could seem heavy, the book is anything but. Brinn weaves in moments of humor, tenderness, and emotional insight that make it impossible to put down. ... This book is a gift—and without a doubt, it will become an important memoir for the sibling sexual abuse community and beyond."

— ELIZABETH BARBOUR, INTUITIVE LIFE & BUSINESS COACH,
SPEAKER, AND AUTHOR OF *SACRED CELEBRATIONS:
DESIGNING RITUALS TO NAVIGATE LIFE'S MILESTONE TRANSITIONS*

TABLE OF CONTENTS

PROLOGUE

I was seven when I first stepped onto a stage in front of thousands of people. I squinted, trying not to pull away from the hot lights assaulting my senses. Even though I could only see a few faces of the fancy-looking businessmen and -women in the front row below me, I felt the entire arena watching.

Dressed in a frilly black-and-white dress with a maroon satin sash around my waist, patent leather shoes, and white socks with ruffles along the top, I felt as though I were suffocating. The bow that my mother had crafted out of matching ribbon and hot glue held half of my thick brown hair up, while the other half lay along my shoulders. My older sister, Charlotte, had made an attempt with a curling iron and hairspray, but my hair had already fallen limp. My hair wouldn't boast natural ringlets on its own until a hormone shift at sixteen.

Hidden under my dress were cutoff jean shorts and two Band-Aids covering a scrape on my knee from climbing the tree at the schoolyard next to our house. The dress had been a battleground, the shorts a negotiation strategy. After thirty minutes of yelling and tears, my mother accepted the shorts and I agreed to tolerate the dress.

I stood next to my brother Jake. Two and a half years older than I, he wore a well-fitting black suit and a red fleur-de-lis tie. His wide grin made his blue eyes look as if they were hardly open. He probably imagined everyone was there just to watch him perform. At ten years old, he'd already occupied center stage for four years as the only boy in his dance company. I'd spent many long weekends watching him at dance competitions, where he won trophy after trophy and showed them off to all the girls. His arrogance would only increase with age.

Next to Jake stood Caleb. His round baby face, crew cut blond hair, and braces accentuated his innocence. At twelve, he was more shy and quiet than the rest of us, but if he was nervous, he didn't show it. We were standing in the middle of the arena where his favorite basketball team played, so the line between excitement and anxiety must have been blurred for him.

My sister, home from college, towered over us all. A fully grown adult reaching nearly six feet in her black stiletto heels, she embodied the self-assured presence of a supermodel ready for the runway. Her hair, makeup, and dark-green, crushed-velvet evening gown looked flawless. My mother, beside her, looked similar, although twenty years older. People often mistook them for sisters, with their matching green eyes, height, and blonde hair. Their differences, though, were stark. My sister, thirteen years older than me, had always been a source of comfort and nurturing, and while my mom had those qualities too, it was usually her direct, forceful nature I experienced.

In contrast to my sister's naturally thin figure, my mom had a curvy, athletic build. Makeup and dresses were not her usual style. Typically, I'd find her in a comfy pair of jeans and a professional top, but she knew how to make an impression when she needed to—when she was meeting with clients or attending one of my dad's business events. With her sequined gown, high heels, and hair freshly colored, she was picturesquely beautiful.

My father stood at the end of our line. He was slender with short black hair, thin lips, and a charismatic smile. His polished dress shoes concealed evidence of a life once lived: a few permanently damaged toenails, stepped on by the cows he'd milked at a dairy farm while putting himself through college.

When I was born, he became involved with multilevel marketing to support his growing family, weaving this new networking career into the fabric of my childhood. For nearly ten years before then, he'd partnered with my mom, and together they'd built a successful photography business. They'd met in college through mutual friends at a church gathering. She, already married with a newborn—my sister—was attracted to his independent and free-spirited energy. He was attracted to her big heart, intelligence, and creativity. They bonded over laughter and their shared values of spirituality and family.

Throughout my childhood, Dad traveled constantly, "building the business," which led Mom to single-handedly raise us kids, all while navigating sales calls, portrait sessions, and editing deadlines of her own.

But I always wanted my dad around. Watching from my bedroom window at night, I'd sit on my bed, my knees pulled up to my chest, willing his car to pull into the driveway. Bad things happened when he left.

For reinforcement, my mom hired international au pairs who received room and board in exchange for taking care of us.

"Brinn is crying again! I don't know what to do!" they'd tell my mom desperately in thick accents. French. Brazilian. Polish.

"Brinn Emily Langdale!" Mom would yell as she charged down the hall toward my room at the back of the house. Hiding under my bed, I tried to melt into the floor.

By the time I was a preteen, we had gone through eighteen au pairs; only one of them stayed for the full year. Family legend said I was the "spoiled brat" who ran them off. "Brat" was what they all called me when I had meltdowns. I'd melt down when I was tired, when Mom or Dad left, when I was angry, and when I was sad. I'd throw big fitful emotional explosions of yelling, screaming, and crying. But I didn't want to be a spoiled brat. I didn't know how to communicate or regulate the intense feelings I was experiencing. My dad was usually the one who could calm me down, but he often wasn't home, leaving me with annoyed brothers and a mother who had no tolerance for my outbursts.

After being paraded across stage, our family exited stage left. The temperature drastically dropped as I left the stage lights, but my face still radiated heat. As I followed Jake, he reached his hand behind his back to help me walk down the stairs. Finally returning to solid ground, my eyes adjusted to the dim lights of the backstage area.

We had completed what felt to me like my dad's proudest moment to date: He'd reached the Emerald Level, having hit a new threshold in earnings. I understood that our walking across the stage honored the accomplishments, and sacrifices, he'd made over the last seven years. Seeing us was meant to inspire those in the audience, giving them hope that they too might someday be able to reach such milestones.

As the four of us followed our parents like ducklings, my dad ushered us to meet a stout balding man wearing a three-piece suit. This must be one of my dad's uplines, I thought. Jake leaned over and whispered, "That guy has his own plane that he parks at his house."

"Whoa," I responded in amazement.

"Rich, I'd love to introduce you to my family," Dad said, lifting his chest slightly.

One by one, we parroted, "Nice to meet you, Mr. Lamas," stretching out our hands and looking him in the eye, just as we had practiced with our parents at home. Manners had always been a foundational skill in our family. We even practiced how to answer the phone and take handwritten messages.

"My, my, my, James, what polite children you have." Mr. Lamas leaned back and placed his hands on his belly, reminding me of Santa Claus.

"Thank you, Rich! We sure are proud of them. Please, send my love to Mindy and the kids," my dad said, beaming as he whisked us away, as if not wanting to take up too much of Mr. Lamas's precious time.

I walked away, relieved, knowing us kids had done our job perfectly. Nothing to see here.

CHILDHOOD

WHAT'S WRONG WITH ME?

My vision blurred as tears filled my swim goggles. The black guiding line at the bottom of the pool seemed to disappear. I felt sick. The type of sick that starts in your head, moves down to your heart, and finally reaches your stomach. The thoughts were inescapable.

I should stay under water until I stop breathing. I want to be forgotten, never to resurface. I just want to die. I just want to die!

Another thought bubbled up inside my head.

Why am I like this? What's wrong with me?

There were never answers to those thoughts. I didn't know where they came from, but they had been happening all summer.

At the end of my lap, I dragged my fourteen-year-old body out of the pool and collapsed on the closest bench. I was shaking. My brother Caleb, who'd been standing on the pool deck as one of my coaches, wandered over and sat down beside me.

"How you doing, little homie?" he asked, giving me a pat on the back.

My body shook as I tried to hold back tears.

"I'm … fine," I said between breaths, trying to calm myself.

Not noticing my distress, he said, "Nice work out there. Keep it up," and stood up to talk to the other swimmers. I felt my body deflate as he walked away.

After practice, Caleb still had to coach the other age groups, so I got a ride home from a teammate's mom.

"Thank you for the ride," I said, repeating the line my mother had drilled into our heads since we were young. I walked up the cement pathway to the front door, passing my mother's brightly colored flower garden and manicured front lawn along the way. I stepped into the house. "Hello," I yelled out of habit, but only silence returned my call.

I dumped my swim bag at the edge of the hallway, figuring I'd pick it up on my way back to my room. My stomach growled. It had been four hours and forty-five minutes since I'd eaten that banana before practice, but who was counting?

Opening the pantry door, I scanned the shelves. Aluminum cans of expired peaches, beans, and tuna stared back at me. Boxed cereal sporting slogans like "lower your cholesterol" and "sugar-free" filled the top shelves. Bending down, I reached for my favorite item, a SlimFast can. I popped the top, and I drank urgently. The chalky chocolate liquid settled my stomach and my mind. At just 180 calories per can, it wouldn't affect my weight.

I stood up, feeling dizzy and lightheaded. *Oh no, was I getting another migraine?* A common question since they'd started plaguing me years before. As I waited for my heart rate to slow down, I assessed myself for the usual signs. Are my hands tingling? Is my eyesight blurring? I continued to wait, fearful. *I'd better drink some water just in case,* I thought. Water's good for weight loss, anyway.

After showering, and concluding that I wasn't getting a migraine, I stood in front of the full-length mirror in my room, my long wet brown hair twisted up in a blue towel on my head. Examining the one hundred and twelve pounds of flesh on my five-foot-six-inch frame, I turned from side to side, pinching the skin around my stomach. *Gross.*

I pulled on my favorite pair of gray sweatpants and a black oversized sweatshirt Jake had given me. A large skull with fiery eyes decorated the front. I had cut holes near the wrists so my thumbs could poke through. Grabbing my watch out of my swim bag, I secured the clasp on my right wrist. Then I took my thick cheetah-print slap bracelet and placed that next to the watch. These were more than fashion statements; over the last few months, they had become a necessity to cover up evidence of my pain.

Throwing myself onto my bed, I stared at the ceiling. My glow-in-the-dark plastic stars stared back at me. I didn't have as many as Jake did on his walls. He'd acquired an entire universe up there, and he gave me the leftovers. Just enough to create my favorite Zodiac constellations: Scorpio for me and Leo for my best friend, Grace.

I surveyed my room. On the wall, a framed poster of *The Phantom of the Opera* hung next to a collage of Polaroid pictures: memories from the last day of school, my friends' birthday parties, and summer camp. The windowsill that ran along the length of the room displayed a scene that appeared straight out of a teen pop culture magazine. There were sparkly purple candles that said "Princess" and three variations of cotton candy–scented room sprays. There was a gel-filled Magic 8 Ball alongside binder paper drawings of hearts, stars, and B + G = BFF. While I never would have picked these items out myself, I loved what they represented. These were gifts, reminders that people cared about me.

Maybe I should write, I thought. *Naw, too much effort.*

A few years earlier, my mom had suggested turning my closet into a writing nook. We took out all my clothes, placing them in my dresser drawers, and filled the space with a plain white desk with wooden legs that fit perfectly inside. On the desk, I stacked notebooks, drawing paper, and magazines. Here, I'd sit for hours, writing poetry and short stories and venting in my journal about boys, friends, and the endless quest to understand why I was such a terrible person. In intense moments when my hands couldn't keep up with my thoughts, I'd scribble nonsensical gibberish scrawls as feelings flowed out of me and onto paper.

In the center of my desk stood a trophy from the summer when I was ten, when I had won the High Point award in my age group. Dozens of colorful ribbons hung from the trophy. Blue ribbons indicated first place, while red, gold, and white signified lower positions. There were also medals for placing well at championships.

Starting at four years old, I had spent every summer swimming for our local team. Even though all four of us kids had learned to swim at young ages, Caleb and I were the two who stuck with it. I watched from the outside as he so naturally got along with everyone on the team, including the parents. He seemed to create his own family from the swimming community. It was obvious to me that it was where he belonged.

I too had a few friends on the team that I'd hang out with outside of practice, but never outside of the summer season. We'd watch movies together, maybe bounce on the trampoline, and mostly just talked about boys. But they didn't know the real me. All the other swim kids seemed to come from *normal* families whose parents were still together and who actually showed up for swim meets and practices.

During swim meets, I'd often stand outside the club's front office holding the phone receiver, its white wire snaking through the open window into my hand.

"Mom, I just beat my personal record!" I told her as I bounced up and down, wet drops from my ponytail collecting on the concrete.

"That's wonderful, honey!" she said. "I'm just running some errands, and I'll be there for your next race!"

I couldn't help but notice that she always seemed to arrive at the swim club mere seconds after my race had ended. And no matter how many times I told her what time practice was over, I'd find myself sitting on the curb outside the club in my wet Speedo, my towel wrapped around me, long after my teammates' parents had picked them up. Countless times, I'd call her either from school or practice only to hear, "Is it time to pick you up already?"

Since my parents had begun the long and messy process of separation and divorce in 1997, when I was ten, my mom spent a lot of her free time processing her grief through activities like kayaking, biking, and Match. com. At that point, my sister was twenty-three, married, and with a baby on the way. Caleb involved himself with sports and friends, which left Jake in charge at home—until last year.

At six years old, Jake had declared that he wanted to be a dancer, and my parents enrolled him in dance classes. Within a few years, he was not only dancing six times a week and competing in local competitions but also teaching himself how to play the guitar, drums, and any other instrument he liked. Now his goal was to be a famous musician.

Last year, he'd left home for a performing arts boarding school in Southern California. It was either that or risk being kicked out of high school for ditching too many classes. Caleb had also left for college in the Midwest, which meant I was alone with Mom. Both brothers were home for the summer, but Jake was always off somewhere—probably getting high with who knows who—and Caleb, holding down two jobs, was hardly ever home.

I jolted, startled by the back door opening at the other end of the house. The familiar sound of keys dropping on the Formica kitchen table signaled that my mom had come home.

"Anybody home?" she asked, directing her voice down the hall.

"Hey, Mom," I yelled back.

Footsteps approached and my door opened.

Smiling enthusiastically, she asked, "How was practice?"

"It was fine."

"Anything else besides fine?" Along with her question came that look in her eye.

She always wanted more out of me—to know the latest happenings between my friends or if any new boys had caught my attention. She had always been interested in my social life, especially if it had to do with boys. She'd had her fair share of relationships before my dad and knew the power of heartbreak, so she was empathetic and could comfort me when I needed it. But there was a lot about my world I kept secret. So much she'd never understand.

"No, just fine," I responded, knowing I couldn't tell her what had actually happened at practice. Most of the time, my mom was annoyingly cheerful, and she never liked it when I was sad or depressed. She thought reminding me of how great of a life I had was the cure to all of my struggles. So I kept my mouth shut.

"Are you hungry? Have you eaten?"

"I had a SlimFast," I said, trailing off.

"Sweetheart, you cannot survive on those. How about I make you a PB&J?"

"Okay," I mumbled.

"Okay?" she asked, raising her eyebrow.

"I mean, yes, please. Thank you," I said dryly.

Our eyes met as I smirked, and she laughed.

"All right, come out and talk to me while I make it." She patted my legs and led the way to the kitchen.

I swung my legs off the bed, followed her down the hall, and sank into a stool on the far side of the kitchen table, facing her as she got the bread down from the top of the refrigerator.

"I can't believe my baby girl starts high school next week," she said with a twinge of nostalgia in her voice.

"Yeah, I know," I said with a slight smile. Part of me was excited. It meant I was growing up and moving forward. But I still dreaded the idea of going. "I'll get to see Grace every day, so that's good."

Grace had been my best friend since we were in the same first-grade class. After that, I repeated first grade as Grace went on to second grade. Because of my November birthday, I'd entered kindergarten at four years old, but at five, I suddenly began sucking my thumb and walking around with my blankie over my head. My mom didn't think I was ready for second grade and held me back a year, enrolling me in a homeschool program—the first of many places that weren't a good fit. My mom attempted to find a place for me in homeschool, public school, private school, and different schools in between, but the result was almost always the same.

"Nobody likes me!" I'd tell my mom. "Everybody hates me."

"Nobody likes me, everybody hates me, I'm gonna go eat worms," she sang. "Big ones, fat ones, ones as big as your head," she continued, poking at my sides, trying to make me laugh.

"Stoooooop it," I whined, crossing my arms and furrowing my brow. "You're not funny," I said as I tried hard to hold back a smile.

One morning in third grade, I refused to get out of bed. My mom kept coming into my room, counting down to takeoff.

"You have fifteen minutes until we leave for school," she warned.

"Mommmmm," I said. "I don't want to go! Nobody likes me. I have no friends!"

"Honey, I don't know what you're talking about," she reasoned. "You were just with Grace this weekend, and you're going home with Amber after school this week. You have friends! Now get up. We have ten minutes before we leave."

Five minutes later, I heard her yell down the hall, "You have five minutes, and you are getting in the car whether you are ready or not!" This time, she was obviously angry.

Defiantly, I lay in bed, staring at the white ceiling dotted with yellow glow-in-the-dark stars.

Bursting into my room, she flung back the covers, exposing my little naked body. Wrestling me into my blue terry cloth robe, she practically dragged me to the car.

Anger fueled my mother as she sped through the neighborhood. I sobbed in the back seat as my brothers attempted to coax me into getting dressed, but I refused.

Too distracted to lead us through our typical morning prayer, Mom pulled up to the school and parked the car. I was confused. She usually filed behind the rest of the cars in the drop-off lane.

As soon as the engine cut, she pulled open the back door and yanked me out of my seat. Stuffing my uniform under her arm, she pulled me across the parking lot. Still dressed only in my terry cloth robe, I struggled against her grip as she hauled me up the steps, through the front door,

WHAT'S WRONG WITH ME?

and straight down the hallway to the vice principal's office, where she threw me inside.

"There! You deal with her!" she declared and stormed out.

The room filled with silence. The vice principal sat in her chair and looked at me calmly. I was slumped on the carpeted floor in my robe, my uniform crumpled up next to me. My face felt puffy and red. I was humiliated.

"I'll leave you to get dressed. Then it's time to go to class," the vice principal said gently but firmly.

My problem with school wasn't just that I didn't want to go. I also had strange stomach issues my doctor couldn't explain, daily headaches, frequent sore throats, exhaustion, and since fifth grade, those terrifying migraines. I'd sit in class, my head resting on my desk, staring at the door, completely unaware of what my teacher was saying. I was waiting, waiting for the principal to walk in to inform me that my parents had died in a tragic accident of some kind. Frozen in place, I'd visualize the principal delivering the news over and over again, leaving me numb with dread.

As I feared everyone I loved would leave me, my perception that nobody liked me extended beyond my friends. Boyfriends, teachers, athletic coaches, teammates—I was convinced they all hated me, or were just pretending to like me. In junior high, I had friends, we threw parties, and there was always someone new to fool around with. But between feeling isolated after summer camp and knowing most of my friends weren't going to my high school, I was worried about being all alone in my new school. Except for Grace.

"Speaking of Grace," I said as my mom made my sandwich, "can I spend the night there tonight? I haven't seen her much since I got back from camp."

"I know, you've been in your postcamp depression; your sister was the same way. It's like you wait all year to go to Colorado just to come back all depressed because you miss your friends. I didn't spend all this money for you just to go get depressed," she joked.

I was sad about leaving camp because it was the most amazing place on Earth. It was the only place where I felt like I belonged. My mom had been a camper there too when she was young, along with my sister and Caleb. It was in my blood.

At camp, we all shared a common background: All of us were raised in a small religious group known as Christian Science. Christian Science is a unique religion founded by Mary Baker Eddy during the 1800s in Boston, Massachusetts. She was a radical woman who, after suffering a spinal injury, healed herself through prayer. She went on to write dozens of books and start both a publishing company and a world-renowned newspaper.

Eddy's metaphysical texts teach that spiritual understanding and prayer can bring about healing and well-being. Christian Scientists rely on prayer rather than conventional medicine, meaning most don't go to doctors. My family did go when we needed to and was fully vaccinated. But we also took herbal supplements at the first sign of feeling sick and gargled with warm salt water for our sore throats. We didn't have a history of health issues in our family, and all my grandparents remained out of doctors' care for most of their long, healthy lives. It felt confusing to be a Christian Scientist who also went to doctors. While I loved camp, when it came to being a part of the religion, it was, in a way, just another community that I didn't fully fit into.

When my brothers and I were growing up, my mom would read us angel stories before bed. These were books where miraculous events occurred without tangible explanations, books where people were rescued in highly unlikely situations or made the last-minute choice to not go on a trip, only to find out that they'd avoided a terrible disaster.

We also experienced mysterious events in our family. One day, my mom, Caleb, and I were heading to Southern California for an event when we arrived at the airport and couldn't find our printed plane tickets. We looked everywhere, searched the car and all of our bags, but they didn't turn up. Finally, after missing the flight, we decided to drive down to Southern California instead. At a gas station, we got out of the car to buy some snacks, and when we came back, the tickets were sitting right on top of the driver's seat.

Around this same time, my mom saw unexplained yellow shapes appear in her photographs. She had items go missing, then found them moments later, inexplicably in another room. When I was growing up, I heard flower vases explode from the other room without anyone else around and saw every single cupboard open in the kitchen when nobody else was home.

These unexplained events further emphasized the teaching in our household that we were all spiritual beings living out a human experience. We were all souls who would go on living after this life, and we'd had many lives before this one. We believed that God and the angels were always around us, supporting us, helping us, and wanting good things for us—all we had to do was ask.

Furthermore, each summer at camp, I heard and saw incredible testimonies of faith. I witnessed prayer and love dissolve fear, disagreements, and frustration, and prayer was the only way the camp directors took care of illness and injuries. And surprisingly, for a fully functioning camp of a thousand kids each summer, there were hardly ever major physical problems to deal with.

Camp was magical, a special place nestled at the base of 14,000-foot mountains in an alpine forest, overlooking a high desert valley. There, I felt fulfilled and at ease, surrounded by people who understood the strange philosophies by which I was raised. I wanted to spend my whole life safely enclosed in this positive, spiritual bubble. But that bubble made coming back home lonely, as I felt even more disconnected from my friends at school and on my swim team.

This gnawing feeling inside me, however, had been there longer than just the past two summers when I'd been going to camp. I knew coming home wasn't the only thing bothering me. I just didn't know what the other thing was.

"I'm going to go run some errands pretty soon, so I can drop you at Grace's in a little bit," my mom said, handing me my sandwich and a glass of nonfat milk.

"Thank you."

Knowing I was going to Grace's brought relief. Even though it was hard to relate to my other friends after returning from camp, I never had that problem with Grace. Although I didn't tell her everything I was feeling, just being around her made me feel better.

MY SECOND HOME

waved goodbye to my mom as I walked up the steps to Grace's house. Knocking on the wooden door, I could hear her dad yelling from inside, "Someone's at the door! Who's going to get it—oh never mind, I'll get it!"

Her dad's large gruff manner always scared me, but after knowing him for ten years, I was used to it.

"Oh! Brinner! It's you!" He opened the door wider and said affectionately, "Come in, she's upstairs."

"Thank you," I squeaked out as I rushed past him, kicking off my shoes and taking the carpeted stairs two at a time.

I opened the door of Grace's room to find her sitting on the floor with scraps of fabric and clothes all around her. The familiar sound of the Dave Matthews Band floated in the background.

"Hey! Whatcha doing?" I asked as I threw my backpack in the corner.

"Well, I have this bag of old clothes, so I thought I'd take some of the material and make them into patches for my jacket." She held up her latest find.

"Always a project," I said, flopping on her bed. It made me a little jealous thinking about all the ways she kept herself busy with hobbies she enjoyed. I wasn't sure I could list much that I enjoyed these days, and she always had plenty.

Grace's room was so familiar to me, it was as if it were my own. Despite being in different grades and having only attended the same school for one year, we still spent most of our free time together. When we were younger, we'd tell people we were twins. We were the same height and roughly the same build, although Grace had blonde hair and deep-brown eyes in contrast to my dark hair and hazel eyes. When I was growing up, my dad said the song "Brown Eyed Girl" by Van Morrison was my song, but she'd always point out that my eyes were more green, and she was the one with true brown eyes. I hated that she was right, but that didn't stop me from arguing my claim.

"It smells good downstairs. What's for dinner?" I asked.

The contrast between our two homes was stark, although it hadn't always been that way. Before my parents divorced, we too had sat down around the dining room table every night. But since the divorce, our dinners had ranged from informal to "fend for yourself," depending on the day. Grace's family, on the other hand, felt consistent.

"Girls! Dinner's ready!" We heard the call from downstairs and hopped up. Grace's brother, Josh, was already at the table. We filled up our water glasses and sat down with him.

With her mom positioned at one end, her dad at the other, and us kids in the middle, hot dishes traveled in a circular direction. I served myself mashed potatoes with gravy, along with a piece of chicken and a small helping of salad. The expected questions about everyone's day began.

Under the table, my knee bounced up and down rapidly. The food tasted good, but my stomach had formed a knot. Then the attention shifted to me.

"So, Brinn, how are your parents doing?" Grace's mom asked in a sweet voice.

"They're doing fine," I responded, hoping no more questions would come my way.

"That's good. And how are your brothers? Is Jake going back to that school?"

"Yeah, he's going back for his senior year. I think he's looking into schools like Juilliard or something for college."

I was proud of Jake. Across from me, I watched Josh piling food into his mouth. A pang of sadness flowed through me as I thought about Jake leaving again in a few weeks. Life at the house before my brothers moved out was never dull. Hip hop, R&B, Phish, and Dave Matthew's Band blared from their rooms at all hours. The phone rang constantly, usually some girl asking for Jake. Then, there was the consistent stream of friends coming and going. Plus, they partied a lot and sometimes would even include me. The energy, while chaotic at times, was fun. This past year had been lonely with Caleb across the country and Jake eight hours away.

"Well, good for him." Grace's mom smiled, satisfied with my answers.

"Brinner! You've hardly touched your plate!" Grace's dad boomed. "You're going to waste away into the wind at this rate." He passed me dishes of food I hadn't asked for.

After dinner, Grace and I ran upstairs.

"So we still have some … you know … right?" I asked as soon as the door had closed behind me.

"Yes! We'll need to buy some more soon, but I think we have enough for tonight."

Grace reached up into her closet, behind some boxes, and she pulled out a colorful makeup container. She pried open the lid, and a familiar, pungent smell wafted into the room.

"Flip the switch on the wall to turn on the fan," she instructed as she lit some incense.

Her parents were a lot more oblivious than mine, but we didn't want to be too obvious. My heart beat faster. I'd been waiting for this moment all day, all week, in fact.

Inside the makeup case was a plastic ziplock bag, and inside the bag was a fresh green bud of weed. It was about one gram, enough for the two of us that evening. But she was right, we'd need to buy some from Josh, or my brothers, to re-up soon.

We loaded everything we needed up into her purse and headed out into the hallway.

"We're going for a walk around the block," Grace told her parents, who were watching TV in the living room.

"Okay, be safe," her mom said.

Once we'd put on our shoes and walked out the door, I finally felt free. The hot summer air still lingered, but the nightly breeze coming off the American River just down the street felt like relief on my skin. I was wearing a tank top with jeans while Grace wore shorts and a T-shirt.

"I don't understand how you can wear pants in this heat."

"It's not that bad," I lied. It was torture. But it felt better than exposing my disgusting legs to the world.

We headed to the park and made our way to our favorite spot in the back, a small shaded area with lots of trees and bushes. Almost nobody ever went back there. As we walked together, I saw a couple of young kids riding their bikes. A memory flashed into my mind. "Remember the first time we smoked? With Jake?"

"Yeah, what were we, like, nine or ten?" She giggled.

"I can't believe we were so young! That's probably how old those kids are," I said, motioning to the kids on the bikes.

"We're just two rebels without a cause," she said absentmindedly.

My mind returned to those early days, back when it was rare for me to smoke. Back when I never knew when I would get it again and when getting high felt like such a big deal. Back when Jake would praise me for my big bong rips and call me Little Soldier when I started coughing after a big hit. It was always so much fun when we did that together. Everything was hilarious, and I didn't seem to have any worries in life.

That night, getting high made me feel normal. I could finally fully disconnect from the lingering thoughts that had haunted me earlier at swim practice. My head felt like a safe place to be again. After circling the block a few times, we wandered back to Grace's house, changed into our pajamas, and settled in on the couch to watch TV. Her parents had gone to bed early, so we had the whole downstairs to ourselves.

Aware that I was wearing a pair of plaid boxer shorts, I tucked my legs up underneath me. It grew late as we watched *Friends* reruns. Then, without thinking, I adjusted my legs, stretching them out across the couch until they almost touched Grace.

She looked down. "What are those marks?" she asked, sounding concerned.

Instinctively, I pulled my legs back underneath me as quickly as I could.

"They're nothing," I said as calmly as possible. "They're, uh, mosquito bites that I scratched so much that they bled. They're all scabbed up now."

My face burned. I knew it was turning red and blotchy, as it always did when I felt embarrassed and ashamed. I fixed my eyes on the TV, afraid to look at Grace. The marks weren't mosquito bites. They were burns from a BIC lighter. I didn't really know why I had done it. Perhaps I thought that if I felt the pain, it would take away the gnawing, empty feeling inside. It worked, but only for a moment and wasn't worth this.

She didn't know about the feelings and thoughts that had been circling inside me, so I hoped she would just drop the subject. Luckily, she stayed silent and returned her focus to the show. I fiddled nervously with the watch on my wrist and my new snap bracelet. So far, they were doing their jobs.

BE A CHILL GIRL

stared down at my lined binder paper. Every problem from the book was perfectly written, just as it was supposed to be. The paper was organized and looked correct. Except there were no answers. Instead, hand-drawn cartoon faces, 3D boxes, and polka-dot flowers covered the borders of my paper.

My fingers fiddled with the second metal ring of the open three-ring binder taking up space on my desk. Mr. Martin was droning on about exponential something or other. The familiar, tight knot in my abdomen had been sitting there ever since Mom dropped me off this morning.

I'd made it through the first month of high school and had figured out just how long it took to walk to the far bathroom and back. There were only eight minutes remaining in class. I knew my math teacher wouldn't let me go. I should have asked earlier.

My body wanted to sprint out the door and disappear through the back field. I imagined Caleb and Jake texting me, letting me know they were outside, waiting to take me far away from here. I'd run out, hop in the front seat of Caleb's big red Chevy truck, and we'd drive away with our music blasting and our joints already rolled.

The bell rang, bringing me back to reality. Mr. Martin was making his daily announcement. "Just a reminder, I am here every day before and after school if anyone has questions about what we're working on."

I rolled my eyes. I'd promised myself at the beginning of the semester that I wouldn't let myself fall behind. But I had been behind for weeks now, and there was no way I could tell him that. Even if I asked for help, I'd probably be too stupid to understand what he said anyway.

I put my backpack on and threw my new faux-leather purse with metal studs over my shoulder. I smiled to myself as I smelled the perfume inside. At the end of the summer, just before Caleb left again for college, he'd taken me to the mall.

"You're growing up now, and every woman needs a signature scent," he explained as we snaked our way through the counters at Macy's. At six foot three, with broad shoulders and bright-blond hair, he stood out in the crowd. I hurried to keep up with his long stride.

Perfume wasn't exactly my style, but I trusted that Caleb had my best interests in mind, so I did as I was told. After exploring my options, I settled on a beautiful blue teardrop bottle that came with a scented lotion. *Cool Water.* I used the bottle before school, and I kept the lotion in my new purse that Grace and I had found at a thrift store. I never knew when I would need to cover up BO or the smell of weed.

It felt gratifying to have Caleb buy me perfume and acknowledge how mature I was becoming. For so long, my brothers had seen me as their bratty younger sister, but since the divorce, Caleb had taken on a more parental role in my life. Until Caleb left home for college, he picked me up from school, made sure I ate dinner when my mom wasn't home, and constantly gave me advice. In fact, both Caleb and Jake constantly gave me advice.

"Just remember to be chill, Brinn," both of my brothers instructed. "Be like Brooke and Stacie. They know how to be chill."

The girls they'd selected as "chill girls" hung out with guys as friends, wore little makeup, and excelled at sports; these girls were not overly emotional and, most of all, did not cause drama.

But the summer before I started junior high, my mom gave me her old makeup kit, and I experimented with some eyeshadow. When I came out of the bathroom, Caleb and his friend immediately noticed the difference in my appearance.

"What are you wearing? Is that makeup?" Caleb barked.

"Yeah, I just put on some eyeshadow. It's not that big of a deal." I shrugged.

"Like hell it's not! You're not allowed to wear makeup! We're going to rinse it off your face right now!" He rushed at me, threw me over his shoulder, and marched outside.

I squirmed, struggling to get away, but he held me tight. Once outside, he and his friend turned on the garden hose, held me down on the deck, and blasted my face with cold water as they laughed.

"How many times do I have to tell you? You don't need makeup! You're naturally pretty!" Caleb yelled.

Sputtering to catch my breath, I broke away. I was drenched and furious, but there was nothing I could do. I ran back to the house and yelled, "Jerks!" while I slammed the door.

From an outsider's perspective, this aggression might have looked like cruel and unusual punishment, but to me, this was love. Even during the quiet moments, I knew my brothers cared about me. Caleb slept on my floor when I didn't want to be alone in my room. Jake asked me to go skating with him. Their attention, even if excessive sometimes, meant they loved me.

Whether I was walking into my room to see all my stuffed animals strung up by their necks or watching them playing tennis with my Beanie Babies out the open window, part of me liked the attention. Besides the time Jake pinned me down and dripped spit all over my face while I screamed, I usually found my brothers' annoying antics fun. Anything that involved my brothers, I wanted to be a part of.

Growing up, the only TV shows my parents allowed came through the five local channels we received from our tinfoil-wrapped TV antennas—which meant that we were raised watching Disney movies and classic musicals on VHS. The four of us knew the soundtracks to *My Fair Lady*, *The Phantom of the Opera*, and *An American in Paris* entirely by heart.

My siblings and I collaborated on choreographing dances and producing plays we wrote. On errands with our mom, we wrote fake tickets to strangers for offenses like smoking or littering. Next door to our house was an elementary school where we skated and played hockey, basketball, and baseball. We often hopped fences and shimmied up trees to sit on roofs at the school. Bruises, scrapes, and torn clothes were common for us.

As young children, Jake and I played together often, creating our own world where we made up games, different sports, and even our own coded language and nicknames for each other, like Dub-Dub and Breezy.

Jake was the wild child. There are pictures of him scaling the floor-to-ceiling bookshelf at age two. He had the most emergency room visits in our family, and after he got kicked out of preschool for biting, my parents enrolled Caleb in martial arts classes so he could defend himself against his younger brother.

Energetic and impulsive but also sweet, affectionate, and brilliant, Jake read incessantly, spoke like an adult, and was relentlessly curious. Along with his lack of impulse control, he possessed a desperate need for adrenaline and a staunch defiance of authority. If my mom told him not to do something, he was already scheming about how to make it happen.

"Jakerized" became a verb in our house. Anything broken or destroyed at the hands of Jake was referred to as "Jakerized." Though it may not have always been a conscious decision on his part, he often tinkered with the house phone, our cassette players, or any writing instrument until it broke. Once something had been Jakerized, it never returned to its original state. In time, I would learn this happened to people too.

Still, my brothers were very sweet when they realized I was turning into a young woman. For instance, when I got my first period in junior high. The three of us had spent the night at Caleb's friend's house, but that morning I was anxious to get home. My mom wasn't at our house, so I called her nervously.

"Mom, I have a problem. I started my period," I whispered uncomfortably.

"Okay, honey. Don't worry. Do you need anything?" she asked in a concerned, soothing tone.

"I don't think so. I have one of those pads they gave us at school," I said as I read the directions inside the Family Life gift bag my teacher had given me in fifth grade.

After I hung up the phone, I knew I was on my own to figure it out. Then my door opened slightly, and Jake's head appeared, followed by Caleb's head stacked on top. The looks on their faces were of concern, excitement, and fear, all wrapped up in one.

"What?" I snapped at them.

"Nothing! We just wanted to see if you were okay." They were both awkward and endearing.

"I am fine," I growled as I rolled my eyes, and they gently closed the door.

That evening, one of Caleb's best girl friends, one of his chosen "chill girls," announced she was taking me for ice cream to celebrate my becoming a woman! I truly felt like the most special little sister in the world.

In addition to raising me to be chill and strong, my brothers protected me. While they could harass me all day, they had zero tolerance for anyone else doing so. Imagine a dad sitting on the porch with a shotgun when his daughter's date arrives at the house—that was the message my brothers strived to communicate. They nearly accomplished it a few times.

One day in sixth grade, I brought home a boyfriend, Robby.

"Have you ever seen a butterfly knife before, Robby?" Jake asked as he switched the blade open and closed, a little too close to Robby's face. Suddenly, Caleb stabbed the knife into the door just to the left of Robby's eye.

That same year, I told Jake that the boys in my class were bullying me, and he instructed me to call the ringleader, Richard, and tell him to meet us at the school. When Richard arrived, Jake grabbed him, pushed him against the fence, and forced him to apologize and promise to never bother me again.

In addition to acting as my knights in shining armor, my brothers encouraged me to believe in my abilities. Jake, especially, thought I could accomplish anything I put my mind to. One weekend morning, he sat down at the piano and began playing the most beautiful music. As I walked by, I leaned on the couch to listen.

Noticing me, he scooted over on the bench. "Here, come and play," he told me.

Even though both of us had taken only a handful of piano lessons from our neighbor as kids, he was confident that if I removed my self-doubt, really let myself go, then my fingers would find the right keys and music would flow out of me. After all, that's what he did.

"Listen to this new one!" he'd often say as he sat on the overstuffed couch with his guitar on his lap, his fingers naturally playing with the strings. "Isn't it awesome?"

I couldn't distinguish the difference between it and the last melody he'd played for me.

"You know, all that stuff you listen to on the radio, none of that's good. They don't even know how to play good music anymore. But I'm going to change all that. I'm going to revolutionize mainstream music and make it good again. I know I'm ahead of my time, but they'll see … they'll see …." He returned his focus to his fingers, speeding up the tempo, breaking into a fast guitar jam.

Similarly, when he discovered rollerblades, he always wanted me to skate along with him. He would spend all day skating, performing mind-blowing tricks, jumping off roofs, while every once in a while I attempted to grind a low curb. He'd hold my hand as I jumped up onto the ledge, cheering me on the whole time.

If I fell, he'd say, "Brinn, you're so cool. None of my friends' sisters are nearly as badass as you."

CHASING STORMS

I jumped into the pool and held my breath as I sank to the bottom. Kicking my legs hard, I emerged back at the surface of the water. The bleachers above the pool were filling in with anticipatory parents. It was our first home water polo game. I looked around expectantly for my dad.

Although my mom wasn't coming, he had told me he'd be here to watch me play. I swam to the edge of the pool and put on my numbered cap, tying it tight under my chin to make sure it would stay on my head. I'd only been playing water polo for about six weeks, but Caleb had taken me to the pool over the summer and taught me the basics. He'd played throughout all four years of high school and was one of the best on his college team. My dad had also played when he was in high school, and now I was proudly continuing our family tradition as the freshman captain of the JV team.

As our team huddled up for our pregame cheer, I heard a shout: "Go, Brinner!"

Glancing up, I saw my dad grinning from the stands. He was dressed casually in jeans and a button-down shirt, unlike the usual shirt and tie that I'd grown up seeing him in. He was quickly making friends with the parents nearby and was pointing out his own child.

My chest filled with warmth, and my posture straightened as I waved. A renewed sense of determination energized me, and any nervousness I'd felt soon melted away. A buzz of excitement filled the air as I turned my attention back to my coach, who was reminding us to have fun.

Yeah, it'll be fun when we win, I thought as my heartbeat quickened.

The buzzer rang, and I sprang from the side of the pool. Years of swimming had prepared me for this moment. Reaching the ball first, I immediately passed it to my teammate, and we were off to the races, trying to get close enough to the goal to score. In the end, we won 8 to 4, and I was exhausted.

"Hey! Great job out there!" my dad said as he pulled me in for a hug. I wrapped my towel around me like a cloak and leaned into his embrace.

"Thanks! It was a lot of fun." I grinned at him.

"Well, it was fun to watch you out there. You're so fast. Obviously, it's in your genes, and I'm not talking about your blue jeans," he said, giving me a wink and a nudge.

I rolled my eyes and smiled. "Exactly. That's the only reason I'm fast."

"Come on, I'm taking you home tonight, but first: a celebratory dinner." He clapped me on the back.

At the mention of dinner, my stomach tightened. My mind scanned my day, accounting for how many calories I'd already eaten. That morning, my mom had made me two frozen waffles with peanut butter and syrup, and then I had actually eaten lunch at school.

Since starting high school, I'd made a habit of skipping lunch; this choice came with two benefits: One, I avoided the risk of gaining weight, and two, I could use my lunch money to buy weed. However, after I'd come to practice after school with a headache several times, my coach began asking if I had eaten lunch. One day, when I said no, she didn't let me practice. Now the thought of eating three full meals in a single day literally made me want to vomit.

I wasn't proud of throwing up after eating, and I didn't do it every day. It had started toward the end of the summer when one of my camp friends told me she'd done it, and she looked great with her slim athletic body and no stomach rolls.

But I knew throwing up was bad for me. It was bad for my teeth, for my body, and for my health. I hated the way I felt when my body convulsed and I gagged. But I just wanted my body to get rid of whatever was inside me! I felt horrible if I ate, and I felt horrible if I threw up, but at least one of those options helped me lose weight.

"Okay, I'll get my stuff together," I said, relieved to have a postmeal plan.

My dad and I walked into the sandwich shop down the street and stood in line, looking at the menu.

He leaned over. "This might take a while. First they need to make the bread. But before they make the bread, they have to—"

"Yes, Dad, they have to grow the wheat, and then they have to pick the wheat, then mill the wheat." He was repeating one of his long-standing jokes that he saved for every time we went out to eat.

I gave him the satisfaction of a half smile. It had been a couple weeks since I'd seen him. I missed his playful energy.

After ordering, we sat down at a small table, just big enough for the two of us. He made sure we were well equipped with plenty of napkins, water, and a chocolate chip cookie for dessert.

"So how are your classes going so far?"

"They're fine. I really like my history class." What I didn't tell him was that there was a really cute boy in my history class that I was desperate to talk to.

"History, huh? You must get that from your old man. Studying the past is the key to the present and the future." I nodded, quietly listening.

Once he'd finished his lecture, he asked, "How are things going with your mom?"

"Eh. It's the same as always. Some days we're really good, and other days, I swear she hates me."

"Come on, she doesn't hate you. She never has and she never will. She's just ... passionate sometimes. I know I've talked to you about this before. She loves you more than anything. She just has a hard time controlling her emotions."

I changed the subject, and he started telling me about his new job at the post office. The financial freedom that was promised with multilevel marketing had never panned out. After the divorce, reality sank in, and he was forced to find another source of income.

"Yeah, it's completely different than anything I've ever done before. But let me tell you, having a consistent schedule where I just have to clock in and clock out, and don't have to bring any work home with me, does have its perks."

We ate the rest of the meal with casual conversation, and afterwards he dropped me off at home. "Bye, honey! Love you!" he called through the open car window.

"Love you too, Dad!" I called back as I turned around to face the house. My mom's colorful hydrangeas and potted flowers were still blooming beautifully. The blue-and-white trim of the house looked perfect, and the tall silk tree spread its umbrella all the way to the front door. My mom always made the outside of the house look like it was ready for the cover of *Better Homes and Gardens*.

As I walked up the front walkway, I hoped nobody was home so I could privately rid myself of the meal I'd just eaten.

***

As the school year dragged on, late summer turned to fall, and suddenly it was mid-October. I walked the halls of school, wandering from class to class, zombielike, wishing I were anywhere but there.

One morning, I pulled myself out of bed, eyes feeling swollen from smoking in the backyard the night before. I didn't smoke at home often, just when I was feeling really low. I brushed my teeth, splashed my face with cold water, and tied my hair up into a bun. Staring at myself in the mirror, I hated what I saw.

My face was too round, and even though I'd had braces, my teeth weren't straight or white enough. My skin was blotchy, and as much as a part of me wished I could cover it all up with makeup, I didn't want to be seen as a girl who tried too hard. According to the chill girl code, any makeup I did wear had to be natural looking. I was walking a constant tightrope of having to look good but also having to look like I didn't care what I looked like.

When I walked into the kitchen, I wasn't in the mood to meet my mom's cheerful greeting. Tension immediately filled the room.

"At least you could say good morning," she said as I walked by.

With a mumbled response, I sat down to eat the frozen waffles she'd made.

"What's your problem, anyway? Here you have a mother who's making you breakfast, providing for you, giving everything you need, and you're just being an ungrateful brat, like always."

"I never wanted this!" I lashed out. "I don't want your breakfast! I don't want anything from you—just leave me alone!"

"Fine, get in the car," she growled. "And if you don't want anything from me, then forget about lunch money!"

I knew I had brought this punishment on myself, but I also thought she cared more about me than getting even. Still, she didn't give me any lunch money and rushed me out the door. I couldn't understand why she got so mad at me when I was already depressed; her verbal attacks just made how I felt even worse. It was as if I were the cause of all her anger. Everything wrong in our relationship was my fault.

Is there light at the end of the tunnel? I desperately asked my journal as I plummeted that night. I didn't see any way out. *What's wrong with me? Why do I hate myself and everything else?*

Despite all my lying and avoiding talking to my mother about my feelings, a tiny part of me wanted her to know how much I was hurting. I felt as though I were screaming at the top of my lungs in a crowded room, but nobody was listening. Nobody even noticed.

But the next day in the locker room before practice, Tanya noticed. Tanya and I had been friends since junior high, and now we were teammates and had multiple classes together. She was strong and not afraid to speak her mind. I knew her ex-boyfriend struggled with depression and had begun harming himself. He even told her repeatedly that he was going to kill himself. When that happened, she told every adult she could about her boyfriend's pain. Now she didn't hesitate to do it again.

"Brinn, what's that?" Tanya pointed to the fresh cuts on my exposed wrist. I quickly pulled my arm to my chest. I had just changed out of my clothes and stood only in my swimsuit.

She stormed out of the locker room, her long micro braids swishing back and forth as she headed straight for our coach. A few weeks earlier, Tanya had seen my cuts at practice and asked me about them. I told her it was just something I had tried when I was upset and promised never to do it again. I'd also stopped burning my leg after Grace saw the burns that summer, but I still didn't know what to do with all my pent-up emotions, so I turned on myself. A couple camp friends had done it first, and I wanted to see what it was like. The relief was an instant, albeit temporary, distraction from the buzzing in my body, so I kept doing it.

I slammed my body down on the bench, too mentally exhausted to fight.

I heard footsteps, and my coach appeared. "Brinn, I'm worried about you," she said gently. "I'm going to call your mom. Go ahead and change out of your suit."

I was slumped against the wall, watching my teammates warm up, when my mom appeared on the pool deck. I avoided eye contact as she approached. My coach joined us, and we all huddled together in the corner, trying to avoid attracting too much attention from the team.

"Brinn, could you show your wrist to your mom, please?" my coach asked calmly.

I reluctantly complied.

My mom gasped with horror. The cuts were fresh, and there were seven. They looked worse than they felt.

"Thank you for calling me," my mom said matter-of-factly to my coach. "I'll take her home now."

Silence filled the space between us as we walked down the hall toward the parking lot. My mom tried to wrap her arm around me, but I shrugged her off. I felt robotic and numb.

On our way home, without saying a word, she pulled into the parking lot of a local park and stopped the car. "Let's take a walk," she gently commanded, and I silently obeyed.

We meandered over to the grass, eventually coming to a stop, and sat down. She pulled me close and held me, rocking me back and forth as she had done when I was young. Finally, I sank into her arms.

"Brinn, do you want to kill yourself?" she asked softly.

"No .... I don't want to die," I whispered.

"Okay." She paused. "I don't understand, why would you cut yourself?" She pulled back, looking at me.

"I don't know, Mom," I said emotionlessly.

Part of me wanted to scream at her, shake her, and tell her I was drowning. But I didn't know why. I didn't know what was wrong with me. I just hated everything about myself and thought it'd be easier if I weren't around anymore. But since I was too scared to end my life, I hurt myself instead.

Over the next few days, my mom spent hours on the internet researching self-harm. She informed my siblings and my dad and scheduled a therapy session for me. But I wasn't interested in spilling my self-hatred to a strange white-haired man who had me draw pictures of my family. After that first session, I told my mom I'd stop cutting, and I never went back.

Everyone seemed to expect me to come right out and tell them what was wrong. But I couldn't even put it into words for myself, let alone speak the truth aloud.

A few weeks later, on my fifteenth birthday, I woke up to our family's classic handwritten birthday banner hanging in the kitchen. My mom made her famous French crêpes with all the toppings. She had planned a day in San Francisco with Grace and Caleb, who'd decided to not go back to his school but instead came home and went to community college.

Together we explored the city, riding the trolley cars, savoring chocolate at Ghirardelli Square, and enjoying the street performers at Fisherman's

Wharf. Before heading home, we all sat down at our favorite restaurant, one of those Asian restaurants that cooks the food right in front of you.

But I was miserable. It took all the strength I had to put one foot in front of the other and fake being happy. Soon I could no longer pretend, and my depression fueled my mother's irritation.

"What's wrong with you?" she yelled on the ride home, after we'd dropped off Grace at her house. "I do all these nice things for you, and this is the thanks I get? A mopey teenager who's not even grateful?"

In my bedroom that night, as I sat on the floor and leaned against the wall, I called Jake on the phone.

He and his girlfriend were in their common room at boarding school. He gushed about how proud he was that I was turning into a young woman. He bragged to his girlfriend about how talented I was at sports, music, and dance. Then she got on the line and congratulated me on turning a year older. I really liked her. She had to be the most chill girl I'd ever met.

After hanging up the phone, the silence of my room filled my ears with static. I wanted to cry, kick, scream, and collapse—all at once.

Energy vibrated through my body as the urge to cut grew stronger. It had been a few weeks since I'd hurt myself, but once I made my decision, I felt calm. I needed that sensation, that relief. I knew the relief wasn't real. It always felt like the dizzy rush I got after standing up too quickly—a little bit of euphoria immediately followed by wanting to feel normal again. That was it. I wanted to feel normal. But what the fuck was normal?

With the box cutter in my hand, I sat down on my floor. Suddenly the door opened. My mom stood in the doorway.

My body jumped, but I couldn't move. Time slowed down as she towered over me, her brain slowly registering what I was about to do. Her eyes narrowed, her lips pursed, and she raged at me through gritted teeth.

"I just gave you an amazing birthday, and this is what you do? What do you have to be so unhappy about!" She stormed out of my room.

I felt stuck to the floor, my knees pulled up to my chest. Unable to move. Unable to speak. I knew her wrath wasn't finished.

I heard footsteps pounding back down the hallway toward my room. What was she doing now? Suddenly she appeared, but her face had transformed. She was no longer my mother. She was a demon-possessed nightmare wielding a large chef's knife. She held the blade up to her wrist.

"You cut yourself, so I'm going to cut myself too! It's supposed to feeeeel good, huh? Well, I want to see how good it feels!" she screamed.

Wide-eyed, terrified, I couldn't speak. Then Caleb barged into view.

"Mom, what are you doing? Stop it!" He grabbed her wrist and forced the knife out of her hand. Frozen stiff, I watched the scene unfold.

Moments later, as we heard a knock on the front door, silence fell over us. It was the neighbors. They had heard my mother screaming and were coming to see if everything was okay. This wasn't the first time they'd come by to check on us.

The next morning, my door swung open unexpectedly.

"Good morning," my mother said in a sweet singsong voice.

I didn't move from bed.

"Do you want to go get coffee?" she said, knowing that was my weakness.

I slowly nodded.

"Okay, get dressed. I'll be waiting," she said excitedly as she left the room. I never knew which mother I was going to wake up to—the one who raged and threatened me, or the one who loved me.

Our tradition of going to Starbucks and getting coffee together had started a few years earlier when I began refusing to go to school. My mother used the promise of a chocolate croissant and an extra-hot mocha almost daily to bribe me out of bed. This ritual continued for years. At some point my mom became the shop's local photographer and her portraits hung on their walls. Caleb also got his first job there, so Starbucks became a family staple.

During non-school days, instead of returning straight home, we'd hop on the freeway and go for a drive. Often, it was dark thunderclouds that drew us up through the foothills of the Sierra Nevadas. Once at higher elevation, we'd pull off the freeway onto an empty road just to watch the silent snow fall around us.

Yet when I became a teenager, my mom and I started taking drives together without a storm to chase. During an argument, or if one of us was in a bad mood, she'd look at me, tilt her head sideways toward the car, and I knew: We were going for a drive.

In the car, we'd sing at the top of our lungs to all the divas of the '90s: Faith Hill, Celine Dion, Shania Twain. Side by side on the open road, we could open up about our lives. My mother's car became a safe space where she often consoled me about my latest romantic upheaval.

"Baby girl, of course you're heartbroken—JT broke up with you!" she'd say, leaning over the middle console to hold my hand while steering with the other. "It's okay! Be sad. Be mad. Feel all your feelings until you have no more feelings to feel. That's the only way you'll actually be able to move on.

"Plus, so much of the hurt you're feeling right now is rejection. That's it. It's your ego that's bruised. And your ego will heal, along with your heart," she assured me with a wink and a smile.

Our driving ritual was the glue holding us together, but it was also the rug under which we swept all our conflicts. Now, as she drove, we sipped our coffee. She didn't bring up the night before. There was no apology; there never was. As always, we just kept driving—windows up, music loud, cruising past every chance to really talk like exits we refused to take.

CLOSE CALL

Eric's text came through at about 12:15 a.m. "Come over. Robby and Richard are here. We stole some whiskey from my dad, and we're gonna smoke."

I almost always said yes to Eric's late-night rendezvous requests, or to anything any guy who held my interest wanted me to do. I knew Eric because he was Tanya's most recent ex-boyfriend. They'd broken up when the school year ended, but we lived near each other and had started spending time together that summer.

At first, we hung out at the school next door or wandered the neighborhood together. Soon we were fooling around in his bed, and I was being *that girl* to Tanya.

Without ever officially dating, because that would cross the girl code, Eric and I found every excuse we could to meet up, no matter what time of day or night.

"I tried to drown myself a few years ago," he said. We were sitting on the back steps of the church halfway between our houses at one o'clock in the morning. "But under water, when I realized what I was doing—I stopped."

When I heard his story, I felt jealous. I too wanted some realization to shock me out of wanting to die. I desperately wanted to feel alive again, but instead, I felt lost. I let my mind wander with the idea of starving myself; I'd just quit eating and drinking until I ended up in the hospital. In my fantasy, once I was in the hospital, then I'd realize that I wanted to live too.

Our late-night talks helped me feel less alone. In fact, every time I hung out with a guy, I felt less alone, and there was always someone I was interested in. Ever since Logan Spencer had asked me to be his girlfriend in the first grade, my romantic relationships continued nonstop, almost as if they were out of my control. Usually they'd start out as friendships, and then over time, the flirting would increase and progress into something more.

Whether it was making out at a party or starting an official relationship, I always had a new crush, someone to obsess over, someone to feel wanted by. In junior high, my mind was constantly occupied by Carlos, Sean, Peter, William, Mason, Matt, John. Even in elementary school, I had a group of guys who constantly alternated between friends and boyfriends. In elementary school, girls like Brenda and her friend, whose name I've forgotten, also came into the mix. But Brenda, her friend, and I had an unspoken rule: to never acknowledge what we did under the covers at night.

I told Eric I'd be there soon, then strategized my plan. I got dressed and placed a large pillow in my bed, in case my mom came to check on me.

Leaving, I closed the squeaky back gate of my childhood home behind me. It was now 12:45 a.m., and Eric was waiting for me. My mom's bedroom lay at the far end of our house, so sleeping or not, she couldn't hear the noise.

I never worried too much about getting caught when I snuck out. Not that my mom wasn't terrifying, or that she'd never check on me—she often was, and she often did. It was simply that once I made up my mind to leave, my body took over and my mind went blank. No more thinking, just doing.

But that night felt different. The moment I shut the gate, a subtle, calm voice from within me said, *If you leave, you won't come back in this way.* That voice froze me in place for half a second. I knew I was being warned. But I was used to brushing off my intuition. I'd been trained to.

Firming up my decision to leave, I booked it, running down the street, around a few corners, and past the church. Then I started walking because I didn't want to be out of breath when I arrived.

Sneaking through Eric's back gate, as I had done before, I could hear muffled punk rock music. My mom would never have let my friends and me make that much noise this late at night, but his parents were different. They seemed to let him do whatever he wanted.

I knocked on the window. Eric's head and shirtless torso appeared, and he slid back the glass.

The smell of stale teenage boy wafted out—along with another smell I recognized. His breath could have practically gotten me drunk.

Even before I could crawl through the window, he handed me a pipe with some herb in it and a lighter. I clicked the lighter and took a hit. The hot smoke burned my lungs and felt comforting against the cold air.

I handed the pipe back to him through the window.

"Move over, it's cold out here," I said as I prepared to climb.

Once inside, I saw the full scene. Robby, the same guy I had called my boyfriend in sixth grade, and Richard, the bully Jake had pushed against the fence, were both shirtless, stumbling around the room, headbanging to the music.

The room was too hot, and I began feeling annoyed. We couldn't even talk over the music, and none of the boys paid any attention to me.

This is stupid. Why am I even here? I thought.

Eric was lying on his bed, trying to get me to join him. "Come on, relax. Lay down with me," he coaxed. I didn't want anyone to know we had been messing around together, so I kept my distance.

I planted myself—upright—on the edge of the bed instead. I watched Robby and Richard dance around like idiots, and all of a sudden, they took off their pants. Now they were dressed in only their boxers.

"Okay, I'm done," I said to Eric. Irritated at how immature they were being, I grabbed my shoes.

The window was above Eric's bed, so I passed by him—he was still lying down—slid open the glass, and put one leg up and over the edge of the windowsill. Suddenly I felt myself being yanked backward onto the bed.

Eric pinned me down with his heavy body. Even though he was only a little taller than I was, he had been training all summer with the high school football team. I squirmed under his weight as he grappled with me. With one arm, he held down the top of my body, and with the other hand, he reached down, trying to undo his belt.

My vision began to blur. Then my mind went blank.

"Hey, man. Get off her," Robby said. He was naked in the corner, taking a break from headbanging.

Ignoring him, Eric kept on trying to wrestle my body into submission. As I resisted, his body felt heavier and heavier. My voice stayed silent as I struggled, my body on autopilot, fighting for survival.

"Dude! Get off her!" Robby insisted, louder this time.

Laughing, Eric released me, and in one swift movement, I scrambled out the window. A blast of fresh air hit my skin. I could finally breathe again.

The moment my feet hit the pavement, I heard my cell phone ring.

Mom flashed on the screen.

I answered, trying to sound calm.

"Brinn Emily Langdale! Where are you right now?" my mom screamed through the phone.

"I'm by the church," I stammered.

"Stay right there! I'm coming."

Hanging up, I bolted in that direction. Within what felt like seconds, her little white SUV tore around the corner. I braced myself as I opened the car door.

"Where have you been, and who were you with?!" She hit the gas, barely waiting for me to get in the car. When she passed our street, my heart jumped.

"Mom, where are you going? I haven't been with anyone; I've been by myself. I just wanted to get out of the house." Panic started to fill my body.

"You've been smoking, haven't you? You're high! I can tell! Look at your eyes! Who were you with?"

The interrogation continued as my mind raced, searching for the perfect explanation. Driving too fast around the quiet streets, she scanned the dark, looking for the person who'd been with me so she could bring us both to justice.

"Yes, I smoked. I had some weed, but I was by myself. I swear! I wasn't with anyone! I'm sorry!" My voice escalated with insistence.

"I am taking you to the police! Our neighbor, he's a police officer. I am going to knock on his door right now! I am turning you in to the cops!" She rounded a corner, tires screeching.

"No, Mom, please!" I said. "I promise I'll never do it again! I am so sorry. I just wanted to go for a walk and try smoking by myself, so that way I would know what it was like without anyone else around. I'm so sorry, I'll never do it again!" I rattled off whatever lies I could think of as I pleaded with her to take me home.

The idea of telling my mom about Eric never crossed my mind. He was in the part of my world that adults didn't enter. The world of hooking up, smoking, drinking, sneaking around, lying, of hating myself and my body and no longer wanting to be here. There was no adult I could confide in. Telling adults anything about the life they couldn't see would only lead to getting in trouble. They'd never understand.

At some point, my mom gave up on the idea of finding my mystery partner, and we made our way back to our house. She apparently also decided not to knock on our neighbor's door at 2:00 a.m. Instead, we simply walked through the front door, and I walked down the hallway to my room. My heart raced as I lay down on my bed. *I hadn't come back in through the gate.*

With that realization spinning in my head, I stared at the glow-in-the-dark stars on my ceiling. Had it really happened? Had I heard the voice of God or angels? Why hadn't I followed its advice?

This thought had felt different than other thoughts. It was as if someone had been talking to me—and if I'd listened, I could have avoided that terrifying situation with Eric. I hated him for betraying me. *I'm never talking to him again*, I promised myself as I rolled over and tried to fall asleep.

LEAVING HOME AT SIXTEEN

I stood up in Tanya's small living room and looked around impatiently. We had just finished watching a movie, and I was bored. The lights were low, and my four friends were still squished onto the worn-out love seat on one side of the room. But the boys had wandered outside, and I could smell a delicious scent wafting through the air toward me.

I walked across the room, stepped through the back door, and felt the cold cement beneath my bare feet. Shivering, I thought, *I need something to warm me up.* I checked the time on my phone: 7:08 p.m.

"Hey, babe, you want some of this?" my boyfriend Chaz said, handing me a pipe. Chaz was a junior, and I was a sophomore. Chaz and I had gone to junior high together, but he had no clue who I was back then. Everyone in the school knew Chaz McMullen, with his short dark hair, flawless skin, and heart-stopping smile, and he had a reputation for knowing a lot of the ladies.

Now, three years later, victory was mine. I had just ended a long-term relationship with Austin, the cute boy from my freshman history class.

Being with Austin made me feel loved and connected to someone in a way I'd never experienced before. He was a best friend, an amazing kisser, and someone I could talk to every day. He checked in on me to make sure I was eating enough and asked me what was wrong when I was feeling low. I stopped having urges to hurt myself and found myself less depressed.

But during sophomore year, I broke it off. While I cared about him a lot, his playful nature became too lighthearted for me; it seemed he could never get serious about school or life, and he was on his way to dropping out.

Chaz was different. He had a job and a car and watched out for his younger brother. We had met three weeks before at Grace's house when a mutual friend introduced us. We both went outside to smoke and somehow ended up spending the remaining hours rolling around, making out on her brother's bed. I was aware of his reputation for sleeping around, but I wasn't interested in having sex.

Growing up, I'd made a pact with myself: to not have sex until I was eighteen. I wanted it to be special, significant. It was the only thing I hadn't done.

At fifteen, when I started dating Austin, I snuck over to his house one night when his parents were out of town. We were so excited about just being together that sex wasn't our goal, but one thing led to another.

"I don't want you to do anything you don't want to do," he whispered in the dark as he kissed my face gently. "Just being here with you is more than enough."

"I want to do it with you because I love you, and I know I wouldn't regret it. But I don't want to start having sex all the time. We can do it this once, but that's it, okay?" I said firmly.

After that night, we stuck to our agreement, and since then, I'd held firm to what I believed sex to be—something special for the future. The idea of sneaking around to have sex, or cramming ourselves into the back seat of a car, was not my idea of special. Plus, it seemed like a hassle to take off our clothes, deal with birth control, and risk getting caught. It just seemed simpler to wait until I was older, and out of my mom's house.

So on the bed with Chaz that first night, sex was off the table. I enjoyed the growing anticipation, slow, sensual movements, and pleasure that came from two people exploring each other's bodies without any added pressure. All I wanted was playful fun, and to me, that wasn't sex.

Now, outside Tanya's house in the cold, I performed some mental calculations. It was Tuesday, so I couldn't stay out late, and I was pretty sure my mom would already be home when Chaz dropped me off.

I gave back the pipe. "No, I shouldn't," I said sadly.

I hated saying no to weed, and I almost never did. What I needed now was some other way to ease the racing energy inside. I needed relief. Turning, I went back inside, heading straight for my backpack. Inside waited a plastic water bottle partially filled with cheap vodka. These were the last remnants of the gift a senior in my French class had bought me the weekend before. Even though I couldn't get alcohol as easily as I could weed, I took advantage of any opportunity I could to drink. It was another way to escape.

Without thinking, I unscrewed the small lid and downed the contents of the bottle. The liquid burned my throat, and my eyes snapped shut as my body shuttered. I walked back down the hallway to the outside. As Chaz met me in the middle, I thrust the empty, crinkled-up bottle into his chest. Confusion etched on his face, he stared down at the bottle now in his hand, then at me. Taking a whiff from the bottle, he coughed.

"Did you"—he paused, putting together the pieces of what had occurred—"just down some vodka?"

I answered with a laugh and swayed back and forth dramatically.

"And what if I did?" I asked, lightly poking his chest and kissing him hard on the lips.

"Well, all right then," he said, sounding a little worried but obviously somewhat impressed.

Waltzing down the hallway, I entered the living room. "I wanna dance!" I announced, disrupting the mellow atmosphere of the space. Everyone in the room stared back at me blankly.

"What did you do this time?" Tanya asked, rolling her eyes.

Tanya was the mom of our group. Throughout the past year, following her parents' divorce, her own mother had been spending the majority of her time with friends who lived an hour and a half away, and Tanya's dad had moved back to Europe. Tanya had a couple of older siblings but was by far the most responsible one in her family.

"She needs to go home soon, Chaz," Tanya said, implying that he needed to help clean up this mess. An hour later, Chaz poured me into the front seat of his two-seater Toyota truck.

As he started the car, I navigated the radio and began singing boisterously and dancing in my seat.

"Food will definitely help," he concluded as he drove to the Wendy's down the street.

After a burger, fries, and root beer, I was feeling much more sober. We stayed in the truck, talking as long as we could before it was time to go. Nervous about seeing my mom, I wracked my brain for a solution.

"I have an idea!" I said. "How about we go back to my place, and we go straight into the hot tub. That way, my mom can't get close enough to me to smell the alcohol! And by the time you leave, I'll smell like chlorine. Then I'll need to take a shower and brush my teeth. It's foolproof."

"Okay, I'm in." He started the car.

We pulled up to my house and let out large sighs of relief when we saw my mom's car wasn't in the driveway. "Yes!" I exclaimed. "Let's go!"

I managed to get away with being drunk that night, but I wasn't always as successful. One night, my mom found me throwing up in the bathroom after drinking alone in my room. Another night, I came home with bloodshot eyes after she called to tell me she needed the car. Once she caught me and Grace smoking a joint in my room. But to my surprise, in those situations, my mom didn't yell, scream, or threaten to ground me for the rest of my life. Maybe she was picking her battles because our relationship had become so strained.

"I just want to move in with Dad! Is that so hard to understand?" I seethed. After two years of just Mom and me in the house, I'd had it with her emotional roller coaster. Convinced she hated me and wanted nothing more than to make my life miserable, I desperately wanted out.

"Your dad doesn't have any rules, which is why you want to live with him. So fine, move out, but just not to your dad's. You should just go to boarding school!"

"We can't even afford to send Jake to boarding school. Remember, *you* used my college fund to pay for *his* school!" I yelled, storming off to my room.

About an hour later, the flare of my anger had dissipated. Wondering if she had calmed down too, I casually entered her room. My mother's room was at the opposite end of the house and had been an attached garage before it was renovated for the au pairs she'd hired while I was growing up. She moved in there after my dad moved out.

This large room had its own entrance and bathroom and housed the laundry room. With the help of her new boyfriend, Gary, she had recently closed her photography studio and set up a home office in her room. Gary was a gentle cowboy from Idaho, and their plan was to become equine photographers, taking portraits of people's farm life on their ranches.

Horses had always been my mom's passion, and I had been riding since I was five years old. In the spring of my freshman year, she called while I was hanging out at Austin's house and told me she'd just bought me a one-month-old horse. The truth was, she was buying herself a one-month-old horse, but saying it was a project to bring the two of us closer together was the perfect excuse.

I enjoyed riding and was good at it. It was a skill most of my friends didn't have, and I was grateful for the confidence it gave me when I was able to connect with, communicate with, and lead a thousand-pound animal. I also enjoyed cleaning stalls, dealing with various issues at the barn, and caring for the horses. But I was more interested in hanging out with my friends and playing sports. Owning horses was my mom's dream, not mine. Deep down, I viewed it as another way for her to indulge her own childhood fantasy and spend money she didn't have.

As I walked into her room, all I could hear was the click of her mouse. She sat at her desk, the light of the desktop computer lighting up her face.

I proceeded carefully toward the desk, walking around it to see what she was looking at. Boarding schools.

Silently, I sat in my usual spot, at the edge of the desk, on top of her piles of paperwork. Without looking at me, she continued scrolling through pictures of brick buildings in faraway cities and states.

Noticing one particular city, I said half jokingly, "There's one in Chicago. Instead of boarding school, I should just go live with Allie."

Allie was my best friend at summer camp. She was the one I missed the most when I came home each summer, and we'd been in near-constant communication, sending emails back and forth over the last few years. She'd recently lost her father to cancer and lived with her mom in an enormous Victorian-style house in the suburbs of Chicago.

Without turning her head, my mother simply replied, "Okay."

I stared at her. Slowly, her head turned, her eyes meeting mine. We didn't blink or laugh. We were calling each other's bluff.

"Are you serious?" I asked. My mom had never met Allie, or her mother, and had no idea where I'd be living.

"Yeah, why not? Go live with Allie," she said with a shrug and casually sat back in her high-backed office chair.

Seven days later, I was on a plane.

In a way, it was hard to leave. For the first time, I was actually enjoying my life. Grace and I both had cars we could use whenever we wanted and a solid group of friends, and I loved playing water polo. And of course, there was Chaz. But as usual, once I'd planted the idea in my mind, I felt no choice but to follow through. I turned off my feelings and stubbornly pushed myself forward.

I spent the next four months in Chicago on a school campus without Allie. She was a junior, and I was a sophomore, and the school campus was split. While she was hanging out with the upperclassmen, I was stuck with the underclassmen half a mile away. Although I was able to make light conversation with some people, I felt I didn't belong. During lunch, I'd wander the halls or try to blend in at the end of a long table filled with people.

As the new girl from California, I heard three main questions: Do you live near movie stars, do you surf, and do you smoke weed? As I could only answer one question with a yes, I always noticed the looks of disappointment when I said no.

Yet at my new home with Allie and her mom, life felt smoother. They included me in every activity, as if I were a member of their family. Her mom loved having a second daughter to dote on, and we even brought home a new puppy. Allie and I spent a lot of time hanging out with her boyfriend, who sold weed, so we quickly became good friends.

At the end of the school year, I was ready to go back to California. I missed Grace and Tanya. (Chaz had only lasted one week of long distance before we broke up, but it was for the best.) At the same time, I was a little sad to leave the comfort of my new home. Allie's mom was a sweet retired teacher who was involved in the church and community. She never raised her voice and thought everything Allie and I did was worth praising. My relationship with Allie had deepened into more of a sisterly bond, but we were both ready to have our own space again.

I flew home for only a few days, then got on another plane and returned to my sanctuary in Colorado. After months of feeling awkward and out of place in Chicago, camp brought a soothing salve to my soul. During dinner one evening, the camp director approached me.

"Brinn, can I talk to you for a minute?"

"Sure," I said nervously, wracking my brain, trying to recall what I'd done wrong.

"Brinn, we've had some changes to our camp staff, and I was wondering if you'd be interested in joining us as a counselor in training for the rest of the summer?"

That spring, I'd contacted the camp director to ask if I could become a staff member like Allie. She told me that since I was only a sophomore, even though I was the same age as Allie, I technically couldn't become a staff member. Now I guess she had changed her mind.

"Oh my goodness!" I gasped. "Yes! I'd love to! Thank you!"

"Great! I'll take care of everything on our end, and I'll be in touch about getting you all the paperwork and everything we need to get you settled. Enjoy your dinner," she said with a smile before turning and walking away. Knowing I was going to stay another six weeks filled my body with excitement and relief. Camp was the only place where I was happy and sober. I wanted this feeling to last as long as possible.

A few days later, the same camp director knocked on my cabin door.

"Brinn, I'm sorry, but I have some bad news. It's about your mom. She's okay, but she's been in a horse accident, and she's in the hospital with a broken back."

Tears welled up in my eyes. I was speechless. Suddenly all my resentment toward my mom melted away.

"I have the phone number for the hospital. Please come with me, and you can give her a call."

I nodded and followed her to the nurse's station, the home of the camp's phone. The director handed me a piece of paper with a phone number on it.

"I'll give you some privacy," she said, leaving me alone in the room.

Silence filled the space. Slowly, I picked up the receiver, pushed the numbers, and waited for the phone to ring.

"Helllllo?" My mother's voice sounded tired and strained.

"Mommy!" I said, bursting into tears.

"Oh, honey, it's so good to hear your voice," she said slowly, her speech clearly altered by pain medication.

"Mom, are you okay? What happened?"

"I'm fine, really. I'm okay." There was a pause. "I was out riding with Gary, and my horse got a little crazy, that's all. But don't worry, I'm being taken care of, and everything's just fine."

"Mom, I can come home. I can get on the next plane and be there in a few hours."

"No, no, no. You're exactly where you need to be right now. You don't need to be here. I have Gary taking care of me. Everything's fine. You stay at camp. I don't want you to come home and deal with all this. I want you to stay there. It's where you belong."

I didn't know what to say. I felt torn. Part of me wanted to run home and fix everything that was broken—our tumultuous relationship and her back. But I knew she was right. I was exactly where I needed to be. I let out a big sigh. "Okay, Mom. I'll stay. But if anything changes, I can come home at any time."

"I know you can. I just want you to enjoy the rest of your summer, Miss Counselor-in-Training."

I smiled. It did feel satisfying to know I had her permission to stay.

"Okay, well, I'll call you tomorrow to check in, okay?" I wiped the tears from my eyes.

"I look forward to it," she said quietly.

"I love you, Mom."

"I love you too, honey."

I hung up the phone and sat back in my chair. The nurse's office had grown dark since I'd walked in. I hung my head, and as tears flowed down my cheeks again, I prayed, "God, thank you so much for keeping my mom safe. Thank you for sending her help and making sure she's okay. Thank you, thank you, thank you."

***

"Welcome back!" Grace threw her arms around me. She and Tanya had arranged to pick me up from the airport at the end of the summer. We loaded my gear into Grace's turquoise sedan and closed the doors. Then a familiar smell hit my nose.

"Wow, smells good in here," I said as I clicked in my seat belt.

"Yup, here's a little welcome-home present," Tanya said from the back seat as she lit the joint and passed it up front to me.

The stark contrast between camp and the reality of my life at home smacked me in the face. I'd just spent two months sober, truly enjoying my life in a spiritual bubble of peace, love, and acceptance, but within minutes, I was back to my old ways. Living at home and trying to stay sober was a fruitless effort. I wasn't even interested in trying. Getting high with my friends felt like the only way I could survive the rest of high school.

That night, I scrawled in my journal. *Why can't I just be a good Christian Scientist? Why do I smoke so much and mess around with guys so much? What's wrong with me? I wish I could take back all the bad things I've done. I wish I could be innocent again.*

Coming home, I entered my typical depressive lull as the deep bonds I'd formed over the summer were now forced to become either long-distance or nonexistent. At only sixteen, I'd been away from home for nearly six months. Suddenly my hometown felt foreign to me.

It was now my junior year, which meant I was supposed to focus on getting into college, but I felt restless and already independent. With access to my mom's car (whose gas and insurance I was paying for with my earnings from camp) and hopes of enjoying Grace's last year before she moved out of town for college, school and my homelife felt confining.

"Mom, Grace's performing at the basketball game, so I was planning on heading there soon, if you don't need anything else," I said.

It had been three months since the accident, and she was still wearing her white back brace, which made her sit up straight.

"Did you do your homework?"

"Mom. I'm seventeen. When was the last time you asked me about homework," I snapped.

"I am your mother. That seems like a pretty reasonable question to ask."

Inside my gut, heat expanded all the way up my chest, and I swear steam came out of my ears, but bitterness left me silent.

I wanted to scream at her, *How dare you ask me about homework! You didn't even help me with college applications! Or getting my driver's license. You don't get to pretend that you're an involved parent now.*

I had been taking care of myself for years, especially after living in Chicago and Colorado, and was resentful of her seemingly sudden interest in mothering. The attentive mother she'd been prior to the divorce had vanished into her own grief and hadn't come back. So many times, she'd left me alone with Jake to fend for myself. She let me go to Chicago without batting an eye. Now she thought she could just throw out parental gestures to make up for her absence. She had no idea all that I was juggling by myself and what I'd been through. It would be easier if she left me alone to get through high school so I could finally leave this town.

"No," I growled. "I don't have homework." I snatched up the keys off the table and stormed out.

"Geez, attitude much?" I heard her call after me. In my mind, I flipped her off.

Luckily, just a few days after my junior year ended, I jetted off to Colorado again to spend the whole summer at camp in the horsemanship major as a wrangler.

Each morning before dawn, we wranglers walked out deep into the quiet horse pasture. Around me, I could see silhouettes of horses patiently standing together in small groups, waiting for their breakfast.

Once we'd reached the bottom of the pasture with all the horses in front of us, with a single crack of the bullwhip, the ground would start shaking. The thundering of sixty horses stampeding toward the barn was deafening. I could see my breath as the first sunrays appeared just over the mountains. I shoved my hands into leather work gloves and got started.

We were a small horsemanship staff, so each morning we each fed, groomed, and saddled about five or six horses before breakfast. If we were lucky and finished early, we could make it in time for the staff's morning prayer circle.

Everyone else stood around in their pajamas, with bed head, just awake enough to hear the day's inspirational words. Then our small group would come charging up from the barn, awake for over an hour and fully clad in our dusty cowboy boots, hats, and jeans.

During the day, I'd teach kids and preteens how to ride horses and do gymkhana events like poles and barrels. We also prepared for a three-day pack trip with horses and took trail rides throughout the mountains.

That summer was filled with peaking 14,000-foot mountains, taking trips to small towns with friends on my days off, and soaking in hot springs. Once again, the freedom, safety, and spirituality I felt in Colorado stood in stark contrast to my life at home.

GETTING CAUGHT

When the buzzer rang, I sprang off the edge of the pool. Kicking hard, I stretched out my right arm and snagged the ball before my opponent could. The yellow ball bobbed between my arms in the churning water. I popped up, water sloshing against my hips as I instinctively assumed my shooting position, elbow back, arm straight. Like a rocket I released toward the net. *Bam!* Direct hit.

It was the fall of my senior year, I was captain of the water polo team, and in two weeks, I would be eighteen. We'd left our school early that day to drive the thirty minutes out to the high school whose team was now losing badly. Playing the easiest team in our league didn't take away my satisfaction in scoring yet another goal. Of all the aspects of myself I doubted, my ability to play sports was not one of them, and I relished my athletic achievements.

At the sound of the last buzzer, my body relaxed, drifting in the water weightlessly before sinking into muffled silence. Bubbles tickled my face as I exhaled, dropping myself to the bottom of the pool. When my toes touched the hard cement, I bent my knees, curled my body and, like a spring, exploded up through the surface of the water again.

In a few strokes, I reached the pool's edge, where I freed my long brown hair from the confines of my silicone swim cap, my remaining dry curls straightening in the water. I pushed myself up onto the deck and joined my teammates in lining up to shake hands with the opposing team.

Caleb, now my water polo coach, clapped me on the shoulder.

"Nice work out there today, Top Scorer."

"Thanks!" It felt good, someone who really understood my efforts recognizing me for them. Caleb, after returning home from the Midwest, had then played two years of water polo at a local community college. Currently, he was coaching my team, working at an upscale restaurant, and perusing a certification in massage therapy.

I toweled off, noticing my summer tan lines were fading quickly. Shielding my uncomfortable body with my towel, I trekked to the locker room.

Just inside, my team had taken over two benches with bags, towels, and clothes strewn around them. As I approached, I saw three teammates huddled together, whispering. Seeing me, they scattered.

That was weird, I thought as I unzipped my bag and found my sweatpants. But then my stomach twisted and sank. I'd just remembered what I'd done before the game. I had been so busy playing that I forgot Becky and I had smoked in my car when we'd left campus. I'd known Becky for a couple years, and we'd partied together on the weekends even though she was only a sophomore. Soon the rest of my teammates filed in through the door, chatting loudly until they noticed me. Heat rose in my face as the realization hit me. *Shit. They knew.*

This was not a team who would be understanding of smoking a little weed before an easy game. This was a team who would make a big deal out of nothing, just to prove a point. I hoped they'd let it go, but doubts filled my mind.

The next day after school, I dragged myself to our locker room to change into my bathing suit for practice. Between the rows of lockers, an eerie silence greeted me.

Where is everybody? I wondered as I walked out onto the pool deck. The pit in my stomach was tightening, turning to ice. A familiar numbness crept up my neck into my head.

Tanya walked through the gate and onto the pool deck. Her curly hair was pulled back tight on her head and her large sunglasses covered almost half her face. Just as she had been since freshman year, never in a hurry to get anywhere, she sauntered toward me.

"Good luck, dude," she said, chuckling as she continued past.

"What are you talking about?" I asked impatiently, playing dumb. My mind raced with possible outcomes, but my body remained calm.

"Tiffany's holding trial. She told Caleb to postpone practice." Tanya continued walking to the far end of the pool deck. Wordlessly, I followed her. She rounded the corner, passing behind the cement wall that separated the men's and women's locker rooms.

As I left the bright sunlight, it took a moment for my eyes to adjust to the shade where my teammates had gathered. It wasn't often that our team assembled in school clothes. Looking at them, I felt as if we had never celebrated victories, or cried through losses, or pushed our physical limitations together. They felt like strangers. I no longer felt like their captain or the top scorer from yesterday's game. Instead, I felt that familiar feeling that I didn't belong.

My eleven teammates sat stoically in sun-bleached plastic chairs, the metal legs flaking with rust. All their talking stopped as I walked up to them. The other delinquent was already seated—with an open seat next to her. When I sat down, I saw that she had tears in her eyes. I was trying my hardest not to roll mine.

"Brinn, we need to talk to you," Tiffany Brown declared, hands on her hips, shifting her weight from her left foot to her right foot and back again. She was their ringleader.

My mouth clamped shut, and I felt my jaw tightening.

"We know you and Becky smoked weed before the game yesterday," she barked. She swung her head emphatically from side to side as she spoke.

All I could do was stare at her. My longing to escape was so strong. I wanted out of this situation, out of high school, out of this town. I was sick and tired of dealing with my mom, with my classes, and with this team.

Freedom was only months away, just on the other side of graduation. After that, I would only have one more summer at camp, and then I'd leave for college, wherever that might be. Maybe Colorado? Or somewhere else in California? Wherever I was going to live, it wouldn't be here.

Tiffany's shrill voice brought me back to the present. "Brinn, this is not how captains are supposed to behave. You're supposed to set a good example—not do drugs on the way to a game!"

None of my teammates, besides Tanya, had any idea how often I got high, or that smoking a joint before a game was the least of my worries. But I knew I had been stupid to smoke around these prudes. Of course Becky had opened her big mouth. She was only a sophomore. I shouldn't have trusted her.

While we could call each other friends for the most part, I had found Tiffany annoying throughout the four years I'd known her. She had spoken very openly about her mom's addiction to drugs, which was the reason why Tiffany needed to live with another family. It was as if she knew she was one wrong move away from ending up like her mom, and that was why she judged everyone who tried to have any fun. The rest of the girls had no clue about real life outside their perfect picket-fenced homes.

Becky whimpered, and I was ready to say whatever I needed to get out of there.

"Sorry, Tiffany," I mumbled. "I shouldn't have done that."

None of the girls understood how little this incident mattered. I couldn't explain to them that my tolerance for weed had become so high, I hardly felt the effects of one joint. Plus, we had been playing against an easy team, and I had scored all the goals! I'd thought my team would be excited by our win. But I couldn't tell them any of that. I knew they'd never understand me.

Just like they wouldn't understand why I'd needed to escape to Colorado for the past seven summers or why I'd left home halfway through sophomore year to live in Chicago. Or why I was so desperate to leave for college or the real reason why Jake had suddenly moved back home. Nobody could understand me—because nobody really knew me. I hardly knew myself.

LIFTING THE VEIL

"I have kind of a weird question for you ..." Caleb began.

He had picked me up from the house and taken me out to dinner. We'd wrapped up the water polo season just six weeks before. Now, stuffed to the brim with delicious taqueria food, we'd just made our way across the restaurant parking lot and were sitting in his red Chevy truck. As he spoke, I could see his breath, like little puffs of smoke.

Silence stretched between us, heavy with his unasked question. Sitting in the restaurant parking lot—that's what he recalls. As I remember it, though, we were on our way to the gym and had stopped at the ATM. But I'd put my money on Caleb's recollection because, as he told me later, he had planned that whole evening specifically to ask me this question.

My body shivered in the cold, and I hunkered deeper into my water polo sweatshirt, fiddling with the drawstrings, waiting for him to start the truck. Caleb sat behind the wheel, eyes downcast.

"Since Jake's been home, has he ever done anything weird to you? Like, has he ever come home high and tried to touch you?"

My heart pounded in my ears. Ice ran through my veins, and I was frozen in place. My eyes stared straight ahead. Jake had graduated from his performing arts school at the end of my freshman year and then enrolled in a music program in the Bay Area. In reality, though, he never went to class and spent all the money he had on drugs. A few months ago, he'd hit rock bottom. Fully addicted to heroin and with nowhere to live, he came home to stay with me and my mom.

It was painful to have him back at our house. Needles had left track marks all over his infected arms, and his sunken eyes and gaunt body didn't even look like his. He spent hours on the bathroom floor in cold sweats, shaking and vomiting. I didn't think it was fair for me to live with a drug addict while I was trying to finish high school, but no one ever asked for my opinion, and I never complained. We all just pretended everything was normal.

But with Caleb's question, I lost language. Suddenly, my body took over, responding with uncontrollable sobs. In the truck, with Caleb by my side, I finally admitted to myself, for the first time, that Jake had molested me for years.

Caleb drove us to his studio apartment, somewhere I'd spent a lot of time, so it felt comfortable and safe. Once inside, we sat on his worn red couch. A single light from the kitchen lit up the small space. Caleb pulled out a wooden box from a drawer in his coffee table. He cracked the lid open and reached in, grabbing fresh herb and papers to roll a joint. Once his art was complete, I heard the lighter click as he passed it my way.

"Brinn, I just want you to know that everything's going to be okay."

I nodded silently. Eventually, I asked, "How did you know to ask me that?"

"Well, Victoria actually was the one who figured it out," he said slowly. Victoria was his girlfriend. They'd been dating for a few months, and we'd all spent a lot of time together.

"Remember when she came over to the house last week?" he asked.

I nodded.

"She noticed a dynamic between you and Jake. I can't really explain it, she just felt something was off. She also saw how Mom's bedroom is on the opposite side of the house, so it made her start to think." He took a deep breath. "Brinn, Victoria was also molested by her older brother, who then died of a heroin overdose."

My eyes grew wide.

"She trusted her intuition about the situation and asked me to ask you if something had ever happened." He let out a deep sigh.

I couldn't believe it. Everything in my life had just changed because Victoria had the courage to listen to her instincts, and then Caleb had the awareness to listen.

"Wow" was all I could muster.

"I know, it's a lot to take in."

In the midst of all my confusion and overwhelm, there was a quiet calmness inside me. On some level, the situation felt divinely orchestrated, as if Victoria were some Earth angel coming into our lives to expose the deep wound that otherwise might never be revealed.

"I'll text Mom and let her know you're staying here, and in the morning we can figure out the next move," he said.

The next morning, I sat on the red couch, and Caleb sat cross-legged on the floor as we sipped coffee and strategized.

"I think it's best if I tell Mom and confront Jake," he told me. "I don't want you to get caught in the middle of anything if Jake reacts badly."

Trusting his lead, I nodded. There was never a doubt that she'd believe me. One look at Jake's history and his present situation made him a likely suspect.

"First I'll call Mom and tell her that I'll meet her at the house. Then I'll call Jake." He planned out loud.

He stepped outside on the balcony to make the phone calls.

His voice was muffled, but I could hear him on the other side of the glass door.

"I know what you did to Brinn, and I'm telling Mom! I'll be there in ten minutes," Caleb growled.

I knew he longed to unleash his wrath on Jake, but Caleb was a pacifist at heart.

"Promise you won't touch him, Caleb?" I asked. I didn't want anything bad to happen to Jake—I was still protecting him.

"I won't. As much as I'd like to, I know that's not the answer."

I waited at Caleb's apartment. As I looked out the window, the day seemed strangely ordinary. People walked their dogs on the sidewalk, and cars moved through the parking lot. Except nothing felt normal anymore.

Wearing yesterday's clothes, I felt dirty, exhausted. It was as though I'd spent all of my energy climbing up the stairs to escape my childhood, only to feel those stairs suddenly morphing into a giant slide, plunging me further and further into the dark unknown, with no idea of when, or how, this terrifying ride would end.

An hour later, the phone rang.

"Mom's irate—disgusted with Jake and concerned about you," Caleb said simply. "Jake cowered when he saw me. No denial, just fear."

That evening, my mom came to see me. From the window of Caleb's apartment, I watched her car slide into a parking spot. She paused before getting out and locking the car door. She had pulled back her thick blonde hair into a large claw clip and pushed her bangs off to the right side.

As a kid, I had often watched her in admiration as she applied her makeup in the bathroom—a touch of natural eye shadow dabbed on by her index finger, then a brush of mascara. Simple. A sweep of powder on her cheekbones and, on special occasions, blush to make them pop. She would stand back from the mirror and suck in her cheeks slightly, turning her head from side to side, examining her work. I called this expression her "mirror face."

"You'll have a mirror face someday. We all do," she said, chuckling.

Now the window caught my reflection. My dark hair, brown eyes, and olive skin matched my dad's. I didn't look like her at all. I had never developed my mirror face.

My mom walked stoically toward the apartment building. She looked smaller than five foot nine inches.

We had an awkward greeting at the front door, as if she didn't know how a mother might act or what she should say. I wasn't sure how much she knew, or what Jake had told her, but I felt confident that she believed me as we sat on the couch together. She put her arms around me and rocked me like a baby.

"Honey, are you okay?"

"Mom, I'm fine," I said with a sigh and a shrug.

"You know, it's okay if you're not fine."

"Yeah, but I am. Really. It's not that big of a deal."

I had told Jake the same thing the month before, when he'd mentioned our past. He had asked me to drive him to his friend's house, and I'd said yes. But I knew I was taking him to buy drugs. Jake didn't have any friends; he only had people who could do things for him. In fact, one of our childhood friends, who'd also been selling him drugs, had just overdosed and died. Jake even spoke at his funeral.

Even though I knew I was driving Jake to buy heroin, I didn't rat him out to Mom. I was still under his spell. I was still the obedient little sister holding all his secrets.

Out of nowhere, he asked, "So you know all that physical stuff that we did when we were kids—did that affect you?"

I told him the only truth I knew.

"I'm fine," I said. "I'm just mad at you because you're doing drugs and wasting your talent, not because of what happened between us." He seemed satisfied with my answer, and we went back to listening to music.

Sitting on Caleb's couch in my mom's arms, I didn't feel as if I'd been molested or abused. In fact, I didn't feel anything at all. I told myself that Jake had never been violent and had never physically forced me to do anything to him. And since I'd never refused to comply with his commands, I felt some blame for what had happened. The word *molest* didn't seem to apply to me.

In fact, at eighteen, if you'd asked me if I'd been abused by anyone in my family, the answer would have been no. I came from a loving family where we gave hugs and kisses and said "I love you" often. But the memories, seared in my mind, flashed in my head often.

I didn't call it abuse when my mom jumped on top of Jake and beat him in a fit of rage in front of family friends on Christmas Eve. Or when, one night, she attacked him with his skateboard instead of her fists. Or when either one of our parents would make us go to the garage and get the paddle so they could punish us.

I didn't know to call it abuse when my parents were arguing and I saw my dad charge out of the shower and pin my mom against the wall as I ran to get Caleb to break them up. Or when my mom tackled me to the ground, hitting me all over before school in sixth grade, or when she slapped me across the face in junior high for calling her a bitch.

Or the time my mom regrets the most, when she left a handprint-shaped bruise on my three-year-old body after hitting me repeatedly. In that moment, I didn't cry. I simply stared at her. No, I didn't call it abuse back then. But I do now.

GAINING STABILITY

My mom waited in the car while I ventured into my first therapy appointment. In an attempt to care for me, she had scheduled a session with the only counselor she knew—Jake's drug counselor. Unaware of the ethical issues involved with the same therapist seeing two siblings, one of whom had perpetrated sexual abuse against the other, I reluctantly agreed to the appointment.

As I waited for the session to start under the dimly lit room's low ceiling, I wondered if there was enough oxygen to breathe.

"Hi, Brinn, I'm Krista. I'm so glad you're here! Please, take a seat," the therapist said, gesturing to the small couch against the wall. I sat down, annoyed by her overly friendly greeting.

She looked like she was in her thirties, younger than I had imagined she'd be. Her brown glasses and matching cardigan reminded me of a librarian's. Her dirty-blonde hair hung just above her shoulders.

After asking a few basic questions, she narrowed in on the reason I was there.

"Can you tell me how you feel about all this happening with your brother? I imagine it's pretty upsetting," she said, a concerned look on her face.

"I'm fine, really. I'm not that angry," I said robotically. "I'm just mad at him for doing heroin and wasting his talent."

"I understand. And it would make sense for you to be upset about other things too," she said in a soft tone.

"Sure, he's done a lot over the years. But I also don't remember a lot about my childhood, so I don't really know." I shrugged.

"Do you mean you don't remember specific memories with Jake, or in general, you don't remember much about your childhood?"

I curled my legs underneath me and considered how to respond. I didn't like answering direct questions about Jake.

"I've never had a good memory. There are things my family and I argue about because I swear they never happened—like going to a baseball game or taking a family vacation. I see pictures and hear stories but have no idea what everyone's talking about. A lot of my memories are fuzzy or just aren't there."

"Sometimes our bodies try to protect us from remembering things that are overwhelming or uncomfortable. There's a technique called hypnosis where we could try to recall some of your old memories."

I felt as if I were about to puke. I had no interest in trying to find memories my body obviously didn't want me remembering.

In the car after that session, I told my mom about the therapist's offer of hypnosis.

"I don't want to do it." I turned away from her. As I looked out the window, I noticed my distorted reflection in the office building's glass windows staring back at me. "It's gross and embarrassing," I said quietly.

"I understand, honey," she said. "Nobody is forcing you to do anything you don't want to do." She reached out to squeeze my hand.

Suddenly she jerked back and threw her hands in the air. "I'm just so mad at him!"

I snapped my head around.

"Aren't you?" she asked, searching my face.

I crinkled my nose and shrugged. "Yeah, I guess so."

"Don't you just want to yell and scream at him? It's okay to do that, you know!"

This from the woman who had always punished me for getting angry.

She drove away, and we both rolled down the windows and yelled, *"Asshole"* into the ether as we passed through the empty industrial park. There was no one on the street, no other cars on the road. Yelling felt good. It was the only ounce of feeling I could muster.

That same week, Caleb and I decided to tell my dad. He'd been living in the same one-bedroom cottage next to a creek since my parents' divorce seven years prior. However, he'd recently married his longtime girlfriend and was planning to move into her house, thirty minutes away, soon.

On the ride over, Caleb and I discussed our plan.

"How do you feel about being the one to tell Dad what happened?" Caleb asked. "It's your story, and I think it might be empowering for you to say the words."

"Okay," I said, letting out a deep sigh.

I trusted my dad, but finding the words to let him in? That part of me, I didn't trust.

Once we arrived, we all sat around the kitchen table, Dad on one end, leaning forward in his chair, his hands clasped together. I knew I was about to break his heart.

After the divorce, we'd spent our time together taking day trips to the beach, flying kites in the park, and driving along the river. I adored him. But now that it was time to tell him the truth, I froze.

"Dad …" My voice broke. Tears filled my eyes. I took a deep breath. Convincing myself to keep going, I stammered, "Jake … he, uh, molested me when I was young."

My father's eyes grew dark and tearful. He winced, and his already thin lips seemed to disappear.

The dad I had known could fill long car rides with jokes and gentle lectures about the rights and wrongs of the world. But sitting in the kitchen that day, he processed the information silently.

"We told Mom and confronted Jake about it two weeks ago," I said.

Eventually, my father spoke.

"With Jake at home, where have you been staying?" His voice was choked up.

"I've been staying with Caleb some nights, but mostly I've been at the house with Mom and Jake," I said. In retrospect, I have no memory of ever returning to my childhood home after Caleb first asked me *that question*. In my mind, I never went home again.

"You can't be there with him," Dad replied calmly.

"Yeah, I'm beginning to think that too," Caleb said.

"You can stay here with me, as long as you need to," said my dad. "I have that mattress in storage, and we'll get you set up in the living room." He gave me a weary smile and patted my hand. "We'll figure the rest out after we get you situated." My body relaxed and eased into the chair a little more.

Knowing that it wouldn't be easy for my mother to accept my moving out of her house for good, Caleb returned to the house by himself to pack up my things. Soon after that, I was sitting on the couch at my dad's when my cell phone rang. The word *Mom* appeared on the tiny screen. I cringed but answered.

She sounded breathless. "Honey, I don't understand why you're doing this. You said you were fine. Why can't you just live here?"

Every muscle in my body filled with tension. I didn't know how to respond.

Her voice broke. "I deserve more time with my baby before she leaves for college."

"Mom, it's not like that," I said, pushing off from the couch and pacing around the room.

"Yes it is!" she said. "You're running away to your dad, like always! It's not like he was around when you were growing up, but now he gets to be your hero? I'm the one who's always been here. I deserve more time! It's not fair!"

My fingers tightened around the phone. It took all of my strength to keep it in my hand and not smash it against the wall.

"Mom, why are you acting like this!

"Me? I am not doing anything, Brinn!" she screamed. "You're the one who's making this so hard! Don't you understand, I can't kick Jake out! He's sick! He could die!"

I hung up the phone, threw myself on the leather couch, and let out a pained cry.

She'd chosen Jake over me. She'd decided to keep him, my abuser, in my home and had forced me, the victim, to leave. Yet now, somehow, she had turned the tables to make me feel as if I were the one wronging her. I was abandoning her. I was tearing the family apart. Even though I could clearly see that I'd done nothing wrong, the guilt she spewed accentuated my ever-present knowledge that I was a bad daughter.

Luckily, I never felt that way with my dad. As soon as I told him the truth, he started researching on the internet about sibling sexual abuse and even went to library looking for books, though he couldn't find any helpful resources. He also delayed moving in with his wife so I could finish the remainder of the school year with greater stability in my life.

Even though it felt strange to move in with him just four months shy of my high school graduation, it was my only option. We made space for a twin bed in the corner of his living room and created a closet for my clothes on a wire rack. My new stepmother recommended a therapist through the group practice that she'd gone to, and my dad arranged for me to have weekly appointments. The ground underneath me was beginning to solidify.

My new therapist was a fair-skinned blonde woman in her late thirties whose name was Kimberly Langford. Right away, I felt more at ease with Kimberly than I had with Krista. I drove myself to the appointment and felt grateful my mom wasn't involved with this new therapist. In fact, knowing there was no connection to my family at all, and that I could say anything I wanted to her, made me feel comfortable opening up.

Kimberly sat in an armchair next to French doors that opened onto a balcony. A spider plant hung from the ceiling, its tendrils cascading into the space beside her head. I sat on the couch, often with my shoes off, my legs curled underneath me, a plaid pillow resting on my lap.

During the first few months of our weekly sessions, I would relay the latest emotional upheavals and arguments between my mother and me while Kimberly provided space for me to process my feelings for the first time. Tears sometimes rolled down her cheeks as she listened. As I was used to shrugging off my emotions, witnessing her raw, true empathy struck me hard. She demonstrated calm but also sadness, anger, and frustration. I had never seen those intense emotions expressed in gentle ways before.

"You talk about not feeling much right now and being numb. That makes sense. Right now, your body thinks you're in danger, so you're in survival mode," she explained.

I fiddled with the corner of the pillow and nodded.

"Feeling a wide range of emotions isn't necessary for survival. Right now, you just need the ability to get out of bed, feed yourself, and get through your day. Feeling intense emotions could inhibit basic functioning, so your body shuts them down."

"I wish my mom's body would shut down her intense feelings," I said, shooting Kimberly a sideways smirk.

She smiled.

I felt that she and I had developed an unspoken agreement: I didn't say too much about the abuse, and she didn't pry. It was all too fresh to discuss in detail—plus, my memories were blurry, and it was hard to remember specifics.

Then, during one of our later sessions, the topic of Jake came up.

"I don't even know what to think about Jake anymore .... He's just such a different person than I used to know. Honestly, I feel like I stopped knowing him when I was fifteen," I said with a sigh.

"What happened when you were fifteen?" Kimberly asked, leaning forward in her chair.

I looked down, avoiding eye contact.

"Well ... when I was fifteen, I was a freshman and Jake was a senior. He had spent the last two years at boarding school but would come home for holidays and during the summer. I was actually excited when he came home. I wasn't used to living alone with my mom, and I missed having my brothers around. They were always blasting good music and having friends over. Life was just more fun when they were home."

Kimberly nodded along.

I exhaled loudly. "He came home for spring break, and everything was fine. We were both off from school, and I wanted to soak in the hot tub before meeting up with my boyfriend. So without really thinking about it, I went out to the backyard and got into the hot tub. But as soon as I got in there, I started to get a bad feeling."

I had never said these words before, and my heart pounded in my chest. I didn't want her to know the truth, but it seemed to unravel, the words spilling out.

"Within a few minutes, Jake came outside and got into the hot tub too. And that's when I knew I'd made a mistake. We were both naked—because that's what we did in my house. I didn't know what to do. I guess part of me thought we could just be normal. That's what I wanted."

My words trailed off as I stared at the pillow on my lap. My face burned, and my throat tightened. Kimberly patiently waited in the silence.

"And then he asked. He asked me if he could try his new tongue ring on me. You know ... down there." My cheeks turned an even darker shade of red.

Kimberly's eyes widened a little as she nodded in understanding.

"But I told him no. That was the first and only time I ever said no to him."

"Wow," she whispered.

"You know, it's weird." I shifted in my seat. "It was as if we'd come full circle. That hot tub was where it had all started when we were little. But twelve years later, on that day when I was fifteen, it stopped." I sighed. "See, I was on my period, and he came into the hot tub and asked that specific question. If I hadn't been on my period, or if he had asked a different question, I don't think I would have had the strength to say no."

"Interesting," she said slowly. "How did you feel after that day?"

I shrugged. "Mostly the same. I still kept the secret. It's not like I was going to tell anyone or make a big deal out of something that had been happening my entire life."

I paused, still considering her question.

"Sometimes it feels like I've had a veil covering my eyes my whole life. And the day Caleb asked me the question about Jake was the day the veil was ripped off. Suddenly, I saw my life clearly. I finally saw how messed up Jake was. I could start to understand what I'd been through. I had been so depressed most of my life, but before then, it was impossible for me to understand why. I think that day when I was fifteen, part of the veil came off."

"It sounds like the veil was protecting you."

"What do you mean?" I asked.

"Well, this thing kept you from recognizing what was happening to you. It kept your family intact and kept you from feeling super intense feelings like rage, confusion, and even excitement and joy. We've talked about your body protecting you by keeping you numb—your body's been doing that your whole life. So maybe it was more like armor than a veil."

"Armor ... yeah, it does feel like armor. I think the armor allowed me to push away my feelings and continue being Jake's devoted little sister. With that armor, I could be normal—for the most part. But that day in the hot tub, when I said no, a crack appeared in the armor. I didn't feel much different. But that no must have been the beginning of disconnecting from him. I started to not want to be around him. I started not liking him. But I still wasn't able to say why."

Anger rushed through my veins. I sat very still.

"And now I hate him. I want nothing to do with him," I said flatly as heat flooded my body.

"I think your anger makes perfect sense. I am angry for you! And it's totally healthy to feel angry right now."

I didn't admit it then, but I still felt scared of him. I was scared that he would threaten to tell everyone that the abuse was my fault or that he would accuse me of lying about what I knew truly had happened. I didn't want to hear his excuses or sweep everything he'd done under the rug. But most of all, I didn't trust I could hold my ground if I tried to speak my truth to him. My voice didn't feel strong enough to combat his. He still held power over me, and now that my armor was disappearing, the only way to protect myself seemed to be to stay as far away from him as possible.

But at least I felt comfortable and safe in therapy. I deemed these sessions sacred. I didn't even smoke weed before my conversations with Kimberly. While for years it had been normal for me to travel with eye drops and perfume in my purse to mask any evidence of being stoned, I still didn't want to show up high. I respected our time together. Plus, I didn't want her to know I smoked weed.

In general, I'd always been a responsible stoner. I paid for my gas and car insurance with the money I'd earned over the summer, had decent grades, was a team captain, and was on my way to attending college. And since water polo had ended, I'd been working after school at a local coffee shop. But I still spent the rest of my money, and nearly all my free time, thinking about getting high, making plans to get high, or being high. That was how it had been for years. That was the way I liked it. And I was good at hiding.

For the last few months, Tanya and I had relied on a system. Often before school, we'd meet on some lonely backstreet and smoke. Always after school, we'd meet and smoke. And nearly every night, we'd meet and smoke.

Smoking helped me distract myself from the reality of my life. Since I hadn't told anyone outside of my family about the abuse, I could pretend my life was normal when I was smoking with my friends, as if life as I knew it hadn't just collapsed. As if the life I had carefully constructed for myself at school and at home, the life that had included Jake as my brother, still existed.

A few months later, it was time to tell Grace and Tanya what was going on. I didn't feel ready, and I didn't particularly want to, but being honest about my life felt like the right thing to do. I planned a visit for Tanya and me to go visit Grace in Santa Cruz, hoping that telling them at the same time would make it easier.

Over the weekend, we took a walk through the forest. When we found a bench, I sat down in the middle of both of them. My heart seemed to be beating on the exterior of my chest, and my stomach hurt, filled with anxiety and dread; tears blurred my eyes. The words just wouldn't make sense. Telling my friends didn't seem fair, as if I were about to ruin their day, their weekend, their childhood memories, especially Grace's. I hated being a burden to anyone, about anything, and here I was, making this whole trip about me and putting a dark cloud over my best friends.

I didn't want to be the one who had to tell this uncomfortable story. I knew I had to tell them the truth, and yet I was unequipped to talk about it or respond to their reactions. I took a deep breath, and fumbling over my words, I managed to say, "Jake molested me … for a long time. Since I was little."

Not too many words were spoken after that. They didn't know what to say. As soon as I told them, I immediately wanted the words back in my mouth. I regretted sharing life-altering news with both of them at the same time. Whenever I'm in groups, I can never quite open up the same way I can in a one-on-one situation. It feels too exposing, and I have less control over what multiple people think about what I'm saying.

I wish I'd told them separately so I could have felt more comfortable talking about what was happening. The plan had been to kill two birds with one stone, but now it felt like it was killing me inside.

We sat in that moment of silence until I said, "So does anyone want to smoke a joint?" As we returned to Grace's dorm, I assured my friends that I was fine. At eighteen years old, they didn't know how to respond to my disclosure, but even if they had known, I'm not sure I was willing, or able, to have those vulnerable conversations with my friends yet.

A few weeks later I received a letter in the mail from Grace, expressing the feelings she couldn't say. She thanked me for my honesty and revealed her gratitude for the support Caleb and Victoria had given me. She encouraged me by telling me how amazing and strong I was, and she told me that it was important to work through the pain and not just suppress it. Although, admittedly, she didn't know what that looked like, she was clear that she wanted me to get help. She also said that it helped explain so much of what I had struggled with in the past, and why I'd hurt myself in many ways. She made sure to say that she wasn't judging or blaming me for anything and that this new information didn't change the way she viewed me or our relationship. She closed by saying how much she loved me and that she would always be there for me, no matter what.

Reading the letter, I knew Grace was being incredibly genuine and sweet, and yet I only felt surface-level emotions. I wasn't ready to let her words infiltrate my armor. Underneath, I was still telling myself that I was fine and that everything was going to be fine. I didn't want to spend time thinking about being molested, and from then on, Grace and I hardly talked about it.

Note: *This chapter depicts twelve years of sexual abuse. If you wish to skip this chapter for whatever reason, please know that it will not impact the integrity of the story.*

MY FIRST MEMORIES

Old memories flashed in my mind. Only a few stood out; others were blurry. It felt foreign for these images to float around my brain. I had never allowed myself to think about them before.

The hot tub. The shower. Different rooms around the house. Bits and pieces of disjointed images tried to come together like mismatching puzzle pieces. The ages didn't match up. The scenes didn't always make sense.

I'd always known it had started outside in the hot tub when we were really young, maybe around four or five? Back then, the hot tub was where our family gathered. All six of us would pile inside the steaming, chlorinated water, laughing and splashing, free to be ourselves, fully naked and exposed. When we had friends over, we'd put on bathing suits. But I always found them to be too tight and restrictive compared to how I felt when I was just with my family.

I instinctively knew that what Jake and I were doing was wrong. But I trusted him, and so I always did what he wanted me to. Plus, when it was just us, I felt special.

I remembered the bathroom where we'd showered together, fairly often. That room didn't exist until I was seven or eight, when my family renovated our garage. But what Jake and I were doing had started long before then, and wouldn't end until long after.

Standing in my blue-and-white floral pajamas, the ones my mom had given me for Christmas that year, I watched her preparing our lunches for school. On the far side of the kitchen, my brothers sat at the white Formica table eating breakfast. As a wave of horror washed over me, nausea swam through my stomach. *What if I'm pregnant?* I thought as my young mind tried to make sense of the sickness I felt. I was eight. I wasn't old enough to know that what Jake and I were doing couldn't result in a baby. But my stomach hurt. My head throbbed. I felt exhausted. I didn't want to go to school.

Sometime after that day, he stopped coming to me, and my memories of the abuse faded into the crevices of my mind. But during my parents' separation and eventual divorce, as Jake became my babysitter, alone with me for hours on end, it didn't take long for the abuse to start up again.

We never talked much about what we did together, but what he did say, I remember clearly.

"You know, other siblings do this too. It's normal. But don't tell anyone about it. Not even your husband when you get married," Jake told me after coaxing me into his bedroom under the pretense of showing me his new CD.

Even then, I knew he was full of shit. I wanted to believe him, that we were normal, and that other siblings did what we did. But I didn't trust him.

When I was about twelve, I was hanging out in my room with a friend when Jake opened my door, just an inch.

"Hey, someone's on the phone for you," he said, his eyes lowered.

"That's weird," I mumbled as I stood up. "I didn't hear the phone ring."

Obediently, I followed him out of my room, down the hall, through the kitchen, through the laundry room, and into my mom's empty bedroom. Then he turned around, his hard penis already out of his pants. Without a word, I did my job. Disconnected. Numb. Armored up. I walked back to my friend in my room as if nothing had happened.

Jake soon became blatant about when and where he wanted sexual attention. Sometimes it happened outside at the school next door, sometimes at our grandparents' houses. He even touched me while I pretended to sleep, hoping he would stop. He often wanted to watch pornography together, and each time I logged on to our shared computer in the kitchen, I found myself bombarded by graphic images popping up from every direction.

Unsupervised, we started smoking weed together, and soon sexual abuse and smoking had entirely replaced the creative games of our early childhood. As soon as Mom told us her plans for the day, and that Jake would be in charge while she was gone, I already knew what he was thinking: *How long would she be gone? Did we have enough time to smoke or only enough time for "other things"?* We'd sit by the front door, waiting until her car had disappeared down the street—then he would take out either his penis or the weed.

The most important rule I developed for myself was this: *Never initiate anything sexual with Jake.* In fact, even when I was dating, I never initiated anything sexual with anyone. I never wanted anyone to think that I desired anything sexual from them. Allowing things to happen to me seemed safer than actively going after what I wanted.

At eighteen, once I started looking back on my childhood, I started to understand why I felt uncomfortable, scared even, to be alone with older guys. It always felt as if I were running from them, then just barely escaping without anything bad happening to me. When I was younger I used to think, *Are they going to ask me to do it too? Can't they tell?* I thought for sure everyone could see the red stamp on my forehead that read "I suck dick."

A FRESH START

I stood in the parking lot and watched my dad's cream-colored 1985 Mercedes-Benz drive away. Letting out an audible sigh of relief colored with apprehension, I turned around to walk back to my new dorm.

All around me, students and their families were carrying boxes, lamps, and bedding. Across the courtyard, Tanya and her family were also saying goodbye. She and I hadn't planned on going to the same college, let alone living across the courtyard from each other, but I was excited to have my old friend close by. I breathed in the fresh air and looked around.

Even though I was only two hours from where I grew up, I felt a million miles away. Just on the other side of the school buildings were rolling hills covered in dry golden grass and rows of grapevines. Cows grazed in these open spaces, and turkey vultures soared high above them. Over the sounds of talking families, I heard birds chirping. I noticed just how blue the sky was here. After four months of staying in my father's living room and two months of sleeping in a cramped cabin with eight other girls in Colorado, it felt grounding to finally land somewhere I could call home.

Over the past six months, the divide between my family—with my dad and Caleb on one side and my mom and Jake on the other—had only continued to grow. My sister stayed out of the conflict. She was still living in our hometown but busy raising her young child and supporting her husband, who'd started a local church.

In an instant, all of our lives had permanently changed. We were now a family in turmoil. The close connection Caleb and I had always shared only grew deeper as he shouldered more responsibility for my well-being. But when we were together, all we could seem to talk about was the fighting within our family. We both needed a break from this looming storm, and I needed my freedom. Moving two hours away would help me start not only a new chapter but also, I hoped, an entirely new life.

Due to my strained relationship with my mom, I only received money for tuition, and even that was a hassle. My dad sent me a couple hundred dollars a month, which wasn't much to live on, so my first priority was to search for a job on campus. The university's outdoor adventure program was rumored to only hire upperclassmen, but given my experience in Colorado, I applied anyway—and got hired. Soon I was hanging out with the rock climbers, yogis, and activists on campus, the ones who used reusable everything and only ate local, raw, vegan foods.

"Are you coming to the talk on climate change tonight?" asked Christina, one of my new coworkers. She was dressed in a dark-brown knit sweater half covering a shirt that read "I love you—yes you" and a flowy beige skirt with matching Birkenstocks. She was one of the sweetest people I'd met, always with a big grin on her face. She seemed to drift, float even, from one space to another, happily enjoying the present moment.

"Yup! I'll see you there," I responded. I didn't exactly know what climate change was, but I was excited that she'd invited me to come with her.

At that talk, I learned about the factory farming industry and its negative impact on animals, our environment, and our bodies. At the same time, I learned about the copious amount of fresh local food that farmers in our area were growing.

"The best way to lower your environmental footprint and help the health of our planet is to focus on a locally sourced vegetarian diet," the speaker said, addressing the crowd of about a hundred students.

Inspired, I thought, *I can do that! I'll become a vegetarian!*

Taking small, everyday actions, like riding my bike to the local market and purchasing food from local farmers, made me feel proud. I felt a sense of purpose, knowing I was able to make a difference in the local economy and for our environment. My new healthy behaviors empowered me; soon they became habits, leading me to greater self-awareness and healthier choices. Finally, I felt I was living *my* life.

One weekend in early fall, Grace came to visit. We went out for a walk, and to smoke, and I suggested, "Let's go out to the sports fields and throw the Frisbee."

Growing up, we'd spent summer days throwing the Frisbee down by the river with our brothers. At camp, I'd played a sport called ultimate Frisbee, similar to soccer or basketball but with a Frisbee.

Grace's older brother had played ultimate Frisbee on his college men's team, and this was Grace's first year playing on her college women's team. As with any other competitive sport, she traveled to tournaments regularly and practiced three times a week. Grace told me about how her team learned offenses and defenses and created strategic plays, how they had team captains, team functions, team meetings, and team roles. From her, I learned that "ultimate" (as she called it) was a community, a family, and a way of life.

Wandering over to the fields, we saw a handful of guys throwing their Frisbee around. They looked more serious than just a few friends getting together.

"Hey, is this a team or something?" I asked as we approached.

"Yup, we're the men's ultimate team," one of the guys answered cheerfully. He was a stout man with a young face, about my height and wearing shorts and a ragged white T-shirt. Walking over, he extended his hand.

"Hi, I'm Colin, team captain."

Grace and I introduced ourselves, and I explained our connection to the sport.

"Nice! We've only been around for a year or so, but we go to tournaments sometimes. We even have a girl who plays with us too—her name's Sam," he said.

"Wow! That's so cool!" I felt as if I had just won the lottery. Ever since Grace had started playing in college, I wanted to play too. It seemed like this might be my chance. "When do you think Sam will be around next?"

"She should be at practice on Monday. I think she has class today."

"Okay, great. Same time on Monday?" I asked.

"Yup, we'll be here. And if you do come out, make sure to bring a light shirt, a dark shirt, cleats, and a water bottle—you'll need it." His smile grew even bigger.

On Monday, I arrived with both shirts, a water bottle, and running shoes. I'd never played a sport that required cleats before, so I didn't know where to find them.

"Hi, I'm Sam," a tall brunette with a friendly smile said as she walked up to me on the field.

"Nice to meet you, I'm Brinn. I heard you're the only girl who plays with these guys."

"I am. They're pretty fun once you get to know them. It can be hard keeping up, but they like it when I stay back and handle the Frisbee instead of running around downfield."

I nodded along as if I totally understood what she was saying.

"Are you girls going to just stand there and chitchat all day, or are you going to come play?" Colin asked in a teasing tone.

Sam rolled her eyes. "Don't mind him," she assured me. "Since we're going to scrimmage, how about I play on one team, and you play on the other. That way we can guard each other, and I can show you what to do."

"Sounds good!" I said, eager to join her.

At seventy yards long and forty yards across, the field looked like a minifootball field. Small orange cones marked the boundaries, and there were end zones at both ends. I knew enough to know that I couldn't run with the Frisbee, and that the only way I could score a goal was by catching the Frisbee in the end zone.

"Hey, new girl," one of the guys said, gesturing to me.

"Yeah?" I responded.

"Try to stay in the middle of the field. That's the best way to stay out of the way, okay?" he said, turning his attention back to the field. I didn't like his tone.

Just then, from seventy yards away, a player on the other team launched a long throw all the way to our side of the field, kicking off the game. We ran to the middle of the field, where suddenly I found myself lost within a vortex of sprinting men.

"Hey! Hey! Hey! I'm open! Throw the disc!" they yelled as they sprinted toward the guy with the Frisbee.

For a moment, I felt lost and confused.

Then Sam ran up to me. "Just stay in the middle for now until you get the hang of it."

As I watched the Frisbee fly back and forth among the players, I realized nobody was running toward the end zone. *Isn't the whole point to score in the end zone?* I thought.

I continued to observe my teammates passing the Frisbee back and forth to each other. Suddenly, I saw an opening. I wanted to lose my defender, so with a little zigzag configuration, I took off downfield, my feet flying over the thick green grass.

My legs knew exactly what to do. Even though I grew up as a swimmer, running had always been a passion of mine. I'd been the fastest girl in elementary school and ran track in junior high. Plus, going for runs around the neighborhood had been a great way to get out of the house and satisfy my never-ending desire to punish my body for what I perceived as being too overweight.

Glancing over my shoulder, I saw the white disc flying in the air above all the players' heads. It was coming down fast. I tracked it—right into my hands—as I crossed into the end zone. GOAL!

The whole field erupted in shouts. "Wow!" "Great job!" "Awesome!" Sam, who'd been trailing behind me, finally caught up with me.

"Nice move!" she said, out of breath as she held her hand up for a high five.

"Thanks," I responded cooly, trying not to show her how excited I felt.

After that practice, Sam offered to take me shopping for cleats, and I gladly accepted. As we walked away, Colin ran over to us. "So we're all going to a tournament in a few weeks. If you wanted to come and play, you're welcome to."

I nodded as he continued, "Since we don't have a lot of players going, we're going to team up with the junior college team that's right up the road. So it would be five or six of us and then five or six of them."

"Okay! Thanks!" This time I actually showed my enthusiasm. As I let Sam and Colin hear my excitement, I felt as if I were beginning a new life, the one I had been searching for.

***

At 7:00 on Saturday morning, we arrived at the expansive sports fields of UC Santa Cruz. A dense fog hung in the air, and we could hardly see the orange cones set up on each of the ultimate fields. By the time I finished warming up, my new cleats were soaking wet.

"Always bring lots of socks to a tournament," Sam had instructed me when I asked her what to pack. This had to be the reason why.

I was sitting on my bag to avoid getting my pants wet when I noticed a group of guys walking toward our team.

"Well, good morning, y'all," one of them said as he walked around and slapped hands with all of my teammates. *This must be the junior college team*, I thought.

"What a beautiful day to play some ultimate!" he said, taking an exaggeratedly deep breath in. "Ahhh, I just love that sea air. Now this," he said, draping his arm around the shoulder of one of my teammates and gesturing widely with his other hand, "this is the reason I came all the way out here from Kentucky. Well, this and the great California herb, of course." He laughed.

I smiled. He was kind of cute with his floppy brown hair that hung right above his bright-blue eyes. He was wearing a funky hat with an orange plastic brim. I had seen quite a few unusual fashion choices on the fields already. Many girls, and even some guys, were wearing brightly colored skirts. I noticed a lot of spray-painted T-shirts. Some teams, who looked as if they had themes, had arrived all dressed up in costumes. I wasn't sure what this sport was all about yet, but I liked it.

I kept on observing the teams gathering around me. Some players stretched on their own, while others took warm-up laps together. On the field, there were players throwing Frisbees and small groups talking and laughing. The mood felt lighter, more playful than the serious water polo tournaments I had competed in throughout high school.

After the first game, I already felt exhausted. The sheer amount of running involved in this ninety-minute game astonished me. While it might have felt less serious than a water polo tournament, ultimate required the same level of athleticism as any competition I'd been a part of.

After the fourth game, everything hurt. My calves had already cramped up twice while I was running, my arches felt as if they were about to give way, and I was afraid to take off my cleats because I was sure all my toes were bleeding.

Hobbling, I made my way over to the sidelines to rest. I had figured out that the cute Southern boy's name was Ben, and now I was watching him and one of his teammates making a direct line toward the cliffs at the far edge of the field. Momentarily turning back to face our team, he held up a small velvet bag and waved it around tantalizingly. "If anyone wants to join us for this beautiful sunset, speak now or forever hold your peace ...." his singsong voice trailed off. I shrugged and decided my body could handle walking over to the cliff's edge.

Halfway through the day, the fog had lifted to reveal the most breathtaking view of the ocean I had ever seen. Now I was walking high up on the bluffs overlooking the small town of Santa Cruz as a deep-blue color spread out as far as my eyes could see. I knew the sunset would be amazing, and even more so if I was sitting next to a cute boy and partaking in his California herb.

Climbing over the edge of the cliff, I saw Ben and his teammate Steve. I sat down hesitantly next to Ben.

"Hey, great playing out there today," he said.

"Thanks. It's my first time, so I didn't really know what I was doing," I said, picking at the blades of grass.

"I mean, I think you knew what you were doing far more so than half those guys out there." He passed me the pipe. "Ladies first," he said, smiling wide. It was a kind smile, one that I could trust.

We made eye contact, and our fingers touched as he handed me the pipe. Chills ran down my spine. I quickly looked away, focusing on the task at hand.

"You know, we practice up at the junior college a couple times a week, and we have another girl who comes out there sometimes too. And there are pickup games on the weekends, so if you want, there's lots of opportunities to play," he said casually.

"How long have you been playing?" I asked.

"This is my third year. I moved out here after high school, and I'm starting my third year at junior college. After this year, I'm transferring right here." He patted the ground. "Then after that, who knows. Maybe I'll even stick around and get my PhD."

"Oh wow, that's cool," I said, impressed by both his determination and his long-term goals.

"Yeah, there's nothing like this where I come from, so why would I stay there when I could come here? It was easy enough to take out student loans and get the classes I need, so why not live in paradise?" He leaned back on his hands, admiring the view of the sea in front of us.

My mind processed his words. Even though he was obviously a few years older than I was, he sounded so grown up, as if he had everything figured out. He knew what he wanted, and he went after it. Suddenly, my cheeks grew warm, and I felt too shy to talk.

"Uh-huh," I mumbled. I looked out over the ocean that was quickly changing colors in the setting sun. *Would someone that put together ever be interested in someone like me?* I wondered. So far this school year, I'd continued my trend of casually dating multiple guys, and I hadn't taken it too far with any of them. Yet recently I'd begun feeling as though I was ready for something more serious, someone I could commit to. I hadn't had a long-term relationship since Austin back in freshman year. Ben's voice interrupted my thoughts.

"So do you have somewhere to stay tonight?" He gestured toward Steve next to him. "We didn't make it that far in the process, but you know, I've come to find that things have a way of working out."

"Yeah, actually, I'm staying with my best friend, Grace. She's on the women's team here and has an apartment on campus. I'll ask if you two can crash."

I pulled out my phone and sent a quick text, to which she responded positively.

"Sweet! Looks like we're roommates!" Ben said.

"I guess so," I replied, laughing.

By the end of the weekend, Ben and I had exchanged numbers and planned to go together to a party that my ultimate team was hosting the following weekend. The theme was stereotypes, so I dressed up very out of character, as a preppy Southern California girl wearing flashy jewelry I'd borrowed from Tanya and caked-on makeup. After the party, as we were walking to his car, Ben said, "So there's a pickup game tomorrow morning if you want to go with me." He suggested shyly, "You could spend the night, and we could go together, no pressure or anything. I can sleep on the couch if you want!"

I laughed. I already felt safe with him, but I wasn't going to sleep with him. I would stick to the rules I had created for myself long ago: Sex was special. I would reserve it for special people and special occasions. It was the only thing I trusted myself to say no to when it came to physical intimacy.

"I'm happy to spend the night and go to the pickup game in the morning, and no, you don't need to sleep on the couch—but we're not going to have sex. When I say I'll sleep over, I actually mean *sleep over,*" I said with a flirtatious smile.

"Works for me!" he agreed, ushering me to his car.

That Friday night date turned into not only a Saturday morning pickup game but also a Sunday morning pickup game. These weekends together quickly became our routine, a routine which grew to include weekday practices with the team at my college and with his junior college team too.

Ben was obsessed with ultimate, and I jumped on the ultimate bandwagon with him, playing any chance I could. He belonged to a community that extended beyond his junior college, a community consisting of older men and women who'd graduated from schools like UC Berkeley, Stanford, and UCLA. They were doctors and scientists who had won college championships, started teams, and founded their own communities. These mentors were not afraid to coach me or to impart their wisdom; in fact, they were excited to see my enthusiasm for the sport. Having seen many college teams form and crumble over the years, they eventually encouraged me to step up and create my own women's team.

The idea of starting my own team was both thrilling and terrifying. On the one hand, I longed to play on a field with people my own size and speed. Playing with and against all-women's teams would help me grow into my full potential as a player, yet I didn't know who would be interested in joining or what practices should be like. I'd never started a team before. While the prospect seemed daunting, with the support of Sam, Ben, and my mentors, I felt ready to take the next logical step forward.

That spring, I started planning small informal practices, inviting Sam and a few other women on campus. We threw the Frisbee around and practiced drills I'd learned from Ben and my other unofficial coaches. One of my mentors donated her collection of Frisbees to our new players so they could own their own discs for the first time. Even though we never attracted enough players to fully scrimmage, our numbers remained consistent, and my faith that our women's team could become a reality was growing.

FEELING HOMELESS

"I am just sick and tired of dealing with you, Brinn!" my mother shouted at me through the phone.

I had offended her by not responding to a text message she'd sent back when she was in a good mood. Her anger had obviously escalated.

"Never in my life have I been treated so terribly by someone. After everything I've done for you, what do I get in return? Nothing. You're just a heartless bitch when it comes to me. Everyone else gets happy, chipper Brinn, but not me."

Fire rose up from my belly and shot through my limbs. But my voice stayed silent.

"You think you had the worst childhood ever, and you blame it all on me," she seethed. "Don't you ever get tired of pointing the finger at me? You need to grow up and see what a spoiled, ungrateful brat you are!"

Fuzzy dots appeared in my vision, and I felt tingling in my hands.

"Mom, I'm getting a migraine. Bye." I hung up quickly. At least I'd discovered an excuse to get off the phone.

A few moments later, my phone buzzed with a text.

"Drink lots of water and be sure to eat something. Are you taking those herbal supplements I gave you?"

I scoffed. One minute she hated me, and the next she wanted to make sure I was taking the vitamins she'd researched and ordered for me. Her unpredictability endlessly confused me.

The walls I had built against her were miles high, but the emotions left within me were even stronger. It was as if our wounds never healed before the next bout. Every infraction between us produced a volcanic eruption.

I felt we were reaching an impasse. Neither of us knew how to maneuver around each other. We each desperately wanted to feel seen and heard by the other, and yet we both felt justified in our resentment. Only looking back can I see that through all of our arguing and provoking, at the very core was our deep longing for each other.

Part of me wanted nothing more than to sweep all the tension between us under the rug and move on, as I had so many times when I was growing up. But I couldn't. That wasn't an option anymore. Too much had changed. Too many truths had been revealed. The only way out of the fire was through it.

As I continued to feel the aftermath of my mother's explosion, I felt obligated to tell Ben about the abuse I'd endured in my childhood. I trusted him because I knew, on some level, he'd understand. Growing up, in addition to his two biological siblings, his parents also fostered children and adopted three siblings who had been addicted to drugs and abused in their biological families. Due to the erratic behavior of the traumatized children inside the home, he lived in chaos and often had to deal with violent outbursts and intense emotional situations.

When I told him about the abuse, he didn't ask too many questions, but he was understanding and kind. I explained why my relationship with my mom was so tumultuous and why my emotions remained raw. I was noticing, however, that big feelings were starting to stir inside me, as if slowly waking from a lifetime of slumber. I never knew when the next burst of anger, grief, or fear would hit me.

As summer approached, my anxiety only increased. When my college friends talked about their summer plans back in their hometowns, I felt homeless. For the first time in eight years, I would not be traveling to Colorado, and returning home felt impossible.

I'd tried visiting home during the holidays, but reuniting with my family proved too hard. On the first Christmas since I revealed the abuse Jake had inflicted on me, my mom still insisted that Jake take part in all of our celebrations. I wasn't strong enough to protest, so I armored myself up, once again. Just like usual, we all pretended that nothing was wrong, even though we were all aware that Jake was still using heroin and that he had abused me throughout my childhood.

To cope with those holidays, I kept my wine glass filled. We'd never had wine in the house before, but this time, Caleb made sure there was something to ease the tension. But pushing my feelings aside was exhausting, and I didn't think I could keep it up. I just wanted normalcy, stability, a home. I longed for my childhood days of waking up in my own room, in my own bed. I missed decorating our house, stringing up lights, and listening to Christmas carols. I didn't want to sleep on Caleb's couch or at my dad and stepmom's new house. I wanted the cozy house that I had grown up in, and the family I had grown up with, but that life was ripped away.

Never again would I feel the comfort of a crackling fire in our living room while we all showed each other the new gifts we'd received. Never would we all spend time with each other, laughing and joking as we sang along boisterously to holiday songs. Never would we feel like a family, together as one. Those days were gone.

Now, unable to return home over the summer and knowing I couldn't return to my dorm on campus until school started again, I asked Ben if I could stay with him. He happily agreed. So I spent the summer living with Ben and his roommate. We'd all grown close, creating our own little family, traveling all over California playing club (noncollege) ultimate tournaments. I wanted to play constantly, and when I wasn't playing, I wanted to throw, and when I wasn't throwing, I was strategizing. As soon as sophomore year began, I officially started the Women's Ultimate Team at my school.

All over campus, I posted recruitment flyers reading "Real chicks play with discs," featuring a picture of a girl diving for a Frisbee. I hosted informational meetings and social events. I organized travel to tournaments, wrote cheers, coached practices, and hosted team dinners. With only a small number of committed players, I automatically turned any conversation with a fellow female student into a recruitment pitch. But I wasn't only recruiting teammates; I was also recruiting friends.

I'd spent so much time playing ultimate and hanging out with Ben that I hadn't made a lot of friends on campus. I also hadn't continued my outdoor adventure job on campus because it interfered with my class and practice schedule. I did, however, find a new job off campus at an outdoor retail store.

"Hey, I'm starving! Does anyone want to go get some food?" I asked one day after practice. Having played so much ultimate, I'd lost weight since high school. Being able to take control, buying and eating healthy food, had also made a big difference in how I felt about my body. That being said, it still pained me to look in a mirror.

Five pairs of eyes avoided mine. "Uh, I have to go take a shower and then do a bunch of homework," one of the girls said, getting on her bike.

"Yeah, me too," another said, gathering her things and putting them in her bag.

"Sorry, I have class," Sam said, giving me a hug before she left.

"That's okay." I plastered a smile on my face. "If you want to throw around in the quad tomorrow, I'll be there in the afternoon between classes. Then, on Wednesday night, there's pickup, and I'm leaving here at 6:30 p.m. if anyone wants a ride," I reminded the group for the hundredth time.

No one seemed to be paying attention.

"See you Friday for practice!" I called out to their retreating backs.

Someone had forgotten her water bottle near where we'd set up our orange cones, so I jogged over, picked it up, and threw it in my bag for her. Gazing out over the empty fields, I watched what was left of the sunset fade behind the hills. A cold breeze hit my sweat-covered skin, sending a shiver through my body. *Why doesn't anyone like me? Why don't I have any friends?* The small familiar voice in my head felt particularly loud that evening.

I took off my cleats and stuffed everything into my bag. Taking one last look around, making sure I wasn't leaving anything behind, I walked back to my dorm. Checking my phone, I saw a text from Ben. My heart lit up as I quickly read it. "I hope you had a great practice! Did anyone new come out?"

Ben had left for UC Santa Cruz in September. Prior to that, we had been solidly together for nine months. However, from the beginning of our relationship, we had agreed that we weren't going to attempt a long-distance relationship. I didn't want to hold him back from enjoying a full college experience, and I also didn't want to risk him rejecting me if I asked him to stay together.

Still, when it was time for him to leave for Santa Cruz, I felt heartbroken. We went a month without talking to each other so he could acclimate himself to his new space, but one night he called me in tears. Professing his love for me, he asked me to be his girlfriend again.

"Oh, honey, I miss you too," I said, overcome with excitement, both flattered and confused. While part of me was happy, I was also in disbelief. I hadn't imagined him spending his first month away at school sitting around thinking of me. I'd thought he'd been out meeting people and making new friends, as I'd been.

By the time he called me, I'd already hooked up with one guy and realized my longtime attraction to women was more than just a secret from elementary school. Seemingly out of nowhere, everywhere I turned, there were beautiful women—on the ultimate team, in my classes, or just walking through campus—and I had no idea what to do with this new attraction.

But on the phone with Ben, my heart ached for the familiar comfort of his love. It didn't seem logical to turn down a safe, stable relationship for the scary unknown. The small voice in my head, urging me to think this through and make sure it was what I really wanted, was silenced by my resounding yes to his question. Of course I would be his girlfriend again!

Although I do believe that all events in our lives happen for a reason, and I am very grateful for the years that Ben and I went on to spend together, part of me has always wondered how different my college experience would have been if I'd made a different choice that day—a choice grounded in feeling empowered to live my own life, with confidence in myself and my future. I can't say my decision to be with Ben was rooted in that place. While I did love and care for him deeply, and have been forever changed by our relationship, at the core of my decision was a deep desperation to be wanted, accepted, and loved.

As I walked back to my dorm, I responded to his text. "No newcomers, but we're getting consistent numbers. I'm going to walk across the street and get a burrito. Wish you were here." I didn't want to tell him about the team not going to dinner with me. He wouldn't understand. He was usually the life of the party.

That night, while I was drifting off to sleep in my dorm room, my phone rang. *Mom* flashed on the screen. Worried that something might be wrong, I answered.

"Hi, honey," she said, sounding sad.

"Hey, Mom, what's up?" I asked, practically holding my breath.

"Oh, nothing," she said slowly. "I'm just worried, that's all."

I contemplated taking her bait.

"What are you worried about, Mom?" I asked almost robotically. Hook, line, and sinker.

"I'm just worried about your brother, that's all." She sighed. "He's in really bad shape, Brinn."

I stayed silent as her voice became more emphatic.

"You know, he just hates himself so much. I just wish you would talk to him and forgive him! Or at least yell at him and tell him how you feel. You shutting him out is so hard on him."

The thought of having any contact with Jake made me want to crawl into a hole and never come out. I would be lying if I said I had forgiven him—forgiveness was a concept I had no interest in entertaining.

She paused, then spoke again, her voice quiet. "I'm afraid he's going to kill himself if you don't forgive him."

I had no words. The guilt I felt was almost too much to bear. But her tactics had worked. I wasn't even angry at her. I just felt deflated.

"I'm sorry, Mom" was all I could muster.

Ending the phone call, I curled into a ball as my armor cracked under the weight of my brother's life. I wept. *If he dies, it's all my fault! I'm the only person who can save him, and I'm choosing not to. What's wrong with me? I'm terrible for wishing him dead, but I can't help it. What a relief that would be—for him and for me. I hate all of this. I wish it would all just go away!*

I picked up the phone and called Ben. He comforted me as I cried, assuring me that what my mom had said wasn't true.

"Baby, none of this is your fault. Your mom is just being your mom. She doesn't even realize what she's saying."

On some level, I knew he was right, but the guilt was hard to shake. I was too exhausted to talk about it anymore, but he stayed on the phone with me until we both fell asleep.

RUNNING AWAY

That December, Ben and I celebrated our one-year anniversary.

"I was thinking we could go to a bathhouse in downtown Santa Cruz next weekend," Ben suggested over the phone. "We'd have our own private spa, just for us. How does that sound?"

I smiled and swooned. "That sounds amazing." I loved that he took events like my birthday and our anniversaries so seriously. I knew he really cared about me.

"Good. Then I'll book it."

On the day of our anniversary, we rode the bus from his on-campus apartment into town and arrived at a tucked-away location that reminded me of a Japanese tea garden. Once inside the spa, I marveled at how quiet it was. Soft, tranquil music played throughout the building, and I could hear the relaxing sound of running water emanating from the many features of the space. A tall, slender middle-aged woman greeted us as we entered.

"Good evening," she said in a soothing voice. "May I help you?"

"Yes, we're checking in for our 6:30 p.m. reservation," Ben said.

"Okay, Ben? For two? Is that correct?"

"Yes, that's us," he said, glancing over at me. I grinned widely. I was looking forward to indulging in this time and relaxing with him. Between school, practices, and tournaments, we could both use a soak in the tub. Plus, I had never been invited on such a romantic date before.

"Follow me," she said, gliding out from behind the desk. We followed her as we snaked our way through the hallway, passing by numerous closed doors. Finally, she stopped, unlocked a door, and opened it wide.

Ben entered, and I followed. Inside waited a beautiful dimly lit shower area with two showerheads facing each other on the walls. Next to the shower area stood a black toilet and matching sink. Just outside on a deck lay a wooden hot tub protected by a circular wooden fence. Growing just outside the wooden fence were trees and jungle vines, colorful flowers, and green ferns. The tranquil music made its way from the lobby into our private suite as well.

After giving us a short tour of the space, the woman left us on our own, closing the door behind her.

Eager to get started, Ben and I undressed, rinsed off in the shower as she had instructed, and tiptoed excitedly to the hot tub. The water was hotter than I was used to, and it took a few minutes to adjust.

"This feels so nice," I said once I was able to fully submerge myself.

"It does feel good." He leaned his head back against the edge of the tub.

Slowly, we drifted toward one another. He reached out, gently caressing my arms, then running his fingers down my back.

"Mmmmmm, I'm so glad we're here," I said softly, letting my hands wander across the water.

He leaned over and kissed my lips, softly at first, then with growing intensity. Suddenly, as if someone had flipped a light switch, I felt repulsed, disgusted by him. My heart seemed to beat outside of my chest. *I'm trapped*, I thought. I frantically searched for an escape.

"I have to pee," I mumbled as I scrambled out of the water.

Inside the bathroom, I felt the cold slate rock under my feet. *Something's wrong! What's wrong?* I could barely breathe. Then I froze. Hot tingles flashed through my body. Rage filled me. *I can't trust him. He's using me for my body. He doesn't even like me or care about me. I hate him!* I was drowning.

Breathing hard, I tried to calm myself. I didn't know what to do. I couldn't go back out there, but I also couldn't stay in the bathroom forever. I wanted to leave this place and run home, but my legs wouldn't move, my jaw couldn't unhinge, and I had no words. I questioned my sanity, feeling logic slipping away.

Eventually, Ben came looking for me. He found me sitting on the toilet. My body jumped when I saw him.

"Hey," he said hesitantly, "is everything okay?"

I avoided eye contact.

"What's wrong?"

I couldn't begin to tell him what was wrong; all I knew was that I wanted nothing to do with him, and I didn't know why.

Ben tried everything to get me to talk, but all I could do was stare into space while giving a few affirming grunts and a quick nod. I was simultaneously hyperaware of the world around me and unable to interact with any of it.

The silent bus ride home echoed our date's abrupt ending. Collapsing on his bed, I pulled my knees up to my chest and wrapped my arms around them as tightly as I could.

Ben moved in and out the room, trying to make me as comfortable as possible. I continued to stare into nothingness, my mind pinballing every which way. Slowly, after what felt like hours, rational thoughts began to form, and my anger at him turned into burning hatred for myself and searing shame.

I'm such a terrible girlfriend. He tried so hard to make our night special, and I couldn't even look at him, let alone talk to him. I'm so fucked up. What's wrong with me? I ruin everything! Now he thinks I am crazy. Maybe I am crazy! Why is this happening to me?

It would take me years to understand why fooling around in a hot tub would cause such a panicked response in me. I was experiencing a post-traumatic stress disorder episode, and my nervous system had gone into survival mode to protect me from a familiar scene. Consciously, I knew I was safe with Ben; subconsciously, my body was reacting to what it thought was dangerous. But back then, I had no idea why I'd run away from Ben, and I simply concluded that I was the problem.

We never talked about that night. I imagine Ben was a lot more aware of how my trauma was impacting me than I was. He saw the connection between my behavior and my trauma, but at the time, I didn't.

A few months later, after noticing my growing crush on a girl in one of my classes, I opened up to Ben about my evolving sexuality. He was understanding and encouraged me to keep exploring my desires, so we agreed to open up our relationship but continue to keep each other as our primary partners.

At the last tournament of the school year, Ben returned to Santa Cruz after Saturday's games while I stayed with my team at a teammate's family's house. In our text conversation that evening, Ben mentioned that his team hadn't played well, and he was feeling pretty discouraged about it.

His last message stated that he was planning on staying in that night and having his "oline over to hang out." Reading that text, I felt as if my guts were falling out of my throat.

The weekend before that, he'd gone to a concert, danced with some girl, and kissed her good night. I felt comfortable with their interaction when he told me, but with this one text, my trust in him turned to dust.

I lay in my sleeping bag wide awake, tossing and turning, convinced that the girl from the concert was named "Oline." I pictured her comforting and consoling him after his long day. I felt betrayed, excluded. *She'd make such a better girlfriend than I am. Of course he wants to be with her instead of me. I'm crazy!*

I felt guilty for caring because if we were truly in an open relationship, then I should be okay with him finding comfort with someone else when I wasn't available. My thoughts circled around and around in my head. I felt confused as to why he wanted to hang out with a new date when he had played all day and needed to wake up early to play again. She must have been really important to him.

After a sleepless night, I dragged myself through the motions of getting ready for the day's game with my team. Shut down and teary-eyed, preoccupied with my own thoughts, I hardly said a word to anyone. I sent the team to warm up without me as my head spun on the sidelines. Then, feeling pressure to show up for my team, I walked out onto the field and lined up with my six teammates. At least I could try to act like the captain I was.

Yet during the game, pass after pass slipped out of my hands, each drop sending me deeper into my self-loathing. The small nonathletic team we were playing against normally wouldn't have been a match for us, but we almost lost the game. The Brinn who had been a strong, loud, charismatic leader, coach, and team captain became a silent, withering pile of anxiety on the sidelines. I just couldn't shake the image of Ben with beautiful Oline.

Ben, who'd been playing on a nearby field, jogged over after his game to watch us. I avoided eye contact. I didn't know which would be harder to admit: all the made-up stories in my head or the fact that we had almost lost to this team.

After the game, too exhausted to cry, I hung my head, and I tried to mumble words. He stood close to me, working hard to comprehend what I was saying.

"You thought I was with someone last night? Someone named Oline?" He seemed shocked while compassionately trying to hold back laughter.

Gently, he explained that "Oline" meant his o-line, his team's offensive line. He'd been hanging out with his team to strategize their offense. As he spoke, the fog lifted, and his words sunk in. I was mortified. I knew what an offensive line was. I regularly used the terms "o-line" and "d-line" when talking about my own team.

How could I be so stupid as to make up wild stories in my head and believe they're true! Why didn't I just pick up the phone and call him or send him a text? Why do I get paralyzed and weak and let my emotions control me? Why do I let my worries about my relationship take over my whole life?

Even a change as minor as Ben falling asleep without kissing me good night could leave me wide-awake till dawn, convinced he didn't love me. I perceived his quiet evenings reading a book on the couch as indications that he was no longer interested in me. Every six months or so, for the entirety of our relationship, these thoughts and feelings would build up inside me, eventually bursting out as I collapsed in an angry, crying mess, certain we should break up. Each time, Ben would talk me down, soothe me, and reassure me that we could work through whatever worries I was feeling.

Drunk Brinn was even more anxious and sensitive to rejection. One weekend at a tournament in Santa Cruz during my junior year of college, Grace and I spent the day on the sidelines spectating. Spectating involved rooting for our favorite teams and drinking copious amounts of boxed red wine—because it had a spout for easy access.

That evening, we returned to Grace's house on campus, near the forest. Her neighbors were throwing a party, and they had hidden a keg of beer in the trees, requiring a small hike every time we wanted to fill our cups. By nightfall, my actions had reached the upper limit of social acceptability. I was snappy, making passive-aggressive jokes to Grace's friends that nobody thought were funny—because they were actual digs. I knew I was embarrassing Grace, but I didn't care.

Back in her room, I sprawled out on her bed and slowly drifted in and out of sleep while everyone else carried on enjoying themselves around me. Suddenly it grew quiet. They must have all snuck out of the room. I sat up, furious. *How dare they leave me? Do they think I won't find the keg? I'll show them!* I rolled off the bed and stumbled to the door.

Determined to prove I wasn't too drunk to drink, I marched through the black forest without a light. Navigating as if the keg had a spotlight on it, I soon found the girls circled around the silver canister.

Grace looked up, clearly surprised to see me. I reached for the tap.

"Brinn, I think you've had enough," she said in a calm but stern voice.

I felt as if she'd punched me in the stomach. It was hard to breathe. I dropped my cup and ran. I fled back through the forest, past her house, and down the hill to the parking lot. Out of breath and doubled over, I squatted next to a car, crying. Shame overwhelmed me. *What's wrong with me? I'm acting like a child! Why can't I control myself? Why do I keep running away?*

Running away yet longing for others to chase after me had been my pattern all my life. In first grade, during my birthday party, with an inflatable bounce house in the front yard and my friends running around everywhere, I felt so overwhelmed that I hid under a table in the living room. The table had a long tablecloth draped around it, so no one could see me. Still, I sat there, desperately wanting someone to lift up the tablecloth to find me. But no one ever did.

I kept running away—from a dance party at the San Francisco Pride Parade, from my friends' houses, and even from an ultimate tournament. Whenever someone told me I was too loud, or that I needed to stop drinking, and whenever I felt Ben or a friend wasn't paying enough attention to me, I would blow up. First I would run away in anger, and then I would sheepishly hide in shame.

No matter what I did in my life, I always tried to be the best. If I wasn't naturally talented at an activity, I simply would not do it. And if I ever faced criticism, my whole world crumbled. Even contemplating the idea of being rejected by someone made me cower at the thought of ever showing my face again.

The fear of not being good enough drove me in other ways too. I would find myself bragging or boasting when it wasn't necessary. Or I would shrink, act small, and stay silent around others. Both extremes occurred when I felt uncomfortable or sensed I didn't belong, which was often. When I was drinking, the former pattern would emerge, and when I was sober, the latter.

Later in my junior year, Ben and I joined a beach tournament in Southern California. It was Saturday night, and we were planning to walk back to my teammate Mia's best friend's house to shower, then walk to the tournament party. By the time we left for the party, however, I'd already taken four shots of rum, drunk three beers, and invited people over after it was made clear to me by Mia that there wasn't space for more people.

I stumbled out of the house.

"Come oooooon, let's gooo!" I called as I ran down the street, away from the group.

Halfway down the block, I felt the urge to go to the bathroom. *I'll just pee in those bushes before the group gets here*, I thought.

"Brinn! Stop! What are you doing?" I heard Ben say. I'd been wrong. The group wasn't far behind me, and they'd seen everything.

"Let's get out of here before someone calls the cops!" Mia said.

Embarrassed, I started crying. As I fell behind the group, Ben stayed back with me. I kicked the curb with my foot over and over again. He placed his hand on my back. "Brinn, stop. You'll hurt herself."

"Get off me!" I yelled, wrenching myself away from him, tripping over my own feet, and almost falling onto the ground.

"Come on, my car's right here. Just take a minute," Ben instructed, knowing where this night was headed. He opened the passenger's side door and ushered me in. He closed the door behind me.

"We'll catch up!" he yelled to the group as he climbed into the driver's seat.

As soon as he closed his door, I roared, *"Ahhhhhhhhhhhhhhhhhhh!"*

Raging, I thrashed in the front seat, punching and kicking the dashboard and windows. Tears coated my cheeks, my long hair caught in my mouth and eyes. I needed to get it out, to release whatever was trapped inside my body.

Ben quietly stood guard, watching as my arms and legs flailed beside him. He sat with me until I calmed down again. Every storm eventually runs out of rain.

Early the next morning, the sun broke through the windows, burning my eyes through my eyelids and waking me up. I winced, dreading whatever was on the other side of my closed eyelids. As I lay in my sleeping bag on the living room floor of my host, whose name I couldn't remember, flashes of scenes from the night before filled my mind. My heartbeat quickened, and my stomach twisted into knots. Before my eyes opened, I wished they never would. I wanted to die. The hangover was brutal, but the realization of how drunk I had been the night before felt even worse. *I'm such an asshole.*

Ben drove us in silence to the beach where the tournament would be held. I stayed in the car, not yet ready to face reality. Eventually, slowly, I made my way out onto the sand.

Passing by the center of the tournament, I picked up a banana and a bagel, hoping they would help absorb the alcohol still in my system. Immediately, Mia confronted me.

"You were so embarrassing last night!" she started in. We walked down to the water together, and she berated me for inviting people over after explicitly being told not to and acting like I owned the place. Silently, I listened, taking in her words, unable to form my own. As my voice seemed to have stopped working, I couldn't respond to her accusations or her feelings.

Right before she turned and walked away, she said, "I hate drunk Brinn. I hope I never meet her again."

The games were starting, but I took off in the opposite direction. *Nobody wants me there anyway. I'm doing them a favor by skipping the games.*

I dragged my body down the beach for over an hour, mentally flogging myself for my drunken actions. By the time I headed back, my perspective had begun to shift.

I can't keep doing this—to myself or to Ben and my friends. I need to make some changes, I thought as I walked. *How do I never do this again?*

Fearful that I wouldn't be able to quit alcohol completely, I formed an agreement with myself. I could continue to drink wine and beer—if I promised to stop drinking hard liquor. The latter seemed to be the real problem for me. I also decided that I needed to apologize to Mia. She deserved more than a silent response. It was time for me to start taking accountability for my actions. I was no longer interested in sweeping my problems under the rug. It was time for me to start living differently.

By the time I returned to the games, Ben was worried sick. I'd been gone for hours, missed all our games, and abandoned my friends.

"I just needed to take a walk, I'm sorry," I explained to Ben. "Where's Mia? I need to talk to her." I scanned the crowd.

I found her on the sidelines with another team, watching them play. I sat down next to her, shoulder to shoulder. "I'm sorry, Mia. I really am. I know I messed up, and I'm going to try and do things differently from now on." I didn't know how to authentically apologize; nobody had ever taught me how. It was painful to admit that I'd been wrong. I felt physically sick trying to own what I'd done.

"Thank you. I appreciate that," she said simply as she watched the game.

"Do you hate me?" I asked, hoping she'd relieve this terrible feeling I had inside.

"No. But I don't think I'm ready to make up just yet. But I do accept your apology."

I sighed. I couldn't blame her. I'd just have to sit with my guilt and shame a little longer.

Once we arrived back home, Ben sat me down. He'd moved into my apartment with me and my two roommates since graduating from Santa Cruz.

"We need to talk," he said. He told me he'd reached his breaking point; he could no longer tolerate my explosive behavior. And not just when we were partying. He was tired of my lashing out at him over unimportant details at home. He was frustrated with the way I didn't address issues head-on and instead stewed for days in a pouty, icy silence. He was finished with the way I could flip from being happy-go-lucky to angry and sulky in a matter of seconds.

He sighed. "Brinn, I love you, and I want to be in this relationship with you. But something needs to change. I can't do this anymore unless you're willing to work on these issues."

His truth stung, and yet it also validated my desire for change. Ben had seen me through so many challenges in my life. We'd been together more than three years, and I cared deeply for him. I respected him too much to ignore his directive. Something felt wrong, deep inside me, and even if I couldn't explain what it was, I knew it needed healing.

At this point, I was in the process of earning two bachelor's degrees simultaneously, working part-time at an outdoor store, running the ultimate team, playing five days a week, training at the gym, and traveling to tournaments every other weekend. I was exhausted.

I had also developed a form of hypoglycemia that required me to eat every two hours or run the risk of passing out. Meanwhile, even though I was now in the best shape of my life, I still hated my body and, in times of stress, restricted my food intake. Debilitating migraines hit me several times a month, and less severe headaches struck me more regularly. I was often sick and even contracted strep throat twice in one month. My body was screaming, but I was only half listening.

After that conversation with Ben, I realized what I needed to do: slow down and stop distracting myself from my feelings with school, ultimate, and partying. So that summer, I forced myself to take a break and look inwards. Instead of playing ultimate, I signed up for an intensive eight-day personal growth training called Leading from the Center at the Authentic Leadership Center. The training had been recommended to me after Caleb went through it the year before. Ben and I also bought tickets to travel for two weeks in Costa Rica for some much-needed relaxation. I called this the Summer of Me. It marked the beginning of my lifelong process of identifying, acknowledging, and healing the many parts of myself that had needed loving attention for so long.

HEALING

OPENING UP

It was Friday afternoon on a hot August day when I pulled up to a mysterious office complex in Sacramento. As I turned off the car, I soaked in the heat and the silence. This was it, the moment I had been waiting for, the program that would fix all of my problems, cure my anger, and teach me how to be better at everything. All I had to do now was find the right office suite.

Walking into the small waiting room, I saw three adults, two women and one man. I guessed them to be somewhere between their late thirties and early fifties. These were my fellow participants, people who would end up knowing more about me than anyone else in my life ever had. We made small talk as we anxiously waited to meet the facilitators of the program, our coaches.

Prior to starting the program, we'd each filled out an extensive personal history and had a phone interview with one of the facilitators. From this information, they'd assigned each of us two coaches who would serve as our mentors, cheerleaders, and chaperones on our eight-day journey.

The program's core concept: Each participant was free to make their own choices about which path was right for them while the coaches provided structure, support, and guidance along the way. We were told that these individuals were nonjudgmental, well-trained, loving volunteers who had no agenda for what *should* happen.

Since my relationship with Ben was in jeopardy, I intended to develop my emotional awareness and learn the skills to communicate and manage my emotions. Furthermore, my painful relationship with my mother still plagued me, and I wanted to find a way to start handling it differently. Logically, I knew addressing my history with Jake would help me in the long run, but even though I'd shared some information about the abuse in my personal history intake form, I didn't feel ready to explore those feelings in depth yet.

Eventually, we were ushered into a large room with tables and chairs lining the back wall. There were also plastic folding chairs arranged into a circle in the middle of the room, and occupying some of these chairs were our coaches.

As the training began, I quickly learned that the small waiting room would be my refuge. Every time we participants had a break, and whenever we needed to write or reflect, we retreated to this room. But the larger space on the other side of the door was where we listened to lectures, worked individually with our coaches, and sat in circles sharing our feelings and learnings.

After we introduced ourselves and discussed the guidelines for the group, we received our first assignment: Go find a spot anywhere in the room, and your coaches will find you.

I felt ready—and nervous—as I ventured to the perimeter of the large room. It felt safer to observe the action from the outside. The stiff office chairs felt uncomfortable, so I found myself sitting on the carpeted floor, against the wall. I pulled my legs up to my chest and wrapped my arms around my knees. Looking back, this was the position of a frightened child, not of a twenty-two-year-old adult.

My coach, Daniel, turned out to be my dad's age. He had left a successful career as an engineer to pursue a doctoral degree in psychology after making his way through a personal growth program similar to this one fifteen years earlier. As he shared his story, I understood that he could relate to the challenges I was experiencing in overcoming my abusive childhood, my pent-up anger, and underlying depression—and I felt comforted by the fact that he had the technical schooling to match his life experiences. My other coach, Mary, was younger in age and was also studying to become a therapist. Soon I felt well taken care of by both of them.

Throughout the weekend, we spent practically all of our nonsleeping hours in that room with our teammates and our coaches. Luckily, the training focused on practical skills such as communication, which Ben had asked me to work on. Together, we participants learned about the importance of listening to understand, as opposed to listening while waiting to speak.

To my ego's surprise, I realized I wasn't as good of a listener as I'd thought, especially when I was upset. My mind began recalling conversations with Ben when I'd frequently interrupted him, rolled my eyes, or just plain stopped listening. I would wait until he paused and then unload my frustrations without addressing the topic he'd brought up. I would make sweeping, bold generalizations and stabbing remarks that I later regretted. Or, more often, as my body took over, I would shut down, unable to speak.

Light bulbs flashed on in my mind as I realized I couldn't communicate how I felt to Ben because I didn't *know how* I felt. All my life, whenever anyone had asked me how I was feeling, I had answered with "good" or "fine." I never explained when I was angry, sad, disappointed, or even confused.

"Brinn, how are you feeling right now?" Daniel asked in between lectures. We were sitting in our small group in the corner—me, Daniel, and Mary.

I sighed, shaking my head. "I don't know."

He gently pried. "Is the response 'I don't know' familiar to you?"

"Sure. It's one of my go-to answers, if that's what you mean. Ben is always complaining that I never know what I want to eat or what I want to do. I'm really indecisive, and I often don't know anything for sure, especially how I'm feeling."

Daniel dug a little deeper.

"Why do you think the response 'I don't know' makes perfect sense, given all your history?" I was growing familiar with what seemed to be his favorite question: "Why does everything make perfect sense for you?"

I thought for a moment as I fiddled with the ring on my thumb. By this point in the training, through all the lectures we'd heard about human psychology, it'd become clear to me that almost everything we do, from how we talk to how we think to how we behave, stems from our conditioning in childhood. So I started there.

"Maybe I don't know how I feel because I could never admit what was really going on with me. I couldn't be honest with myself about what was happening in my life, so how could I be honest with anyone else?" It made sense now—I'd defaulted to phrases like "I don't know" and "I'm fine" because I'd learned to ignore my feelings and had never wanted to explore what was happening inside more deeply. I didn't even know that was an option.

Daniel explained that when we live through traumatic events, our brains protect us from being overloaded with heavy, uncomfortable emotions. Our brains shut down more often and more easily, making our thoughts and feelings foggy and unclear, and preventing us from focusing too deeply on painful experiences. This technique allows us to survive, whereas walking around overwhelmed by strong emotions is not conducive to survival. To help us survive—that's also why our brains block out traumatic memories, and probably why I had such a hard time remembering my childhood.

I slowly nodded in understanding. I remember my first therapist talking about this same concept, but this time, it clicked in a way that made more sense.

"In fact, the prefrontal cortex," Daniel said, pointing to his forehead, "the part of the brain that is responsible for logical reasoning, shuts down when we are in flight, fight, or freeze mode because our bodies are preparing for danger. This is why people sometimes behave in ways that don't make sense, or say outlandish things, or shut down completely when they're upset—because the logical parts of their brains are offline."

"So is that why sometimes when I'm really upset, it's hard for me to talk, or I feel frozen, like I can't move, or I run away and hide?"

"Exactly," he said. "And if big emotions were shamed in your house, and your family told you those emotions shouldn't be happening, it makes sense that you'd grow up shutting down what you were feeling."

I didn't know whether to cry tears of sadness or joy. For the first time in my life, I felt seen, and my experiences validated. Maybe I wasn't crazy. Maybe there were reasons for my behavior. The more I learned about how the human brain worked and developed, the more my life made sense to me. My body had been, and still was, protecting me from the dangers inside my childhood home, and from remembering what had happened there too.

Later that day, another facilitator described the concept of negative core beliefs. This facilitator began by explaining that when we are young, we believe everything in the world happens because of us. Children see themselves as the central causes of the events around them because they're trying to make sense of the world; they're creating meaning from their life experiences the best way they know how. If Dad is angry, it *means* it's my fault. If Mom and Dad divorce, it *means* I did something wrong. If I am crying and Mom doesn't comfort me, it *means* I shouldn't crying. This is how children's brains function until about age ten.

The problem with this child logic is that we misinterpret the *meanings* of others' actions and behaviors. And if the child grows up without corrective experiences to override those negative thoughts, then the child draws negative conclusions about themselves, building their life on a foundation of negative core beliefs.

I stretched out my legs and started thinking back to my parents' breakup. While I'd never felt as if their divorce were my fault, I did remember feeling like a financial burden to them. I knew that conversations about money caused tension between them, so whenever they bought me clothes or food, and when I went to camp, I felt I was the cause of their financial problems, which to me represented the reason for their divorce.

The facilitator continued, explaining that some of the messages we received as children were direct messages: "Get good grades" or "Stop crying, or I'll give you something to cry about." These words are explicitly clear. But research shows that the words we use convey only 7 percent of our communication; most communication occurs through body language and tone.

What? Only 7 percent of communication is words? I scribbled this surprising information down in my notebook. *I wish someone had taught me this sooner*, I thought as the gold nuggets kept coming.

For example, consider someone saying, "I love you." They can say those same words with different tones and body language, and the meaning will feel different every time. This is why we question certain people's motives, why we feel uneasy when someone says yes when we think they really mean no, and why so many miscommunications occur over text or email, the facilitator explained.

Heat rose in my face, and I recrossed my legs. A pit grew in my stomach as I recalled my text message miscommunication with Ben about Oline. I slowly inhaled, attempting to refocus on what the facilitator was saying.

The messages kids receive about themselves often come in the form of adults' actions. For example, if Dad comes home every night and zones out in front of the TV, he may never say anything negative, but his actions still convey a strong message. Young humans are detectives, constantly searching for messages—and believing that each message means something about us. If our parent looks distracted and gives one-word answers when we're talking, we take that to *mean* that our parent is disinterested, no matter what words our parent uses. In contrast, if our parent gives us eye contact, listens to us without interruption, and asks us follow-up questions, then to us, that *means* our parent cares.

When we receive these messages enough times, we start to believe what they mean. If Dad zones out in front of the TV every night, we believe we don't matter because he doesn't acknowledge us. We're not good enough for his attention. These actions and behaviors lead us to make conclusions such as *I'm not good enough; I'm unlovable, broken, a burden, not safe; I'm not deserving;* and even *I'm alone.* These become our negative core beliefs.

Tears welled in my eyes, and I quickly blinked them back. My heart hurt, knowing I identified with almost the entire list of negative core beliefs that the facilitator had just rattled off. My body shuddered as I realized that on some level, I was convinced that I didn't matter, that I was a burden, unlovable, and ultimately alone in the world. Were these negative core beliefs why I acted the way I did? Was this why I felt so miserable? I longed for answers to my questions.

MEETING BRINN EMILY

*B*ang ... *bang* ... *bang.*

I was sitting in one of the plastic office chairs when a memory surfaced. I was nine years old, my face soaked with salty tears, and I was hitting my head against my bedroom door. *If I bang my head long enough, someone will come.* My long dark hair crisscrossed over my eyes and stuck to my wet, hot cheeks. My family had long since lost interest in my sobs and begun to ignore them. Beyond me, all was quiet. I had heard my mom and brothers leave to go to my uncle's for a family gathering, and my dad was in his room at the other end of the house.

Once I realized no one was coming to help comfort me, it clicked. I was alone.

I stopped crying, stood up, went into the bathroom, and washed my face. I made my way down the hallway, through the kitchen, and into my mom's bathroom. I dug around in her drawer and pulled out a light-green compact. I surveyed my face, strategically covering the red splotches with powder.

"Dad ..." I asked in a small voice, my eyes cast down. "Can I go to Unkie's house?"

"Sure," he responded casually, "let's go."

We drove in silence. Arriving at the party, I kept my head down, ashamed, but I desperately wanted to be a part of my family. On the outside, my family seemed to get what they wanted; I had stopped crying and returned to the family like a good girl. But the victory came at a price.

This memory surfaced within my consciousness as Daniel explained how negative core beliefs can evolve from both little incidents that build up over time and from pivotal events in childhood. As more and more memories came into focus, they began fitting together like the pieces of a puzzle.

I recalled times when my mom and I had argued about my not smiling enough, not showing enough happiness or gratitude, not cleaning enough—all her little nitpicky critiques of my personality, my actions, my clothes, my choices. For years, I'd been walking around feeling alone, like a burden, not worthy, not good enough, not smart enough, not lovable, not pretty enough, and knowing I was way too much for my mother to handle. No wonder I had been depressed and self-loathing all my life.

"Now that you're more aware of your negative core beliefs, which rules and patterns in your life do you see as the results of those beliefs?" Daniel asked our group. Our assignment was to reflect and write about the patterns we saw in ourselves.

As I sat in the little entryway contemplating my childhood, I realized I'd based rules for myself on my negative core beliefs, and these rules dictated how I lived my life. To gain greater clarity about how my beliefs, rules, and patterns of behavior related to one another, I wrote them down using a diagram my coaches had given me.

Negative Core Belief	Rule	Pattern
I'm not good enough / I don't matter	Always be the best or Don't try something new because you might fail	Exhausted, overachieving, too competitive or Don't try and quit or fail
I'm a burden / I'm not worthy	Don't ask for help, don't rely on anyone	Confused, lost, frustrated, exhausted, lonely, disconnected from others
I'm too much	Don't be emotional	Hold everything inside, disconnected from myself and others, people-pleaser, explosive
I'm unlovable / I'm alone	Stay in relationships, no matter the cost. Can't be single	Martyr, people-pleaser, fixer, worried everyone hates me

My head reeled as I internalized this new perspective on how my childhood beliefs had shaped the entirety of my life experiences. As a little girl, I had taken the information around me, gathered up the messages I received, and made unconscious decisions about the person I was.

Furthermore, as the qualities my parents and siblings viewed as acceptable and unacceptable became clear to me, I became quiet, complacent, and chill so that they would accept me. I stopped speaking up and instead internalized my anger, turning it on myself. I held in all of my feelings, pretending I had none, until they exploded.

The self-harm, self-hatred, running away, outbursts, silence, substances, toxic relationships, eating issues, anxiety, depression, and suicidal ideation—they were all starting to make sense. The more they made sense, the more understanding and compassion I felt for my younger self.

During the training, our facilitators encouraged each of us to acquire a picture of ourselves as a little kid. I asked my mom to send me a specific picture, the image I envisioned whenever I thought about my younger self. When I received it, I saw my Inner Child with her perfectly combed chin-length, thick brown hair. The front of her hair was pulled to the side and held in place by a homemade hot-glued bow matching the dark-green top she was wearing. She was smiling, showing off her straight baby teeth, and her tiny hands were folded in front of her. She looked adorable and innocent. Her name was Brinn Emily.

The next day, Daniel and Mary asked me to depict a real-life scene that illuminated one of my negative core beliefs. Choosing a scene that encapsulated my relationship with my mom, I focused on how I'd felt when Caleb and I told her about the abuse. It wasn't an actual memory, more a compilation of memories that together pointed straight at these core beliefs: *I don't matter and I am alone.*

This was a role-play scene, and one of the facilitators would play my mother. We were to stand in front of the group and act out the short scene I'd written. As I watched two other participants in the program act out their scenes first, fear filled my body. My core belief that I was a burden, too much to handle, put me on full alert. I didn't want my story to make anyone feel uncomfortable.

Shaking on the inside, I felt all my feelings turn numb as I walked to the front of the room. Daniel and Mary stood beside me, asking if they could place their hands on my upper back to support me. I agreed with a nod of my head.

"Are you ready, enough?" Daniel asked gently.

I took a deep breath. "Ready as I'll ever be."

As if on a movie set, someone said action, and my "mother" eagerly approached me. She wore a floral apron, which was out of character for my mom, but I understood the intention to portray a maternal vibe.

"Honey, how are you? Are you okay?" She leaned toward me with a look of concern. "You're okay, right?"

My arms crossed in front of me, and my heart began to race. A familiar fog swirled through my mind. Unable to think, I shot out an automatic response: "I'm fine."

She pressed on. "I know you're okay, but Jake, he's not well. We need to take care of Jake right now." I saw her look of concern—for him, not for me.

Then suddenly, out of the depths of my soul, I roared, *"Fuuuuuuuuuuuuuuuuuuuucccccccccccckkkkkkkkkkkkk yoouuuu!"* Unable to hold the weight of my body, I doubled over, sobbing.

I released grief, sadness, abandonment, and anger. I released my rage at my mother for desperately wanting to believe I was okay because it would make her life easier. It was so convenient for her for me to be fine, just as I had been fine my whole life. I released the built-up pain of years of wearing a brave mask. Finally, I was allowed to not be fine.

After my cathartic release, Daniel whispered, "Brinn can you take a step back and see this hurt little girl?"

With my eyes still closed, I stepped back. "I see her. I see her chin-length straight hair, her little bangs just above her eyebrows. She's wearing jeans and a T-shirt. She looks so sad and alone."

With Daniel's encouragement, in my mind, I scooped her up and into my arms, rocking her back and forth. I kissed the top of her head.

"It's okay, Brinn Emily. It's okay. You're okay," I promised her. "I need you to know none of this is your fault. You don't deserve any of this pain. You're so brave, courageous, and strong. You do matter. Your feelings matter. Your thoughts matter. And you are not alone anymore. I'm here, and I'm not going anywhere. I will protect you and keep you safe. Everything's going to be okay."

So she was the part of me who felt so terrified of the world. The one who felt small and insignificant and was convinced she wasn't good enough. The part who became explosive or shut down when her feelings were hurt, and the one who felt deep shame about her emotions. She was the one who clung to relationships and felt so afraid of being alone. But all she had ever wanted was to feel understood and loved for who she was.

Brinn Emily didn't deserve what happened to her in her childhood, and now, as an adult, it was my job, my responsibility, and my honor to notice when she felt alone and scared. Now I could soothe and console this amazing little girl who had endured so much. By showing up for my younger self who had been hurt, scared, and alone, I would reparent her. I would give her the love, care, and support she hadn't received from her own parents when she needed them most.

While I visualized caring for Brinn Emily, the tension in my body disappeared, and a sense of peace washed over me. But as my mind quieted, the realization that sixteen people were watching me sank in. Fear and shame quickly replaced the calm I'd felt.

"Do you want to look up and check in with your group mates?" Daniel gently asked. All of me wanted to bolt out of the room. Instead, I took a deep breath.

Preparing for the group to reject me, I winced as I peeked through my eyelids. But there in front of me, all eyes shone back with love and empathy.

Allowing this group to witness my deepest emotions, see the truth about me, and validate my experiences healed my Inner Child more than any individualized therapy ever could. I was learning that big emotions are meant to be seen by our community, not bottled up and saved for when we're alone.

I also learned I could heal my pain by rewriting the negative beliefs I held about myself. In order to change my life, I didn't need my mom to change or to apologize; healing could come from myself. When I rewrote the script I'd been replaying in my mind and saw clearly who I *actually* was, that's when the first inclination toward self-love emerged.

THE DIFFERENT PARTS OF ME

"Imagine walking on the sidewalk with a little kid. But suddenly, they run into the middle of the street. How would you react?" Daniel asked me.

I was sitting in one of the uncomfortable office chairs beside my two coaches. There were other chairs in our small circle, each representing one of the parts of me that we were learning about: my Inner Critic, my Nurturer, my Inner Child, my Free Child, and my Adult.

My Inner Critic, who felt like a male persona in my head, was the easiest part for me to identify. He was the loudest voice in my head, the one constantly judging, criticizing, and pushing me to be better in every facet of my life. No matter what I did, or didn't do, this Critic was never satisfied. I felt exhausted by his relentless attacks, punishing me for never being good enough, smart enough, pretty enough, funny enough, or spiritual enough, and for never living up to my potential. I just wished he would go away!

"I'd probably chase after the kid and take their hand so they wouldn't put themself in that situation again," I suggested.

"That sounds reasonable. If you were their parent, you might scold them for running into the street. And if you were a harsh parent you might shout, "Never run into the middle of the street again!" His tone softened. "But what is the *feeling* underneath the parent's strong reaction?"

My brow furrowed as I considered the perspective of a parent watching their child run into a street.

"Fear," I said. "They're scared something bad is about to happen, and they're trying to protect the kid from getting hurt."

"Exactly," Daniel said triumphantly. "That's the same exact thing your Inner Critic is doing to you."

Admittedly, I felt a little strange talking about, and with, these voices in my head. But before learning their names and roles, I had felt even more confused by my internal chaos. Usually, I felt not only as if I had more than one part of myself but also as if these parts were in conflict with one another, pulling me in different directions. Learning this Parts Work model helped me understand my inner world more clearly.

"So you're saying the part of me that beats me up all the time is actually trying to protect me?" I asked, skeptical of the inner dialogue that had been so cruel to me.

"That's exactly what I am saying."

Daniel went on to explain that before the development of civilization, humans lived perpetually in survival mode. Their brains had to watch out for danger at all times. The people who looked for danger survived, passing on their genes to the next generation. Those who didn't look out for danger didn't survive and didn't pass on their genes. Thus, humans evolved to have a part of the brain that worked constantly to protect them.

But protecting themselves from danger didn't only mean watching out for wild animal attacks or avoiding getting hurt. It also meant belonging to a tribe. Being loved by our parents and community is a crucial part of our survival—in fact, when we're born, we rely completely on them.

While in our modern world, our safety has increased, our brains remain hardwired to look for emotional and physical danger. When we are young children, our parents give that part of us direction, and as we grow, we begin to look out for ourselves—through our Inner Critic.

But there's more to our Inner Critic than just pure survival skills. We've built our society on a foundation of Critic Culture: We praise achievement, success, being the best, and not settling for less. Working hard, glorifying busyness, and sacrificing our mental, physical, and emotional health for status—our Inner Critics drive millions of us toward these norms.

Looking around the small circle of chairs, I felt encouraged. This was my chance to get to know this critical part of myself and find out who he really was.

Across the circle, I eyed the empty chair labeled "Critic." Feeling doubtful and a little silly, I finally asked out loud, "Critic, why do you push me so hard?"

Then I moved and sat in the Critic chair. Suddenly the answer became clear.

"I want you to do well in life. I want you to be successful in everything you do. If you work hard and do all the things I ask of you, then maybe you'll be happy."

Tears welled up in my eyes. My Critic criticized me because he wanted the best for me? I could hardly believe it. Just like a military drill sergeant pushing a new recruit hard for positive results, my Critic wanted me to succeed. Yet the air in the dimly lit room had grown cold. I grabbed my sweatshirt, for both warmth and extra comfort.

I felt a familiar tightness in my throat as I thought back to the past semester of college, when I had finally earned straight A's for the first time in my life. I sat in bed with my laptop on my lap staring at the line of A's on the screen. *Well, you only got straight A's because your classes were easy. You weren't taking any math or science classes, so it doesn't really count.* Thanks, Critic.

Even though I was on track to graduate with two majors, taking a full load of upper-division classes, working part-time, taking on internships, and running the ultimate team I had created—all while maintaining an active social life and deepening my romantic relationship—I still wasn't good enough for my Critic. But at least now I had some perspective.

Standing up from the Critic chair, I settled into another one across the circle. It might have been my imagination, but the room seemed warmer, a little brighter, and somewhere inside myself, I felt hope.

I was sitting in the Nurturer chair, a foreign concept, yet one I found comforting.

"It's natural to feel less aware of this part than your Critic," Daniel explained. "We live in a society where we're not taught how to be nurturing to ourselves."

I nodded along, wracking my brain for an example of someone who was noticeably kind to themself. I couldn't find any.

"Adults tend to shut down children who feel good about themselves early on because they're usually outspoken, stubborn, or less compliant. Plus, we often label people who feel good about themselves as selfish, arrogant, conceited, or worse. And it's especially true for women."

I remembered my group of friends in middle school. It had seemed to be the cool trend for each of us to talk about how fat, ugly, and dumb we were while gushing about our amazing friends. We learned early that girls could praise others but not ourselves.

Now my Inner Nurturer felt weak and measly compared to the body-builder strength of my Critic. This circle of chairs felt lopsided. I needed to build up my Nurturer so she could start building me up too. So I practiced.

At first the words felt uncomfortable, and I stumbled as I spoke. It took me a few tries, and a concerted effort to not roll my eyes, but I eventually stated, "I am Brinn, a vibrant, energetic woman who is happy, wanted, and lovable." It felt awkward but satisfying at the same time, to say something nice about myself for once.

During one of the lectures, the facilitators explained that by intentionally repeating positive thoughts, we can create new pathways in our brains. In becoming a deeply ingrained habit, negative self-talk wires our brains to focus on our flaws. But we also have the potential to forge new ways of thinking that are caring and supportive, noticing what is right instead of what is wrong. We create new neurological pathways whenever we try something new, but they only solidify with repetition. I needed lots of practice with these new thoughts so the small pathways could build themselves into neurological highways.

"Increasing the strength of the Nurturer isn't just about saying nice things to yourself, it's also about developing the ability to self-soothe," Daniel told me after we'd created my personalized positive affirmation.

"What's self-soothing?" I asked.

"Self-soothing is how you comfort yourself when you're upset."

I began to think about all the ways I sought out comfort. Whenever something upsetting happened, I would immediately jump to call Grace, Ben, or my mom. I never wanted to be alone with my pain. I didn't know what to do with myself or if I could even handle my strong emotions without going crazy. So instead, I vented—or turned to smoking, restricted my eating, had sex, zoned out on the internet, or even picked fights. I always needed something to distract me from whatever was causing me pain. It had never occurred to me that I could soothe myself in healthy ways.

In preparation for an Inner Nurturer meditation, I left the plastic office chair for a purple slingback cushion on the floor. I tucked a soft baby-blue blanket around me and closed my eyes. Quiet instrumental music drifted through the air. A gentle voice spoke, whisking me away into my imagination.

"Take a few deep breaths in and out of your body. Relax into the support around you."

I sunk a little deeper into the cushion beneath me.

"In your mind, imagine someone kind, loving, compassionate, encouraging, and empathetic. Someone wise and nurturing. Now, connect to their energy. Think about what they would say and how they would comfort someone in pain. Give that energy a color and let that colorful energy wrap you up in a blanket. Get clear on this nurturing energy so you can recall it whenever you need it."

At the time, the person I envisioned was my stepmom, Maria. She had been a grounding force in my life since I was twelve, and I'd always appreciated her kind, nurturing presence. Throughout years of doing this work, however, my image of nurturing has shifted. Over time, I realized that the same person who had been one of my biggest critics growing up had also been my softest comfort.

My mom's voice now flows through me when I picture soothing Brinn Emily. I am finally able to recall countless times when my mom took me in her arms, rocking me back and forth and singing me lullabies. These days, I often speak out loud to Brinn Emily, and when I do, it sounds as if my mom's voice is speaking. "Brinn Emily," she used to say in a gentle singsong tone, with a slight emphasis on *Emily*.

Then I wrap my arms around myself, as if hugging my own little girl. I speak to Brinn Emily the way I would speak to any other child who is frightened, in pain, or struggling.

Saying things like "It's okay, honey. I know you're having a hard time right now and that's okay. I'm here with you. You're not alone in this."

The physical effect of speaking out loud to myself and receiving a hug is potent. I immediately calm down and feel at peace. Of all the methods of healing I've learned, self-soothing is one the most powerful because I will always be with me, a guarantee no one else on earth can make.

***

"Join us!" the group cheered.

Blinking, I rubbed my eyes. Since finishing breakfast, I'd been continuously absorbed in emotionally processing and rewriting my negative beliefs with my coaches. But now the powerful August sun hung low in the sky just over the horizon. Squinting, I registered the scene.

In the back parking lot of the office complex, my energetic group mates and our coaches played four square on a chalk-drawn court, joyfully skipped through a game of hopscotch, and casually passed a soccer ball on the grass. *What is going on out here?* I wondered as I watched others blow bubbles in the wind. Everyone else wore tutus, silly hats, and brightly colored, translucent scarves, and there were more for me to try on too.

My body tightened with familiar avoidance. As a child, I had been somber—I had felt too old for silly games. But bouncing through this adult playground, I saw a spark I wanted. Grabbing a princess tiara, a pair of oversized sunglasses, and a stick of chalk, I joined in.

Together we laughed, sang, and cracked jokes, allowing ourselves to be completely ourselves, completely in the moment with one another. I finally felt like I belonged.

Afterward, we debriefed.

"How was that experience for you?" my coaches asked.

"It was a lot of fun!" I responded, still catching my breath. "A lot more fun than I thought it would be. Usually I don't get into that sort of thing unless I've had a few drinks, but we were all sober." Then I grew quiet, unsure of what to say next.

"I noticed something else came up for me right in the middle of having a great time. It was weird, but I suddenly felt a little depressed. I'm not sure why."

Their heads nodded in understanding. Daniel asked me his classic question, "Why does it make perfect sense for you to feel a little sad after playing like this?"

I turned the pink sunglasses over in my hands as if inspecting them.

"Maybe because I didn't do this as a kid," I said. "Or at least, I don't remember doing this. I grew up so quickly after the abuse started. It robbed me of a childhood filled with carefree joy." My eyes burned with tears as the wheels of my mind turned.

While other kids were playing and enjoying their lives, I was doing grown-up things. I was sneaking around, holding secrets, being sexual, and smoking by nine years old. All that is how I was programed to have fun. I could no longer relate to the ways other kids played.

However, there was one area in life where I let this part of me, my Free Child, shine. This part who was fun, spontaneous, adventuresome, passionate, excited, joyful, and creative, I felt her come to life when I played ultimate. On the field, I felt focused, present. My body moved without thinking, in a flow state. Instincts took over as there was no longer space for worried thoughts.

Often during less serious tournaments, I played fun games with the opposing team and dressed up in costume. However, when it came to letting myself fully laugh, expressing myself without fear, engaging in a creative project, or letting life go unplanned, the free part of me ceased to exist.

We all crave the qualities of the Free Child, the other half of the Inner Child, but fear locks this part of us away. We grow up learning that our responsibilities and practicalities don't and can't involve fun. For me, substances had become the only way to unlock this part of me.

That afternoon with my group mates, I learned I could experience joy without substances, competition, or winning. I realized that enjoying myself meant making myself vulnerable. I felt the most free when I let my guard down, stopped overthinking, and allowed myself to be completely present with others.

After that conversation with my coaches, I decided on a new collection of goals: to allow myself to play more, laugh more, make more silly jokes, and let my creativity flow without judging myself. I wanted to show up fully in my life, in every way.

As I integrated these new experiences of connecting with my many parts, I saw how each part impacted me. It was clear that my Inner Child and Inner Critic spoke to me the loudest, while my Free Child and Inner Nurturer had softer voices. But learning about the Adult part of me helped me sew my many parts all together.

As Daniel and Mary explained to me, the Adult acts as the manager of the self. As if all the parts are sitting around a circular table having a board meeting, ideally, the Adult makes final decisions. This part gathers information from the other parts and makes choices based on how we want to show up in the world. It's the Adult who takes the necessary steps in order to achieve our dreams and goals.

I found that my Critic and Inner Child often *masqueraded* as the Adult. I thought I was making logical, mature decisions when really it was the other two who were in control. For example, my Inner Critic might push me to stay up all night working on a paper *(because it needs to be perfect)* and then go straight to the gym the next day without any rest *(because I need to be in better shape)*.

As a student-athlete, that might seem like a logical, even responsible decision. However, if my Adult and Nurturer were present, they might suggest getting a few hours of sleep and waking up more refreshed to finish the paper the next morning. They might also say it's okay to take the day off from the gym after a strenuous night. In the bigger picture, sleep is vital to mental and physical health, and missing a few points on a paper, or not going to the gym for one day, is not the end of the world.

Since my Adult was harder for me to identify, I found it helpful to try connecting with how this part *felt*. As I reflected, I realized that when I am in my Adult space, I feel grounded and secure. I do not feel anxiety or fear, and I am not shut down. I speak clearly about my feelings and opinions without attacking, blaming, or judging myself or others. I make hard decisions that serve me in the long run, even if they don't immediately seem fun or easy.

When I thought about how much I'd grown at the Authentic Leadership Center, I found that my Adult was the part of me who'd registered for the ALC training in the first place. She was the voice inside who knew I wanted to change. She wants to help me become a better version of myself, but unlike the Critic, the Adult doesn't do that with tough love. It just does it with love. In fact, I began to see how my Adult and my Nurturer were actually quite similar. Although the Adult is more pragmatic and logical and the Nurturer is more loving and empathetic, I decided that I want my Adult to also be loving and empathetic. So my Adult quickly became my Nurturing Adult, which combined the qualities of both parts into the version of myself I wanted leading my life.

At the end of the eight days, I was ready to celebrate! On the last day, there was a small graduation ceremony, and our coaches encouraged us to invite our loved ones to commemorate our hard work. I invited my mom, dad, stepmom, Caleb, Grace, and Ben. I also invited my sister and my nephew, but they weren't able to join us.

During the celebration, four of us participants shared our experiences. My heart beat with excitement as I stood up. As I spoke, my words flowed naturally and rapidly.

"When I first started this training, I thought that by the end of it, my whole life would be wrapped up in a nice little package with a bow on top. I thought all I needed was to get through these eight days, and I would be healed and happy. What I've realized, however, is that this is just the beginning."

Overwhelmed by emotion, I felt my eyes filling with tears, and I took a sip of water.

"This training was an incredible way for me to start my healing journey. It shifted how I saw myself, my past, and my future. So far, I have learned that I am wonderful. I am powerful. I am good enough and perfect just the way I am. I realized that due to certain situations in childhood, I held on to limiting, negative beliefs about myself. These beliefs held me back from accomplishing my goals and from connecting closely with people the way I want to. I am now in the process of letting those limiting beliefs go and rewriting my internal story so I can lead a life that aligns with the person I strive to become."

I closed by thanking my coaches, my fellow participants, and the family and friends who had shown up to support me. I felt free—the best natural high I'd ever experienced. I was grateful and proud to have given myself this opportunity to dive into my healing work. But as I'd said, this was only the beginning.

THE METAPHORICAL BAND-AID

After ALC, I felt liberated and confident. My life was far from perfect, but as I entered my last year of college, I felt excited by the possibilities ahead and looked forward to whatever was coming next.

In four short years, the ultimate team I'd founded was finally blossoming. While we didn't have the lineage of experience that other schools relied on, we did have grit. We were scrappy, and due to our low numbers, we had great team chemistry.

In many ways, we were becoming unstoppable. Other teams now formed strategies aimed at shutting down our top players. That year, our peers from across the country nominated my cocaptain and me as two of the top ten overall players nationally. Having dedicated so much of myself to this sport and this team, receiving this honor felt incredible.

California represented the most competitive region in the nation, which meant our team regularly played against well-established programs like UC Berkeley, Stanford, and UCLA. They all had reputable A-level and B-level teams, and some even had C-level teams as well. Meanwhile, at our practices, we were lucky if we could assemble enough players for a seven-on-seven full-team scrimmage, let alone have enough people for a B team.

But we kept on playing better and better. Our first year, we finished fourteenth in the region. The next year, we jumped to seventh place. Our third year, we ranked fifth. Fifth in the toughest region in the country put us just one spot away from qualifying for the largest tournament of the year: College Nationals.

Now if only we could move up one more spot to place fourth in the region this year, we could qualify to play with the top teams in the country. Advancing one rank felt doable. While our team remained small, we were committed, and my senior year, we set our minds on qualifying for Nationals. In solidarity with one another as we worked toward our goal, the whole team agreed to early-morning weight training, track workouts, and three practices per week.

One frigid January afternoon in the last semester of my college career, I met a teammate at the track for a workout. As I stood in the cold, wishing I were elsewhere, my body felt especially sore and stiff. I bent down, stretching my legs, slowly swaying my torso back and forth. Then I stood up and began jogging.

Ouch! I felt a twinge of pain shoot through the center of my heel. *What was that?* I thought. *It's nothing, shake it off. You're fine. You'll warm up soon.*

The next morning, I attempted to get out of bed and stand up, but my foot objected loudly. After a few days of hobbling, I decided to seek out the wisdom of the internet. I learned that the bottom of the foot is one large tendon called the plantar. Plantar fasciitis is tendinitis of the plantar tendon. Reading all the reports I could, I concluded that was the condition I was experiencing. It was a setback I refused to accept.

I began a strict regimen of anti-inflammatory medication, stretching and icing my foot daily, sleeping in a foot brace every night, and using a walking boot along with crutches. I also stopped (mostly) playing and became an enthusiastic cheerleader and coach on the sidelines. Still, months later, right before our Sectional tournament, my pain level remained high.

"I don't know what to do," I said to Ben on the couch one day while I was icing my foot. Ever since ALC, the connection between us had felt a lot more peaceful. I'd been using the communication models I'd learned, continuing to check in with the different parts of myself and self-soothing when I felt overwhelmed. But none of my tools could help me accept the idea of not playing in the tournament our team had worked toward all year.

"The team's counting on me to be on the field. Our strategy revolves around me playing. There's no way I can let everyone down. I'm just not interested in sitting out the big games."

"How about you talk to a specialist? Someone who knows about athletic injuries. They might be able to help," he suggested.

I secured an appointment with a former athletic trainer for the Oakland A's professional baseball team. I figured he would understand my dilemma.

"I know what you need," Dr. Orland said without looking up from his chart. "One cortisone shot will clear this right up. You'll be back playing in a few days, no problem."

By then, I was feeling desperate. Not playing wasn't an option. I hadn't dedicated my entire college career to this sport, and to this team, only to sit on the sidelines at the very end. That was not going to happen. Without much thought, or research, I blindly followed his advice to numb my pain.

"Ready?" he asked.

I took a deep breath, nodded quickly, and closed my eyes. The gigantic needle went straight to the epicenter of my injury. Excruciating pain shot through my heel, spreading through my foot and up my body. Every muscle tensed as I attempted to breathe. Pained noises escaped my mouth as I tried to mask my feelings.

The shot worked. I easily played through Sectionals, and my foot felt completely normal as we qualified for Regionals. One step closer to Nationals.

But soon after Sectionals, the national governing body of college ultimate sent out an alert. They had decided to rearrange the qualifying spots for Nationals in order to even out competition around the country. They announced there would be only *three* spots from the West Coast instead of the previous *four*. Our team now needed to beat two teams in order to qualify.

Beating one team to place fourth in the region felt doable; beating two felt impossible. We had three extremely strong teams in our region—UC Berkeley, Stanford, and UC Santa Barbara—and with this new system, we would have to knock out one of them. Still, blinded by ambition, I pushed us forward, encouraging more practice, more sprints, and more focus on Nationals.

Within those two weeks, the pain in my foot had flared up again, and so I returned to the doctor. He gave me the same directive: a cortisone shot to the heel. In a desperate attempt to cling on to what was left of my college athletic career, I said yes. I couldn't allow myself to sit on the sidelines and carry the burden of letting everyone down, even if that burden was only in my head. Apparently I'd forgotten how to connect with the Nurturing Adult part of myself who knew my value was more than just being a good athlete. I endured the temporary pain of the injection in order to be able to play pain-free one last time.

As if playing on borrowed time, that weekend, I played with more heart and determination than ever before. We were the underdogs—we had nothing to lose—so we cheered louder, ran faster, and fought harder than anyone else on those fields. And we did it all with only a handful of players too.

In our second-to-last game, against UCLA, we were tied and out of time: Next point wins. I caught the Frisbee right outside our goal line, inches away from scoring. I was just about to throw it to my teammate, when smack! My hand stung where I had been hit.

"Foul!" I yelled.

"No way! I didn't even touch you!" my opponent said, throwing her hands up in frustration.

I took a deep breath and walked around in a small circle to calm myself. In ultimate, there are no referees. Part of the game is learning how to call your own infractions and dispute others' calls. It was one of the ways I'd learned to develop my voice.

"Your hand hit me when I was trying to throw. I'm calling a foul. Either you contest the foul or you don't," I challenged her.

"Contested foul," she growled.

The clock started. Immediately, I threw a high-release backhand into the end zone over a group of offensive and defensive players. I held my breath, praying my Hail Mary would work. My teammate jumped high above them all, grabbed the Frisbee out of the air, and landed back on the ground. Cheers erupted! We rushed the end zone, tackling her in excitement. We'd won.

We were now officially in fourth place. One of our goals had been met, but we couldn't celebrate yet. We were elated but exhausted and terrified of our next game. We were playing UC Berkeley's A team, and they also had a B and C team at the tournament. That meant they had ample players to keep fresh. After our last game, we hardly had players who could walk.

In the end, we lost. Yet when Berkeley scored that final point, tears of joy streamed down my face. We all cried and hugged each other, more than the winners did. We had reached our original goal! We had ranked fourth in the toughest region in the country. If the rules hadn't changed, we would've qualified for Nationals.

I cried because for me, it was over. I was leaving the team to whom I had given all of myself for four years. We all cried because we knew our team, as we stood right then, would never play together again. And because we had left everything we had on that field. We had done our absolute best.

It felt like a wonderful ending to our beautiful underdog story. We were proud. We had fought our hardest as a team, and we knew that every one of the teams on their way to Nationals deserved to be there.

* * *

The next weekend, Ben and I celebrated Memorial Day at a fun, low-key tournament. To my surprise, my foot wasn't hurting, so I laced up my cleats. As I casually walked across the field, I fell suddenly, screaming and clutching my foot. I felt as if it were being ripped open from the inside out.

From all directions, people rushed over to see if I was okay, and someone carried me to the sidelines. Confused and panicking, I lay helpless on the grass.

"You should go to the hospital right away" was one person's advice.

"Well, since it's Memorial Day, it might be better to wait until tomorrow," said another.

I decided to wait, but it was hard for me to function. Eventually I visited four specialists who gave me four different diagnoses. Some said I had partially torn my Achilles tendon, another said I had chipped cartilage, which would require surgery, and others said I had collapsed my arch and torn my tendon. All those diagnoses were probably correct to some degree. Interestingly enough, after doing some research, I found out all these diagnoses matched the potential side effects of repeated cortisone shots to the same foot injury. The doctor had never warned me about any negative side effects, although honestly, if he had, I don't know if I would have listened.

I'd been headstrong in ignoring my long-term future for a short-term gain. I not only disregarded the information my foot was telling me in the first place, but I refused to look into the risk of taking multiple shots within two weeks. In my gut, I knew it was risky, but as I'd done so many times before, having made up my mind, I pushed forward anyway.

My determined attitude in pursuing my goals, coupled with my fear of letting my team and myself down, had pushed my foot over the edge. Yet again, instead of facing my pain head-on and coping with it responsibly, I'd masked it. I had stuck an enormous needle in my foot as a metaphorical Band-Aid—twice! Despite my awareness of my negative core beliefs, my Inner Critic, and all the other different parts of myself, I still thought the right thing to do was push through. Even after making progress at ALC, I remained the queen of tightening up my armor and putting on my mask.

I hadn't planned for college to be the end of my ultimate career. That year, I'd been recruited by the best women's team in the world, by women who had been my idols. Before this new injury, my dream had seemed only a few months away: I would move to San Francisco, join that team, find a well-paying job, and travel the world playing ultimate.

Now I realize that sticking to that plan would have required me to keep my mask on. Pushing myself to continue competing would have only continued distracting me from the messages my soul was trying to communicate. Part of me, even then, knew I had to continue facing my past and keep healing the wounds of my childhood. I needed to stop running.

Walking away from the ultimate community was one of the hardest choices I've ever made. I not only let go of a potential new life of success, but I also left a community that had adopted me when I was just eighteen. This community gave me a long-term secure boyfriend, steady jobs, stable places to live, roommates, best friends, coaches, and mentors. They grounded me by giving me a passion on which I could finally focus my energy. They taught me leadership and gave me experiences that would shape my career. Plus, they helped me get in the best shape of my life.

But none of these mattered when my body and my mind still felt broken. I needed real change and deep healing. It was time for me to stop hiding from the questions that were growing inside me. Who was I besides a team captain and an athlete? Who was I outside of a relationship? Who was I without a mandatory practice schedule and regular social gatherings with the same team? My soul was begging me to slow down, take off my mask, and look around. She was holding up a mirror, and I finally felt ready to see the real me.

STEPPING INTO THE WORLD

While in college, I double majored in environmental studies and cultural geography. When people asked me the obvious question, "What do you want to do after you graduate?" my response was "Travel and save the environment."

Truthfully, I had no direction. Nonetheless, my mantra remained the same—travel and save the environment. One month after graduation, my mom called. My Aunt Sally, whom I hadn't spoken with in years, had contacted her after seeing my graduation announcement. She was inviting me to Brazil for a two-week biology excursion on the Amazon River! My postgraduation intention was starting to manifest!

Ben drove me to the airport, both of us in tears. We were breaking up, for good this time. It was a natural parting, and we both felt at peace with our decision. But the reality was, I was leaving my boyfriend, my friends, my job, my team, my apartment, and the town that felt like home. I had no idea where I was going to live or work, and if I thought about any of that for too long, it was overwhelming. But I felt there was nothing I could do about my future. All I could do was focus on what was right in front of me.

I'd arranged to meet my aunt at the airport after my first connecting flight. Wondering if I could recognize her after all these years, I saw her instantly. She hadn't changed a bit. She was wearing baggy brown hiking pants with a plain gray T-shirt. Her salt-and-pepper hair was pulled back in a long braid that reached the small of her back. Her makeup-free face smiled warmly when she spotted me. "Brinn! I'm so happy to see you," she said, embracing me.

For the next fourteen days, we traveled up and down the Rio Negro, spotting colorful macaws, bright-green parrots, and countless other birds. There were python sightings, and monkeys, iguanas, caimans, tarantulas, sloths, and pink dolphins.

As we traversed the flooded forests in our canoes, the photosynthesizing tree trunks and blooming orchids were unlike anything I'd ever seen. The humid wind blew through my hair, and the sound of insects and frogs lit up the dark nights. Wrapped in the smell of freshly fallen rain, these moments felt like dreams.

From Brazil, I flew to Quito, the capital of Ecuador. I'd reserved a hostel and immediately met other young travelers from all over Europe, Australia, New Zealand. It was easy to meet people in the common room and join different groups who were exploring the city. As someone who had taken French in high school, I knew hardly any Spanish but had learned enough to buy a bus ticket from the bustling city of Quito to the tiny little town in the middle of the Andes called Salasaca.

On the bus, I sat down next to an older woman with shiny hair the color of the night sky. She wore a colorful poncho and had only a few front teeth. We communicated mostly by exchanging friendly smiles and nods. She understood I was American and traveling to Salasaca and was very shocked to learn I wasn't married.

About four hours later, she elbowed me, pointed, and said "Salasaca."

The bus was slowing down, and I looked out the window. I saw a few dilapidated shops on a dusty road, but that was it. I looked back at her, puzzled. "Salasaca?" I asked.

She nodded her head. I swallowed hard. Part of me wished I just could stay here, next to her, and ride the bus forever. And if she hadn't told me it was my stop, I very well would have done so. She was an angel on my journey, guiding me to my next adventure.

In college, I'd felt the most disconnected from my spirituality. It wasn't something I talked to Ben or my friends about, and I wasn't involved with camp or church anymore. Yet, alone in a foreign country where I hardly spoke the language, faith became my north star.

I thanked her, stood up, and swung my overstuffed backpack onto my shoulders. After stepping down onto the curb, I watched the bus pull away in a cloud of exhaust. I looked around. Plastic toys hung in the window of the shop next to me. Baskets of purple and red potatoes, onions, and something that looked like broccoli sat on a wooden table. A faded picture of smiling women drinking Coca-Cola was peeling off the wall.

I took a piece of paper out of my pocket and re-read it. *Look for the blue library. When you get there, go to Pachamama Hostel.*

I scanned the area. There were no blue buildings and nothing that looked like a library or a hostel. Laughing to myself, I thought, Well, it's time to use the most classic Spanish phrase I can think of: ¿Dónde está la biblioteca?

I practiced the phrase a few times in my head before gathering the courage to walk into the store. When I did ask the man behind the counter, he just shook his head. My body deflated. Walking out, my Inner Critic scolded me: *You should have prepared more and gotten more information from the school before you left.*

What are we going to do now? my frightened inner child asked.

I took a deep breath. Just then, an old tattered sign high up on a telephone pole caught my eye—Pachamama Hostel—with an arrow that pointed down a dirt road. "Oh thank you, God," I whispered. "Thank you." With tears of relief in my eyes, I hitched up my backpack higher on my hips, pulled the bottom of my light blue tank top down, adjusted my hiking shorts, and started walking down the dusty road, ready to find Pachamama Hostel.

As I walked, I passed half-finished cinder block houses and groups of women with babies secured to their backs with colorful fabric. I noticed they wore similar outfits—long, thick black skirts and billowy white tops with various small, embroidered bright yellow and red flowers. Each woman's shirt was a little different, yet they all wore their straight, dark hair long, topped with a wide-brimmed black hat. The young girls with them however, wore blue jeans and T-shirts with labels like Nike and Abercrombie & Fitch.

After about ten minutes of walking, I still didn't see anything that resembled a library or the hostel. Every few minutes, however, a pick-up truck with a full bed of people would drive past me. I'd read online that in Ecuador, it was common for pickup trucks to act like taxis.

Curious, I watched another truck drive by. And then another. Finally, I worked up the courage to wave one down. When they actually stopped I was surprised, relieved, and apprehensive.

"Pachamama hostel?" I asked, hesitantly.

"Sí," the driver said, and he motioned for me to get in the back.

I loaded up my backpack into the bed and then crawled up after it. I took a cue from the three men sitting on the edge of the bed and sat myself down on the small ledge. The truck lurched forward and I braced myself, grabbing the steal siding. A cloud of dust swirled behind us as we headed down the road.

Sitting on the bed of the pickup truck, I watched in amazement as the world sailed by. At almost nine thousand feet in elevation, the day was perfect. White puffy clouds were set on a clear, crisp blue background. Snow-covered mountains and volcanoes surrounded the valley we drove through, and I could see a thin line of smoke drifting from the top of one of them. Lining the road were large spiky cacti and small shrubs. Chickens pecked the ground on either side of the road, and at one point, we passed a donkey and her nursing baby.

I can't believe this is my life, I kept repeating to myself, and sometimes out loud, too. *Even with a strange man driving a truck into the unknown, I don't even care what happens to me; I can die happy now.*

All the pain and suffering that had come before seemed to fly away in the wind. Never had I felt more free and self-reliant. Never had I been more proud of myself for taking calculated risks and trusting my instincts. I didn't have a man to rely on or a friend to ask for advice. All I had was me, God, and the Universe to continue showing me the way, and this time, I was listening.

Soon we reached the top of a hill and pulled up to a large brick house with ceramic shingles.

"Pachamama Hostel." The driver pointed out the window to the house.

"Gracias!" I shouted back, jumping down from the bed of the truck.

A blonde White woman about my age swung open the door. She was wearing an oversized white button-down hiking shirt, long, baggy khaki shorts, and converse sneakers.

"You must be Brinn." She gestured to me to come inside.

Stepping out of the sun, I noticed the temperature drop as soon as I walked onto the tile floor. Looking around, I saw beautiful archways that led to different parts of the house. On the wall hung a large woven tapestry depicting the valley where we were standing and the snowcapped volcanoes above us. Small clay figurines adorned a few of the wooden shelves, and a large wooden table set stood in the middle of the living room.

"I'm Lara," she said, sticking out her hand.

She had a firm handshake but soft skin and a smile that seemed to gently illuminate the dimly lit room. She explained that she'd been there for a month and had been the one emailing with me about the school's volunteer program. Originally from Holland, she was taking a gap year after university. It sounded as though she'd been almost everywhere in South America, not to mention that she'd lived in China during her studies. Now she was nearing the end of her travels. Next, she planned on moving to San Francisco, where she had family, and getting a job in finance.

As the days passed by, we spent more time together, and I became even more impressed. Two years younger than I was, she'd already accomplished so much. She was confident, knew what she wanted, and passionately pursued her goals. When I heard her talk, it was apparent that she'd developed a deep affection for her students and for the elderly American man who'd founded the school. She empathized with them, had quickly become a dedicated supporter, and stayed well after the original month that she'd planned to stay.

At first, whenever I asked about her love life, she seemed to avoid the topic. So I went on and on, telling her all about Ben and our relationship and how I was finally on my own for the first time in my life. I also made a point to share that we'd been in an open relationship so that I could explore my sexuality with women. When I said those words, she shot me a look, a look that communicated so much.

That night, we talked all night long on the couch in the living room, and just before sunrise, we shared a kiss. That kiss led to us becoming inseparable for the next month. We'd walk up the hill to school together, write our English lessons together, walk down to the market together, take the bus into town together, and cook our meals together. In such a traditional culture, we didn't show our relationship in public, but at our hostel, we were together.

After my first week at the hostel, out on the back balcony, looking up at a sky full of stars shining bright, she turned to me. "What do you think about coming to Columbia, Cuba, and Mexico with me? After that, we can fly back to San Francisco together."

"Yes! That'd be amazing," I said, excited that my dreams of traveling the world were coming true. But I was already running out of money. Luckily, I was able to borrow some from my dad and Caleb, with the promise of paying them back when I returned.

Together, Lara and I navigated countries, riding buses, trains, planes, and taxis. She proved to be a wonderful travel companion; I felt safe with her. She seemed fearless but held firm boundaries and often made the best of challenging situations. Like the day we needed to leave Ecuador because my visa was set to expire that night. We left before dawn and took a taxi, then a train, then a bus to get the border of Colombia. However, less than thirty minutes away from the border, as the sun was starting to set, our bus stopped in the middle of the road with no intention of moving forward. There had just been a mudslide up ahead, and no traffic was getting through.

Lara immediately instructed me to get off the bus, grab our backpacks, and walk onto the highway. She carefully navigated the fallen mud, rocks, and debris with a smile on her face. Once we made it across the slide, she walked up to a taxi that was waiting in traffic on the other side and paid him to turn around and take us to the border crossing. We made it just in the nick of time.

After our trip, I returned to my dad and stepmom's house, convinced my stay there would be short-lived. Lara was also staying with family in the Bay Area as she looked for a stable job. I was determined to meet her in San Francisco.

Yet after one month of being back, reality hit me hard. I still had no idea what I was doing with my life. And diving back into a relationship was not the answer. I'd always heard about the wisdom and growth that could be gained from being single, but I'd never given myself that opportunity.

During my almost five years with Ben, I'd wanted to break up with him several times but never had the courage to follow through. This time, the moment ending the relationship crossed my mind, I acted. Trusting my gut, I followed my heart and never looked back. My decision felt empowering.

Curious to learn more about myself, I was excited to find out what other decisions I would make, and what activities I would enjoy now that I was single. I had always focused so much of my energy on relationships, acting like a chameleon to fit how others wanted me to act. In order to grow as an independent adult, I had work to do—on my own.

HEALING IN MY HOMETOWN

Sitting on my bed in the guest room at my dad and stepmom's house, I examined all of the floral prints and antiques that surrounded me. My latest batch of job applications had led nowhere. My eyes stung, threatening tears again. Sadness had become my sullen companion.

Taking a deep breath, I recalled my exercises from my ALC training. It was time for a check-in. I pulled out my journal and began to write.

Brinn Emily: I'm sad. I don't know what to do. I'm so lost. I miss him.

Adult: Who do you miss?

Brinn Emily: I miss HIM!

Adult: Ben?

Brinn Emily: I miss him too.

Adult: Who else do you miss?

Brinn Emily: I miss my dad.

My body released silent sobs. I had to be quiet, as my dad was in the house. I'd never felt this way before, but the feeling was clear. Brinn Emily desperately wanted her dad to hold her and soothe her. I craved for him to give me the comfort I hadn't received as a child. Despite the terrifying memories my mother had left inside my mind, she'd nurtured me far more than my father had.

My dad had shown his love through acts of service and long conversations. He taught me how to change a car tire and how to check my oil, and I could always count on him to impart a valuable life lesson.

I had always admired my dad and listened intently as he shared his views on the world. From him, I learned what was acceptable and what was not. In our talks, I always stuck to appropriate topics. Perhaps the role I played with him shaped my interactions with all men: I remained quiet, calm, collected, controlled—until I'd snap. But I never snapped with my dad. I let it slide whenever a racist, homophobic, or sexist slur slipped out of his mouth disguised as a joke. I bit my tongue when I wanted to scream.

Don't rock the boat, stay agreeable, and whatever you do, don't be an "emotional woman" like your mom. The subconscious messages he had instilled and I'd internalized in my childhood still floated in my head.

Yet my sadness grew stronger and stronger. I yearned to show my dad my tears, to have him comfort and hold me while I cried. My Inner Child felt terrified of showing him these strong emotions for fear of rejection. But my Adult wanted a real, authentic, vulnerable relationship.

As I listened to my dad moving around in the kitchen, I longed for him to knock on my door and ask me what was wrong. But I knew that knock would never come. If I wanted to fulfill my need, I needed to take a risk.

After what felt like hours of indecision, I pulled myself out of bed. Without bothering to wipe my tears, I opened the bedroom door. With my eyes fixed on the plush white carpet, I sensed he was sitting at the head of the kitchen table. Without speaking, my twenty-four-year-old body crawled onto his lap. I put my arms around him and wept.

I cried for all the lonely nights I had spent staring out my window, wishing he would come home. I cried for the times I needed protecting and he wasn't there for me. I cried for every time I needed to be strong and every time I pretended to be fine.

His tears poured from me too. For the violations that had occurred, for the loss of his son, for the loss of his daughter's innocence, and for the helplessness he felt. I cried all the tears he could not show me he cried.

His arms held tight around me, gently rocking me back and forth. Finally, my tears dried.

"How about I make you some hot chocolate with a little brandy?" he offered.

Nothing sounded better than my dad's special remedy.

Afterward we talked, and he really listened. I told him about my fear of my emotions and of being "too much" to handle. I explained that I had been trained to be quiet, obedient, and "chill." I spoke of not feeling good enough, striving so hard to be the best, and feeling like a failure. I wanted to tell him about my longing to feel protected and comforted by him, but those were thoughts I was not yet brave enough to speak out loud.

Exhausted by the end, I was incredibly proud of how we had both handled this emotional release. That night was a salve that soothed my wound of abandonment. While it didn't cure everything, I will always treasure that healing moment.

After six months of working a full-time job at a coffee shop, I saved enough money to move out. Moving from my dad and stepmom's house in the suburbs to downtown felt like living in a whole new city. I was finally within walking distance of grocery stores, restaurants, parks, and rivers—and most importantly, my brother's yoga studio. Caleb had opened the studio a few years before. Now that I lived close by, attending his classes became my new normal.

By working full-time, practicing yoga, and returning to ALC, I slowly began to form my own community. The intensive training I'd completed the year before had become the gateway to my healing process. But remnants of my childhood haunted me, especially around the holidays. No matter which family or friend tried to include me, I never felt I had a normal Christmas; instead I felt empty and alone.

One Christmas Eve, I was on the phone with my mom.

"Brinn, he's a part of this family too," she said after informing me that Jake would be at her house the following morning. "You don't even have to talk to him. Although it would be nice—it is Christmas after all."

My mother was once again choosing Jake over me. He hadn't shown up the last few Christmases, but when he decided to surface, she always gave him what he wanted. Somehow I felt as if it were my fault that we couldn't be a normal family on Christmas. This phone call felt like a slap in the face. Did she even care that he'd hurt me? Was nobody paying attention to me, *again*?

My blood pressure rose. My vision blurred. The beginnings of a migraine seeped into my brain.

"Just don't go," my stepmom urged me. "You can stay here, and we'll have Christmas morning together. Caleb and your sister are coming over anyway, and you can see them then."

I knew it was my choice whether to attend or not, but the idea of not spending Christmas at my mom's with the whole extended family felt unfair and heartbreaking. And I was bitter. For so many, this time of year felt festive and colorful. Meanwhile, I spent the holidays anxious, irritable, and depressed.

In the end, I went to Christmas morning at my mom's but made sure to avoid Jake the whole time. While he physically respected my space, energetically, I felt his presence, almost like he was watching me. Like if I let down my guard for a second, he'd immediately sense it and try to talk to me. Luckily, that didn't happen.

"All I want for Christmas is a picture of my four children together," my mom reminded us, again, as she ushered us outside to where her camera was set up.

As we filed out the door to catch the natural late-morning light, my sister pulled me close.

"Stand on this side of me, that way you're not next to *him*," she whispered. Feeling a sudden sense of protection made my body soften.

We stood in formation, me, Charlotte, Caleb, and Jake, all arms around each other, smiling, as if we were a normal family of four. It was a moment that my mom could feel good about putting up on her fridge. One that showed only one side of a family that used to be.

Jake had begun to appear in my dreams too. I had nightmares of him stalking me like a predator while I feared for my life. I would wake up with a start, unable to move my body or catch my breath. Another sign of PTSD, Daniel explained. Just like when Ben and I were in the hot tub, and all those other times when my body would freeze or I'd run away. Luckily, now these episodes only occurred during dreams.

One night, after waking up from a nightmare, I found myself stuck to my bedsheets. I felt terrified, unable to speak or move. The room was pitch black.

As I lay frozen, Daniel's voice entered my mind. "Wiggle your toes," the voice instructed.

I methodically moved my toes back and forth. Slowly, I was recalling my humanness. Movement came to my fingers as well. Yet the dark was holding me hostage. If I could only reach up and turn on my lamp, I would feel better.

But my body felt like deadweight. *Come on, Brinn, come on,* a voice whispered in my head. Just get to the lamp. It took every single ounce of effort I had, but I lunged and clicked the switch.

Bright light splashed into the room as I collapsed back onto the bed. Breathing heavily, I lay there, amazed at how much relief I felt. A small giggle escaped my lips. This was a moment to celebrate! With techniques I had learned in therapy, I had overcome my body's response to fear, shutting down. This stuff was working!

I know now that my Adult self was the part of me who remembered to move my toes and fingers. It was my Adult who had the strength to reach for the lamp. Before then, Brinn Emily would have stayed frozen with fear, potentially all night. After that night, I didn't have regular nightmares anymore.

But while Jake stopped appearing in my dreams, he remained a presence in my life. A few months before Caleb's wedding, Caleb sat me down for a talk.

"I know you haven't spoken to Jake in a while," he said. "But since you'll both be attending the wedding, would you be willing to talk to him beforehand?"

I hadn't had a full conversation with Jake in several years. My heartbeat quickened. "I don't know. I'm not sure how I feel about that." I fidgeted with the ring on my thumb.

"I'm not asking you to reconcile or dive deep into what happened. I just don't want any drama at the wedding. Maybe if you two talk, it'll help things be less awkward."

The idea of talking to Jake made my stomach queasy. I respected Caleb and understood his perspective, and I appreciated him not forcing a reconciliation or forgiveness, unlike my mother. Still, while I was open to talking with Jake, I wasn't rushing to make it happen.

Soon after Caleb's request, Jake called me, leaving a voice message. Hearing his voice made my skin crawl. His tone dripped with condescension, and I felt all of his suppressed emotions just under the surface. He said he wanted to talk but didn't mention Caleb or the wedding. Feeling scared, I reluctantly responded with an email saying I was open to talking but was curious about his intentions in wanting to speak with me.

As soon as our email communication started, it was clear our defenses were up; we were both intent on expressing our feelings of having been wronged. Jake claimed that all he wanted was reconciliation, but I felt anger in his tone and words. He blamed me for the fracture in our family and for my refusal to discuss the past with him or anyone else. He felt as if I had betrayed him, throwing him to the wolves. He went on to state how much rage he held against me, and eerily, he described watching my life from afar. However, he still held firm that his only intention in reaching out was full reconciliation.

Speaking words of truth, I responded to every part of his email. I called him out on his aggression, and I found the inner strength to stand up for myself. I told him directly, for the first time, that he'd molested and abused me for years. I explained that when I was eighteen, I hadn't been able to talk with him about my feelings because I hadn't processed them yet.

And that's when he softened. He acknowledged his attitude, stating that he didn't want to lead with anger. Within a few hours, he had shifted from spewing hatred at me to claiming that his sole motivation in life was to resolve the greatest crime he'd ever committed and dedicate himself to my healing.

While his softness was touching, I was wary of his quick turnaround and his bombastic language. Words had always been his favorite tools for manipulation. But we agreed to meet.

Wanting moral support and a witness, I asked Daniel to attend the meeting. I knew Jake still had power over me. His tactics had the ability to sway anyone's perspective. I would need to remain levelheaded and centered.

Daniel and I sat in his office waiting for Jake. After some idle chitchat, the door opened and Jake walked in. He shook Daniel's hand but kept his distance from me. It was obvious he was trying to hide his nerves. It was the first time in six years that Jake and I had been together without our family present. The two men sat next to each other on the couch, and I sat across from Jake in a separate chair. I felt uncomfortable yet grounded. Having Daniel there with me was a lifeline.

Tears flowed down Jake's cheeks, and he covered his face with his hands as he cried. After taking a few deep breaths, he said, "I know you've probably wondered why I did what I did, and it's something I ask myself too. I just know that our parents allowed for so much openness and nudity. There were just so many times they weren't around."

Red flag. He had opened by blaming our parents. I wasn't going to follow his narrative easily.

"Jake, if that's the case, why didn't Caleb do the same thing to me?"

"Brinn, I don't know. You and I were like partners in crime. We did everything together. It just made sense for some reason. I never ever thought about it negatively impacting you. You never seemed to mind or tell me no. The one time you did say no, when we were older, I was mortified and stopped." His voice trailed off.

It's hard to recall the details of the rest of the conversation. In the end, we agreed to be civil at the wedding. He asked for a hug as he was leaving, and I reluctantly gave in. I didn't like touching him, but in this particular context, a brief hug felt appropriate.

After Jake left, Daniel and I debriefed. Daniel commented on my ability to stay present while speaking my truth. He asked if I had seen any red flags, and I listed Jake's lack of full ownership of his actions and his inability to see how his actions negatively affected my mental health, especially as a teenager. Daniel offered his professional opinion: He agreed with my assessment. He'd been struck by the multiple tactics of manipulation Jake attempted to employ, the tactics on which I had picked up.

For the next week, I walked around in a daze. Raw, messy emotions clouded my mind. Besides Daniel, nobody knew the magnitude of the conversation I had just survived. I felt adrift in the world, with nothing anchoring me to reality. I went to work, putting on a happy mask, never sharing my inner world with my friends from the coffee shop. Living a double life, dissociating from my painful experiences, and compartmentalizing my feelings were survival skills I had honed and perfected.

On the wedding day, with Grace and Tanya by my side, I felt strong and confident. There were so many friends and family at the wedding that, besides posing in pictures, Jake and I avoided each other the whole time. Talking beforehand had reduced the anxiety of not knowing what to expect and relieved me from feeling blindsided by seeing him again. We were both able to focus on what was important, which was celebrating our brother and his new wife.

GOING DEEPER

In that first year after returning from South America, I not only worked at the coffee shop but also taught environmental education to elementary school students and conducted fieldwork with an arborist. Still, part of me was curious about life in the corporate world.

My friend from yoga class worked at a prestigious environmental lobbying firm and encouraged me to apply for a paid internship. *What if policy and politics are hidden passions of mine?* I wondered as I applied in December. To my surprise, I found myself filling out hiring paperwork in January, and soon my new boyfriend was taking me out to dinner to celebrate.

One month prior, I'd noticed him on the dance floor at my favorite downtown venue. He matched me in height, wore a beanie over his curly blond hair, and sported a scruffy beard. At the end of the night, he asked for my number and we shared a kiss.

Within a few weeks of us planning our first date, I was mentally planning our wedding. I thought about him constantly while calling and texting him often. After one month, I said "I love you," and the next week, he broke up with me.

Sitting on my bed in the guest room at Caleb's house, I stared blankly past my now ex-boyfriend. My jaw clenched shut. I felt frozen.

"I just need to do my own thing because summer's starting," he said.

He was a thirty-six-year-old raft guide who lived in a yurt forty-five minutes away. I was a twenty-five-year-old living with my brother and his wife, and I still had no clear plan for life after my internship.

"Hey … say something," he urged me.

When I didn't respond, he stood up and walked out, ripping my heart apart with each step. I felt crushed. Hadn't he just asked me to meet his mom? Hadn't he been the one pushing for us to become official after just a few weeks? Confusion swirled in my mind.

I called in sick to work that day and told the college ultimate team I was coaching that I couldn't make it to practice. I didn't care that I was letting people down. He consumed all of my thoughts.

I manically sent text messages and reached out on social media, begging him to talk. After not hearing from him, I strongly considered driving to his house and showing up at his work. I was convinced that if I could just talk to him, I could fix whatever mistake I had made to cause him to leave me.

Nights passed without sleep. What had I done to screw everything up? Was it because I had said "I love you?" Was it because I asked him to not interrupt me when I was talking? I knew I shouldn't have said anything.

After seven agonizing days, he responded.

"Please never contact me again unless there is a genuine emergency like you're pregnant or something."

I couldn't figure out which hurt more: the loss of our relationship or that final rejection.

But at least I knew these feelings were familiar. I often felt rejected, even within my relationships. Whenever my partner didn't call when I wanted them to, or say the exact thing I wanted to hear, or stayed home instead of seeing me, I would spiral. My fear of rejection was so closely tied to my fear of abandonment.

Not only was my love life in shambles, but I was also starting to hate my new job. From day one, I had felt immensely out of place working on the third floor of an office building across the street from the capitol. I had never worked in such a formal environment. Our clients were actively shaping California's, and therefore the world's, environmental policies. The executive director of the Nature Conservancy was on my supervisor's speed dial.

Within my first month, the stress of the job began giving me nightmares. Dread became my morning companion, and the novelty of applying mascara every day soon wore off. My desire to step up and "figure it out" quickly waned. I had no place in a world that felt so inauthentic. Every meeting came paired with discussions of whom you could tell this information to and whom you couldn't. There always seemed to be a crisis, and I felt overwhelmed, like I was constantly failing.

On the outside, I appeared to walk confidently in my striped Calvin Klein pencil skirt suit. But in reality, I folded under pressure, made significant mistakes, and berated myself constantly. Shame and guilt followed me everywhere.

A few days after my heart had been broken, I reluctantly dragged myself out of bed to attend a meeting for a yoga festival Caleb was hosting. I was one of the main volunteers for the festival, but I was not looking forward to presenting like an actual human being for this meeting.

I was tilting my head back, trying to take in the full view of the high ceilings of the vast festival venue, when I heard "You're Brinn? I am so happy to finally meet you in person!"

Suddenly, I found myself wrapped in a sweet hug, embraced by strong, masculine arms. It was Tom, the person with whom I had been emailing about logistics, except he wasn't the fifty-year-old man I'd pictured in my mind. The person looking back at me resembled a young model who'd just stepped out of an outdoor magazine photo shoot.

His shaggy brown hair fell just above his dark eyes. His broad tan shoulders and defined muscles showed that he took very good care of himself. I couldn't help but stare, but I couldn't speak to him either. My mouth had forgotten how to work again. And as far as my broken heart, I could hardly remember the last guy's name.

"*Who's Tom?*" I blurted out at Caleb as we exited the event hall. Caleb laughed as he explained that Tom was a yoga teacher who was moving to Colorado to build hiking trails in the Rocky Mountains. My heart fluttered at the idea of him spending time in an area I knew and loved. Caleb put his arm around my shoulder. "Sorry, little homie. Better luck next time."

Nevertheless, at the end of the yoga festival, Tom and I went on our first date. The night before, he had walked me to my car, and I offered him a ride home. As we drove and talked, he happily stated, "My favorite part of the festival so far has been meeting you."

My heart stopped beating for a moment, and I ran a red light. A shy giggle slipped out of my mouth as I attempted to respond. After dropping him off that night, ironically, even though I was no longer heartbroken, I still didn't sleep a wink.

This time, my mind raced with thoughts of the future, not the past. *What if he's my person? We have so much in common—yoga, hiking, and spirituality! Thank goodness things didn't work out with what's his name.* Bright-yellow sunrays soon shone through my window as renewed energy flowed through me.

The Buddha says, "If someone makes your heart pound, your hands shake, and your knees weak, that's not the one. When you meet your soulmate, you'll feel calm, not anxiety or agitation." In retrospect, I should've listened to Buddha.

Tom and I spent the summer getting to know each other over weekly long-distance phone calls and letter exchanges. Our jobs were coming to an end in the fall, and we decided to travel together in Southeast Asia for three months.

At the end of my internship, the company's founder took me to lunch at the five-star restaurant across from our office building. He wanted to review my year and ask questions about my future.

Sitting across from a man who earned more money in a month than the full amount of my student loans, I said, "I've learned politics isn't the right place for me. I see myself doing something more holistic, like reading people's astrology charts." He must have thought I was crazy.

Yet instead of feeling proud that I had been honest, I heard the voice of my Inner Critic shaming me for acting stupid and naïve.

I felt lost, as if someone else held the map to my life and I wasn't allowed to see it. I didn't yet trust that the map of my own life was in my hands. I still couldn't trust myself at all.

After all, as I'd begun to realize at ALC, I'd spent decades diminishing my own feelings, thoughts, and reactions. Growing up, I'd been forced to ignore my intuition and instincts; everything Jake did went against what I knew was right, so how could I trust myself? Countless times, I'd heard the quiet voice in my head direct me one way, only to find myself doing the exact opposite. The pressure I felt to act against my intuition had led to self-loathing, criticism, and incredible indecision.

After nine months at the lobbying firm, it was clear to me that I needed more help. Plus, I was really starting to enjoy learning about psychology and longed to have a more of an understanding about myself and others. I even volunteered to be coach-in-training for the first-level ALC training and felt the rewards of being there for the new participants.

The week after my internship ended, the week before Tom and I were scheduled to leave on our trip, I enrolled as a participant in ALC's level-two program, Going Deeper. I hoped that taking my healing journey to the next level would help me overcome the crippling insecurities arising not only in my love life, but also in my career.

"Brinn, I want to tell you something," my new coach Liz said to me quietly before our first team meeting. I was back, sitting in one of the uncomfortable plastic chairs of ALC. With my small team of two coaches and one other female participant, I felt supported and equipped to continue my healing journey.

Liz pulled me aside. "I can relate to what you've been through," she said gently. "I too was molested by my brother." Her eyes were steady and clear. If she could figure out how to move forward in her life, enough to then help others, then maybe there was hope for me.

They say healing is like peeling an onion—there are many layers. At first, there's the outer shell, which we can peel back quickly and easily. From there, the layers become thicker and harder to access. They require more focused time and attention to remove. But no matter what, we must start with the outer layers.

In my first ALC training, Leading from the Center, I had revealed the outer layers of my childhood. I processed pent-up emotions, dissected negative core beliefs, and began rewiring my brain with a new narrative about who I was.

My relationship with my mom had emerged front and center, but I hadn't talked much about Jake. At the time, that wound was still fresh. It had only been four years since I'd realized that I'd been abused. I realize now that I needed to increase my nervous system's capacity first in order to cope with the intense feelings and memories that lay beneath my outer layers.

So now, three years post–Leading from the Center, I was ready to uncover the center of myself. My new goals revolved around healing codependency and building up my self-worth and confidence. On the outside, I was twenty-five, but on the inside, I still felt as if I were twelve. When it came to knowing what I wanted to do for a career, I felt like a deer in headlights, frozen, utterly unsure of my next move.

Throughout Going Deeper, my cohort and I peeled back the layers of our deepest emotions, actively processing whichever ones emerged. When our rage exploded, we took a plastic baseball bat and hit it against a mat. When our sadness stirred, we cried, wrote poetry, and burned it in a metal can. When our joy surfaced, we laughed with relief. The alchemy of expression transformed our pain into powerful healing.

A few days into the training, Liz asked me, "Brinn, are you innocent?"

That word, *innocent*, stung my body. I couldn't connect with a single time in my life when I'd felt innocent. Never had I experienced the luxury of not feeling guilty, ashamed, or responsible for someone else's feelings or experiences. The bliss that other adults referred to when they reminisced about their innocent childhoods had always been lost on me; I'd assumed it was merely a form of ignorance or naïveté.

Now I felt grief, despair, anger. How dare Jake rob me of my innocence!

Surrounded by my team and cocooned in blankets and pillows, I cried tireless tears for Brinn Emily. Not only had my younger self survived so much, she also hated herself for it. She felt as though it was her fault she wasn't innocent, her fault she didn't trust herself, and her fault she was lost and confused. But my Nurturing Adult knew there was another truth, a truth that spoke to the sweet, loving little girl who was just trying her best to love and be loved.

"How would you feel if we did a role-play scene and you spoke your truth to Jake?'" Liz asked.

I took some deep breaths and wiped the tears from my eyes. I nodded. "I think I'd like to."

We brought in a man from the other group and asked him to play the role of my brother. His direction was to sit and listen. Straightening my spine, I sat up in the chair and leaned slightly forward, my hands clasped together on my lap. I was ready.

From a place I didn't know existed, I spoke with unapologetic clarity. "Jake, I am innocent. What happened between us wasn't my fault. It was all on you. It was your secret to carry—not mine." Anger stirred within me. I grabbed the side of the chair to steady myself and spoke emphatically. "I am not your sex slave. You can't do what you want to me any longer. I'm taking back my childhood and my power. You can't rob me of myself." My conviction was strong—I believed every word I spoke.

The eyes staring back at me held steady. He said not a word. There was no need. This was all for me.

Afterward, I felt lighter, more grounded. In control. Taking inventory, I checked in with the different younger versions of myself. I spoke with my four-year-old little girl, my eight-year-old tomboy, my thirteen-year-old goth girl, my cowgirl who rode horses, and my athlete. Every single one of them knew they were safe, innocent, pure, and whole, filled with light and love.

It didn't seem real that these role-playing conversations could cause such a shift, but that's why we call this healing work magic. It's almost unexplainable. In the right environment, when we are willing and ready, our lives can change in an instant.

At the time, I couldn't imagine continuing on with life without healing my past. My trauma had harmed my adult life too much. I had seen it damage my relationships, my work and family dynamics, my daily choices. I recognized that by not going deeper, I'd been holding myself back, and I was the only person who could move myself forward.

At ALC, surrounded by people nearly twice my age, I continually heard "I can't believe you're so young. Imagine if I had done this work before marrying and having kids." But when I heard statements like these, the hairs on the back of my neck stood up. My stomach twisted, and I felt heat in my chest.

Yes, I was proud of myself for making healing a priority, but it wasn't a luxury for me. It was a necessity—a fact I tried not to resent. Part of me hated that I had to do this work! I wouldn't be here if my life hadn't been so fucked up! But each time I inched forward in my healing, I gained greater acceptance of myself and my experiences.

Acceptance was the key to releasing myself from my internal battles. It quieted my *Why did this happen?* and soothed my *I wish life had been different*. It also validated my truth, challenging my minimizing *It wasn't a big deal*. Accepting the reality of my past brought my Adult to the present to figure out how I could navigate my future. After acceptance, the only question remaining was *So what am I going to do about it now?*

By the time I completed this training, I had gained even more abilities and practiced integrating them into my life. I started pausing throughout the day to check in with my different parts. I asked how my Inner Child, my Critic, and my Adult felt and journaled each of their responses. I hung a feelings chart on my refrigerator and looked at it often to build my emotional vocabulary and encourage me to articulate how I felt.

I committed myself even more deeply to Brinn Emily. I realized that every time I broke a commitment to myself, I was breaking a promise to her. I had spent decades letting her down by pushing her aside and showing her that she wasn't deserving of healthy habits, that she wasn't worth taking care of.

Now I began viewing her as if she were my own daughter, our relationship just as tangible. I said "Goodnight" and "I love you" to her every night before bed. I took her picture and framed it, placing it on my bookshelf in my room. I made her photo the background of my phone's screen so that she was always with me.

Even committing to little habits like brushing my teeth twice a day, flossing, washing my face each night, showing up for yoga, meditating, making my bed, and preparing healthy foods for myself, these all became acts of love for my little girl. Self-care began to mean *I care about myself.*

I was becoming the safe, reliable Adult my Inner Child had always needed. Following through on my word, especially on days when I didn't feel like it, meant building trust with Brinn Emily. And building trust with her was my first step toward building trust with myself.

ANXIOUS IN ASIA

A week after Going Deeper, Tom and I were flying over the Pacific Ocean, traveling eight thousand miles away from everyone we knew. We'd agreed to backpack through Thailand, Cambodia, Vietnam, and Laos for three months for what was supposed to be a fun adventure, but we began arguing on the flight, and it didn't stop there.

Tom had never left the country before, and instead of leading the way with my travel experience, now that I was in a relationship with a man, my insecurities took over, and I stopped trusting myself.

"Take time and space away from each other *before* you actually need it" was the advice one friend gave me before we left. "Traveling with someone twenty-four hours a day is taxing, no matter how great the relationship."

"Yeah, of course" was my logical Adult answer.

I knew healthy relationships required each person to pursue their own interests and live their own life, but my anxious Inner Child didn't understand logic.

"Hey, I'm going to go down to the beach," Tom said as I lay down on the bed in our hotel room. The words alone hurt my heart.

I crossed my arms and tried to act as if his decision didn't bother me. "Okay."

"Is that okay?" he asked cautiously.

"I just don't get it. Why does it feel like you just want to be away from me all the time?" I whined.

"I just need some space."

"I know, I know, you just need space. Sorry for being such a burden," I cried.

Tom walked out the door, leaving me alone with my tears.

As my anxiety raged, I became needy, sad, and dejected. Unconsciously, I was creating the situation I feared: pushing Tom away. He felt unable to meet my unrealistic expectations and found himself torn between my needs and his own.

I wanted him to want to be around me all the time. I could be around him all the time, so why couldn't he be around me? I was used to ignoring my own inner call for time to myself, and I unconsciously expected others to do the same. I hadn't known healthy boundaries before, and to Brinn Emily, any amount of separation could only mean he didn't love me.

Even though I had worked so hard in ALC just a month prior, being in a new relationship brought all my attachment wounds to the surface. I tried to journal and self-soothe, but I felt overwhelmed with Tom's need for space, and he couldn't give me the reassurance I longed for.

Soon my insecurities turned me into a self-conscious mess who couldn't make decisions and who relied on him for my security, even though I was the more experienced traveler. His lack of compassion toward my anxiety fueled my anger—it never occurred to me how frustrating I must have been to deal with.

During one of our good days, we sat on the edge of the Mekong River in Phnom Penh, Cambodia. The turbulent brown water spanned wide across to the other side of the city. Plastic bags, Styrofoam cups, and wrappers of all kinds lined the banks. Locals were out jogging, walking, sitting, and talking. It was hot and muggy, so we'd decided to take a break, resting on the cement ledge and watching the boats pass by.

I was lamenting the fact that I still had no idea what I wanted to do for work. After the last year at the lobbying firm, it was clear politics wasn't for me. I also couldn't see myself teaching environmental education as a career, and my Inner Critic told me I wasn't smart enough for a job in environmental conservation.

Out of nowhere, Tom asked, "So why aren't you a therapist?"

My face couldn't hide my bewilderment. He said it so casually, as if I had obviously thought about the idea before. In the same breath, he continued, "I know it's a lot of schooling and hours. That's probably why you're not doing it, right? Just too much school?"

The thought of being a therapist had never entered my mind.

There have been several times in my life when I've felt guided by certain people—as if they'd been divinely placed in my life to have a specific conversation with me, at exactly the right moment. Now I remembered how in my senior year of college, during a conversation with Ben about his going back to school, he'd said to me, "You know, you too could go to grad school one day."

With that one sentence, he opened a door to higher education that hadn't felt accessible to me before. For some reason, I'd never thought of graduate school as an option—perhaps because I was raised by a family who expected me to go to college but never mentioned education beyond that.

Here I was again, years later, with Tom granting me permission to travel beyond than the future I'd thought possible, first to attend graduate school and then to become a therapist. I had to admit, the idea felt exciting! While I struggled to imagine myself in a professional career, that moment planted a seed within me—even if my Inner Child still felt it was too bold of a dream to dream.

A couple of weeks later, my fear of being abandoned became a self-fulfilling prophecy. Tom announced he wanted to travel by himself for the remaining month and would meet me in Thailand at the conclusion of our trip.

Due to the declining dynamics of our relationship, it made perfect sense to separate. In fact, I didn't even want to spend time with him anymore, but I still felt just as crushed as I had when the rafting guide had left me all alone. Again, I found myself in the throes of heartbreak, unable to shake my feelings of rejection, hurt, confusion, and fear. All the parts of myself screamed as my brain frantically sought to sift through the chaos in my body.

I can't believe he's leaving! But why is this so soul crushing? Some of my favorite travel memories have been when I was alone. I should really get my act together and make a plan. But I can't! I don't even know where to start!

Soon my nervous system had shut down my brain entirely. All my logic seemed to have disappeared. I was in pure survival mode, unable to help my twenty-six-year-old self function with any higher reasoning than that of a ten-year-old who believed that any rejection was her fault. Desperate for a safe adult to turn to, I called the person who had rescued me before.

"Caleb," I said, hardly able to get words out between sobs.

"What's wrong? What happened?" he asked.

"I'm fine. Really, I'm okay. I just don't know what to do." I tried to calm myself and explain the situation so I would stop worrying my brother.

"Tom is leaving without me in a few days, and I have to decide where to go and how to get there. The train seems like it'll take too long, and the buses don't look safe. I'm trying to figure it out." I could barely choke out comprehensible words.

Luckily, Caleb, who had led worldwide yoga retreats, was not only an experienced traveler and professional tour coordinator—he was also my protective older brother. He immediately shifted into action mode and bought me a plane ticket to Laos. He also arranged for his tour leader in Luang Prabang to pick me up from the airport and take me to the hostel Caleb had booked.

I felt simultaneously relieved, grateful, and ashamed of being so distressed and needy. But I knew I could always rely on him. Nobody else in my life had cared for me as consistently as he had, and for his generosity and support, I remain eternally thankful.

MOTORCYCLE RIDE
TO MUANG SING

Boarding the plane to Laos, I spotted a young woman my age carrying a yoga mat. When we started talking to each other, I found out that Sara was an art therapist who worked with children. She was taking a break to travel in between finishing graduate school and starting her career. I couldn't help but take this meeting as a sign from the Universe, nudging me in that direction. Once I met with my driver, we gave Sara a ride into town, and Sara and I exchanged contact information.

Our friendship grew quickly. After touring the cute town of Luang Prabang together for a few days, Sara and I decided to venture up into the mountains. We packed our bags and made our way to the local bus station. Halfway into our bus ride, when we stopped for a bathroom break, I spied a large pile of crickets people were munching on. Interested in adding another exotic insect to my dining list, I mistakenly took a few bites.

After a long twisting bus ride into the hills, Sara and I finally reached the small town of Luang Namtha. As if on cue, as soon as we had settled into our hostel room, my body began to betray me. Typically I have an iron stomach and a great immune system, but not this time.

Suddenly, with the rumble of my digestive tract, I ran to the bathroom, where liquid spewed from both ends of my body—at the same time. The only toilet was a hole in the ground, flushed by pouring a bucket of water down the drain. And the shower had no hot water.

After twelve hours of what felt like hell, I finally left the hostel in search of basic nutrients. My legs felt weak under the weight of my body as I slowly made my way down the street to meet Sara, who had left our room early that morning. Luckily, I managed to hold down a fruit smoothie.

On our bus ride to Luang Namtha, I had read about a seventy-five-mile round-trip motorcycle ride to the Chinese border town of Muang Sing. I'd settled on making this my goal for our trip; it sounded like a beautiful, peaceful ride through the mountainous jungle and a great way to see local villages along the path.

"You know, I am feeling a lot better," I told Sara, trying to convince both of us it was true. "If you're still interested, we could try and make it to Muang Sing today."

Shocked, Sara replied, "Really? Are you sure you want to do that? It's getting kind of late, and it might be better for you to just rest."

"No, no, no, I'm fine," I assured her. "I've been cooped up all day, and I just want to get out. Plus, sitting on a motorcycle is easy. It's not like I'll be hiking up the mountain."

"I guess that's true," she said skeptically. "How about we go see if motorcycle rentals are still available and take it from there?"

"Deal."

We finished our smoothies and trudged back to where we'd seen a sign for motorbikes. A chill crawled down my spine as we walked. Neither of us had planned for today to be as cold as it was. All the tour information we'd read had ensured us that we would have beautiful warm weather. I began to feel unprepared, wearing the only pair of jeans I'd brought and a T-shirt with a thin long-sleeved flannel on top.

But the rental process was quick and easy, and soon Sara and I were riding out of town. Within the first mile, Sara crashed her bike and sprained her ankle. Along with everything I'd been dealing with that day, her injury should have been enough for me to turn around too.

"You can keep going without me if you want," Sara said in a pained voice as she rubbed her ankle. "Really, I can make it back to the hostel on my own. It's no big deal."

I hesitated. *Maybe going on by myself isn't the best idea. Plus, I don't want Sara to feel like I'm ditching her. No! I can't turn back, I have to keep going.* Feeling torn, I pushed forward anyway.

The ride was incredible. I passed little villages of thatch and mud homes. I drove through washed-out parts of the road, navigating twenty-foot-wide and one-foot-deep potholes while zigzagging up the mountainside. At one point, I rounded a corner to find a herd of cows blocking my way. Slowly, I weaved my way through, cautiously aware of the cliff's edge to my right.

Just when I was beginning to worry about how late it was getting, the trees opened, the road leveled off, and in the distance I glimpsed enormous mountains marking the territory of another country. I had made it!

I drove through Muang Sing at dusk, taking in the tiny town's handful of shops and restaurants. I was hungry but knew I didn't have the luxury of stopping to eat—the sun was already setting. Without even stopping my bike, I flipped a U-turn and started my journey back to where I'd come from.

Anxious thoughts filled my mind, but I stubbornly charged forward, just as I had for so much of my life. The deeper into the jungle I rode, the faster the light faded and the temperature dropped. My long-sleeve shirt wasn't providing much protection from the wind. Tom had been on my mind for most of the ride, and at this point, my thoughts turned to anger and frustration. *I can't believe what a jerk he is! He's so unsupportive and selfish for leaving me alone in a foreign country. How could he do that to me? BAM!*

My body crashed against the gravel road as I watched the motorbike slide on its side and slow to a halt twenty yards ahead of me. My breath was short as pain filled every cell of my body. As my vision focused beyond my bike, I saw headlights slowly driving toward me, not too far away. Bile had risen in my throat, and I swallowed hard.

When the truck drew closer, the vehicle stopped and two young Laotian men jumped out. One came over and carefully inspected my injuries while the other investigated the condition of the bike. Clearly, they didn't speak English, but the sounds of their voices communicated concern. Upon seeing my scraped-up, bloody knee, the man beside me exclaimed loudly, "Oh!"

He ran over to his truck, obviously looking for something. While I waited, memories of first aid classes surfaced, and I started to self-assess, checking my pain levels and moving my hands around my body searching for broken bones—luckily, I found none. As my body began to shake, I forced myself to take deep breaths.

The left side of my jeans had almost completely torn off at the knee, and blood ran down my leg. My hands were scraped tender, as I had used them to brace my fall. Other than that, I seemed okay.

Bringing me fresh water, the man helped me to his truck, easing me onto the tailgate. He used the water to wash away the blood. Feeling restless and disoriented, I started hobbling around in circles, unsure of what to do next.

The man grabbed his cell phone, which miraculously had service. He dialed a number and spoke words I could not understand before handing me the phone. The voice on the other line was kind. "Hi there, my friend is really worried about you. He is headed to Muang Sing in his truck and wants to take you to the hospital there."

Not knowing anything about the Laotian healthcare system and concerned Sara would be worried if I didn't return, I choked back tears and declined the offer. "Thank you, but I have to go back down the mountain."

"Are you sure?" His tone pleaded with me to change my mind.

"Yes, I'm sure." My mind was set in spite of the pain.

I handed the phone back to the driver, and words were exchanged. Again, he handed me the phone. The voice on the other end said, "Okay, there is a staffed lookout point just up the road, and they might have some bandages for your injury. My friend will take you there, but after that you'll be on your own."

I said "Okay," silently praying that the driver and his friend were in fact trustworthy. Within moments, the two men loaded my bike into the truck. Slowly, we drove up the mountain.

The lookout point was an outpost with a little hut on the side of the road. Two men sat around a fire, leaning in for warmth. It was now pitch-black outside. The only light came from the fire and a lantern sitting on a small wooden table outside the lean-to hut.

When the two men with me explained my story, the men at the fire immediately produced gauze, bandages, and water. With a pair of scissors, they cut off my jeans at the knee and poured warm bottled water on my leg. The bruising and swelling had already begun. In the firelight, I could see a rainbow of colors forming around the gashes. After the men dressed my wound, they handed me the phone again.

"The driver of the truck still wants to take you to the hospital. If you don't go with him now, you'll have to ride the motorbike back down the mountain on your own." His voice was frank.

I repeated my stance, "Thank you, but I can't go to the hospital. I just need to get back down the mountain."

In my mind, I had no choice. I was afraid to go to the hospital. I didn't know how much it would cost or if I would be able to communicate with anyone.

Suddenly, an empty pickup truck rounded the corner on its way down the mountain. My newfound friends flagged down the truck and explained my story. Within minutes, they loaded my bike and me into the bed of the truck.

I thanked everyone emphatically, hoping my gratitude was understood. Crawling into the back of the truck bed, I slouched against the cold metal. I felt the vehicle lurch forward as we started moving. Knowing I was heading back toward town, I felt tears burst from my eyes.

"Thank you! Thank you! Thank you!" I repeated, out loud, to no one and to the Universe, as I sobbed.

After what felt like an eternity, the truck finally rumbled back into familiar territory. We arrived at the bike rental shop and unloaded the bike. Upon inspection, I was informed that due to the crash, the brakes on the motorbike were broken. I had been saved. If I'd ridden down the mountain, with gravity pulling me through the dark jungle, I would have found myself in an even worse, and possibly deadly, wreck.

ON MY OWN

The next day, Sara and I limped our way to the bus stop, both of us feeling very grateful to be alive. With her sprained ankle and my football-sized bruise around my knee, we were anxious to return to the familiar town of Luang Prabang. There, the moment I found an internet connection, I emailed Tom about the accident and told him how I was faring. Impatiently, I waited.

Why hasn't he checked his email? Why doesn't he care? Why isn't he coming when he knows I need help?

After three days of agony, I sat on the patio of a French cafe, checking my email for what felt like the hundredth time that day. My body lurched forward when I saw his name at the top of my inbox. Holding my breath, I clicked on his message.

Hi Brinn,

Sorry for the delay, I've been in a small town up by the Chinese border called Muang Sing. I am sorry to hear about your accident. I hope you're taking Ibuprofen and icing.

See you in Thailand,
Tom

My jaw dropped. Heat crept up my neck and seeped into my face. Anger. Embarrassment. Shock. I felt sick.

"Asshole!" I whispered.

Then shame overwhelmed me. I blinked back tears. Why did I think he would come? How stupid could I be? Of course he's not coming. He doesn't care.

As much as part of me hated him for not rushing to my aid, another voice gently whispered, *There's a reason for this.*

I knew what this gentle part meant. My highest self, my guiding intuition, was affirming that I was going to be okay on my own. The subtle calmness in this voice felt different from my Adult. This voice came from somewhere deep inside me; it hardly even passed as a thought. But I knew. Starting to trust my intuition meant starting to trust myself.

The idea of being on my own terrified me, but it had to be this way. This challenge would force me to step up and become the Adult I often sought in others. I had to trust myself and my own inner guidance to lead me.

Sara continued on with her travels a few days before I did, so I soon found myself planning a solo trip back to Thailand. I had to decide between taking a slow boat, a fast boat, or a bus. There were pros and cons for each option, but ultimately, I chose the slow boat down the Mekong River.

Before saying goodbye to Laos, I had a recurring thought to revisit a bookstore Sara and I had explored together. Even though this visit would necessitate a trip across town, I listened to my thoughts. On the last evening before my departure, I slowly, painfully, hobbled my way there.

The entrance to the store was wide. Floor-to-ceiling bookshelves lined both sides of the room. Without any idea of what I was looking for, I felt myself drawn straight to the middle shelf on the right. A medium-sized pink book with *Awakening Intuition* on the spine was nestled in among the other books. As if I saw a spotlight shining on it, I knew this book was the reason why I was there. A smile crept across my face. I had listened to my inner voice, and this gift was my reward. I was already repairing my trust in myself.

After paying for the book, I walked out and into the sticky air.

Thank you, Universe. Thank you.

The next morning, a taxi dropped me off at the water's edge to board the boat to Thailand, a journey that would take three days to complete. The boat resembled a long, skinny elf shoe built from colorful planks of wood. It had one story with a roof overhead and enough room for about twenty-five passengers.

The local passengers and a few tourists like me sat on old van benches that the captain must have salvaged from an abandoned vehicle. The weather had grown colder, and there wasn't much protection from the periodic wind and rain besides a plastic sheet we could pull down from the roof.

As I sat on my worn-out light-blue vinyl seat, I felt as if I were traveling on a school bus. At night, we made port in two different towns, but for three days, that seat became my sanctuary. Wrapped in my sleeping bag and wearing all the clothes I had brought, I read my book. Every few chapters, I paused, took out my journal, and wrote down my thoughts.

Insights rose quickly into my awareness. It had stopped raining, so I rolled up the plastic tarp to watch the jungle pass by. *What lesson am I supposed to be learning out of all these challenges?* As if answering my question, my mind flashed back to when I was fifteen.

If you leave, you won't come back this way—this thought felt burned into my memory. I was standing at my back gate, leaving home to go meet Eric and his friends. The quiet voice in my head had been right. I didn't come back through the gate that night.

I need to start trusting myself more, I thought. That night when I'd snuck out to Eric's house was just one of countless times when I'd acted against my inner knowledge. And it had all begun with Jake. I had always known what we did together was wrong, yet for twelve years, he pressured me to shut down all my instincts. Furthermore, whenever I expressed that something was wrong, my family would tell me that my feelings were wrong. So I grew up not believing, and not trusting, my internal experience.

I'd always had an inner compass, but I'd learned to recalibrate it to fit other people's directions, even when those directions were wrong for me.

Stretching my legs across the bench seat, I nestled deeper into my sleeping bag. Reading my new book helped me find my own true north. It was full of examples of people using prayer and listening to their inner guidance; even if it seemed like a crazy idea at the time, the story always worked out in the end.

The author encouraged practice when it came to building a relationship with our intuition. Listening to ourselves is like building a muscle. If we never use it, it won't become very effective. But if we start exercising that muscle with small challenges, it'll grow stronger, and our trust in its power will increase. So if we think of calling someone, call them. Or if the thought occurs to us to go to a specific place, then go there. Sometimes the problem is simply that our mind overthinks, getting in the way of the path that is lit up right in front of us.

I began reflecting on the motorcycle accident, thinking about how I could have made other choices if I hadn't been so stubborn. Even after becoming horrendously sick and seeing my friend crash her bike and sprain her ankle, I had ignored all the signs of risks ahead. I'd forced myself to take the bike trip alone, putting myself in an unsafe situation, just as I'd done in college when I'd pushed myself to compete with an injured foot and countless other times when I'd tried to control the outcomes of events and relationships.

In fact, this whole Asian adventure now felt forced! Tom and I hardly knew each other and could hardly afford the trip. We had had no business traveling together for three months. I realized that I'd crashed in a moment of frustration with Tom, like when I'd slammed my already infected thumb onto the sink while yelling at Tom in my head in our hotel bathroom in Bangkok. I was making myself miserable by ruminating about a person who, for all I knew, wasn't even in the same country as I was anymore.

Scrawling these feelings in my journal, I began writing without edits, without judging my words, and practically without stopping. Seeing myself reflected back on the pages made my flaws clear, and easier to digest.

At first, it felt as though I were writing the same old story I'd always lived: codependency, anger, anxiety, fear of rejection. It was so frustrating to watch myself continue the patterns I'd tried to overcome at ALC. Even after Going Deeper, I still felt out of control.

As I stared at the choppy brown water of the Mekong River, embarrassment filled my chest. I thought about all the ways I had been consumed by my own ego. How I expected people to read my mind, to constantly think about my feelings while disregarding their own. When Tom had wanted to spend time by himself at the beach, I hadn't been thinking of his needs, only of mine.

In relationships, I took my partners' words and actions so personally, transforming reasonable conversations into emotional blowouts. Instead of being the authoritative leader I was in other areas of life, I withered into an indecisive, helpless, small dependent child. I jabbed at my partners with passive-aggressive sarcasm, which eventually escalated to resentment, anger, and judgment. My Adult was nowhere to be found.

My Inner Child, Brinn Emily, longed to be swept off her feet, loved unconditionally, and fawned over. She craved being seen and heard, no matter how intense her emotions. She wanted people to know exactly what she needed without her expressing it—because only then would they prove they actually cared about her.

But if she sensed disconnection, alarm bells sounded and she defaulted to dramatic emotional displays. Any attention, even negative attention, was better than no attention. Yet over time, these volatile patterns in my relationships had become exhausting.

After my Critic had sufficiently flogged me for all my flaws, I began to write about the person I wanted to be in my relationships. I sought to become strong—in my convictions, my voice, and my decision-making. I wanted to be independent, to have my own friends, hobbies, and alone time. It was important to me to learn to accept people instead of trying to change them, to learn not to take everything they did or said so personally.

I wanted to communicate more effectively and let go of unrealistic expectations I had placed on my partners, because those only led to disappointment. And most of all, I needed to feel secure in myself. That way, if my partner did leave or need space, I would be okay, no matter what.

I sat a little taller in my seat. Processing my thoughts and feelings through writing felt helpful. *What else do I want in a relationship? What qualities do I desire in a partner?* I began writing a long list.

I wanted someone dependable, someone who would be emotionally and physically present when I really needed them. I wanted someone comfortable with open communication and someone with the ability to adapt to my needs; someone free with affectionate words and touch and appreciative of the good I would bring to their life; also, someone who would be willing to work through relationship issues and be patient if I wasn't able to change overnight.

My hand started to cramp up, but I continued. I wanted someone who understood my humor and with whom I could laugh freely: a dance partner, a travel buddy, and a fellow moviegoer. I needed someone with whom I could have safe, passionate sex and someone I felt comfortable disagreeing with and speaking my mind to without fear of their leaving me out of insecurity. Most of all, I longed for emotional depth and a soft place to land.

After I was finished, I reread what I had written. It was liberating and empowering to read which of my behaviors I intended to change and which qualities I longed to call into my life. Writing made my growth feel tangible. I was finally beginning to manifest the life I wanted instead of just living with the life others had given me.

Yet even after all this reflection, Brinn Emily still hoped Tom was out there, somewhere, doing his own self-reflection, ready to reunite with me and make the relationship work. After all, she just wanted to be loved.

Arriving in Thailand, however, I did not find the romantic reunion I had envisioned. When Tom got there, a few days after I had, it was clear he had no romantic interests in me. We still had another week together before flying back, and we managed to get along. But as soon as we returned home, Tom said he didn't want to see me again, and my anxiety skyrocketed.

A few weeks later, after I shared about my challenges in my relationship with Tom, a friend asked me, "Are you learning the life lesson, or are you living it?"

Meaning, are you simply aware of the life lesson, or have you actively incorporated the lesson into your life? Are you ready to live the answer by letting go of the unhealthy behavior so you can step into something new? Or are you just repeating the same behavior, and encountering the same lesson over and over again, because what we resist persists.

I wish I could say all the beautiful lessons and insights that I discovered on the boat, and before that, during ALC, blossomed straight into practice, but they didn't. What I've learned over the last fifteen years of healing is this: Healing is not linear—it's more like a roundabout.

When you're in a roundabout, you can get stuck and go around and around, with fear that you might not ever get out. But eventually you find the exit and move forward, until you hit the next roundabout. This new roundabout looks the same and feels the same as the previous one, but it's not. This time you're farther down the road, and with the knowledge and wisdom of the last roundabout behind you, you can exit this one more quickly and with more grace and strength.

Viewing these challenges that I'd faced in my relationships—and in my relationship with myself—as valuable life lessons gave me hope that perhaps through studying and practice, someday I'd be able to not just learn the lessons but live them into existence.

ABUNDANCE

Having returned from Asia, I spent my first week in Caleb's guest room praying for a miracle. It was the beginning of a new year and what I hoped to be a new chapter. I had recently turned twenty-six, and I had no job, no permanent housing, and $1,000 to my name. Fortunately, my leg had fully healed from the motorbike accident, with the exception of a lifelong scar.

Two months before the trip, I'd written *$5,000* on a yellow sticky note and stuck it to my bedside table. That was the amount that I envisioned having in my bank account before leaving. My plan was to spend $4,000 traveling and return home with $1,000. The day I left for Asia, I had $4,978 dollars in my checking account.

The idea of writing down my monetary goals came from Michael Phelps's autobiography. He spoke about how he'd write down his goals for new swimming records, and time after time, he kept reaching those goals. So I tried it for myself, and I found that I was able to manifest the amount of money I'd written down.

One of the gifts I'd received from Tom during our time together was the opportunity to learn about his spiritual practice. He taught me about the importance of keeping an altar: a small intentional space filled with inspirational, personally meaningful objects.

Now, clearing a space on top of the medium-sized bookshelf in Caleb's guest room, I laid down a colorful scarf he'd gifted me from one of his trips. I gathered a few stones and crystals I'd collected and propped up my handwritten affirmations, phrases like *You are a human having a spiritual experience; I am a loving, vibrant, energetic woman who cares deeply about others;* and *I accept and welcome all parts of me.* I found a tea light candle in one of the bathroom drawers and placed it in the center of my altar.

Sitting down in front of my new altar, I took a long, deep breath and closed my eyes.

Thank you, Universe, for all I have received in my life. Thank you for the ability to travel, to work, and to have connected relationships with my friends and family. Thank you for giving me presence in my body, and thank you for my overall health. Thank you for this place to live, for my financial security, and for all the abundance coming my way.

Growing up, I'd been taught that all prayers begin best with gratitude. Being grateful for what we already have in our lives puts us in a position to further receive whatever it is we desire. If we start from a position of lack or wanting, then our words further enforce what we don't have. But when we affirm the abundance that already exists, we align our beings with abundance. A small part of me usually remains skeptical that future events will actually transpire in my favor, but somehow my life always seems to have a way of working out.

Within one week of returning to Caleb's house, I'd landed three part-time jobs and my own place to live. I'd initially contacted the nonprofit where I had taught environmental education. They immediately rehired me, and on my first day back, I met Patty. Patty was a mom of two boys, an environmental consultant, and a city planner who ran her own business out of her home. We only met briefly, moments before I watched her captivate a group of fifth graders by enthusiastically explaining the water cycle.

"Are you looking for part-time work right now?" she asked me after the lesson.

I couldn't believe my luck. "Actually, I am. What do you have in mind?"

She was in need of an environmental consultant to help with her extra workload. She was offering flexible hours, a high hourly rate, and job training. I walked away thinking, *Thank you, Universe, for all the abundance coming my way!*

My third job was at Caleb's yoga studio. He graciously hired me to work the front desk on Monday and Wednesday evenings. Wednesday night happened to be the only time that his studio offered Kundalini yoga.

The only thing I knew for certain about Kundalini was that it was different from all of the other yoga classes I'd tried. Every Wednesday night, the attendees made their pilgrimage to the studio from all over the city. They didn't attend the other classes during the week, and they wore a lot of white clothing. They spanned all walks of life: old, young, American, and international. But they all shared a gracefulness, a sweet, caring way of walking the world.

Each class, the teacher arrived early with her small team, setting up the room with white rugs, Indian instruments, and drums. The environment felt more like a temple in India than a yoga studio in California.

For the month or two prior, before I'd even started working at the studio, I'd felt my inner guidance pulling me to try this class.

"Brinn, I am so happy you're working the front desk! Are you going to stay for class?" the teacher asked me on my first Wednesday evening.

I had known Prakti for a few years through my brother. She was a tall fair-skinned woman with long blonde hair that she'd let naturally turn gray. But tonight her hair was wrapped up tight in a white headscarf.

"Uh, no, not tonight, sorry. I have to do something right now, but I'll be back to lock up the studio after!" I swear she could see right through me as I practically ran out of the room.

"Okay, see you in a bit!" She smiled as she glided away, settling onto her faux sheepskin rug at the front of the class.

One week later, same time and place, she asked, "Brinn, are you staying for class? It'll be a good one."

This time, I had already committed to my inner voice. I was staying.

After I checked everyone in, I rolled out my mat at the back of the class. The lights in the room dimmed low, and as if on cue, all talking stopped.

A deep, quiet rumble began to build momentum, turning into the loud clang of a gong. As if sitting too close to a speaker at a concert, my body vibrated with intense frequency. The sound pierced my heart. Emotions swirled in my chest until, finally, tears burst from my eyes. I was releasing the grief and sadness left over from my relationship with Tom. My heart ached, not just for him, but for the shame I'd felt about how I'd acted. I just wanted another chance to try the relationship all over again.

Eventually the room fell silent, and Prakti began chanting in an unfamiliar language. Next, we moved on to a series of exercises. Arms up, arms down, stand up, sit down, twist left, twist right, breathe in, hold, exhale, hold. Repeat.

Every week, we engaged in some combination of chanting, singing, dancing, laughing, walking, crying, and hugging, and always a lot of unusual movements. Each class, my mind and body felt twisted and drained, wrung out like wet towels. I emerged refreshed—sometimes exhausted, but cleansed and feeling light. Kundalini challenged me mentally and physically. I was in love.

Back when I was a swimmer, I would push myself just enough to feel tired and then stop. I would often wait at the wall, catching my breath while other swimmers, the faster ones, pushed on. I remember feeling sulky and jealous, wishing I could be as good at swimming as they were. It never occurred to me that they were good because they were the ones who kept trying.

On my yoga mat, with my eyes closed, it was just me, for me. I didn't have anyone holding me accountable. I didn't feel the pressure of letting people down. I didn't have anyone to compare myself to and no other teammate to blame but me. I decided how much I was going to show up and how far I went inward.

One more second of this and my arms will literally fall off! I am serious! Stop!

When the mental talk in my head grew louder, I learned to dig in and keep going, using newly practiced healthy tools—not just pure grit based on fears of not being good enough.

Now is when I would strengthen my breath, focus my mind on the chanting, and stay present.

"*Sat Nam. Sat Nam. Sat Nam.*" As I listened closely to the mantra, the screaming of my Inner Child slowly lessened until I felt peace inside my mind.

My Inner Child didn't yet believe I would stay present with her throughout mental, emotional, and physical challenges, but my Adult was beginning to show her that with trust and practice, we could overcome any challenge together.

Through this practice, I became more in touch with my body. The migraines and headaches I'd experienced regularly since I was a kid began decreasing. Even daily habits such as drinking coffee and smoking weed no longer seemed as appealing. Overall, my anxiety eased as I felt more secure in myself.

I noticed that my nervous system was the calmest it had ever been. I was no longer as jumpy, and if something startled me, my heart rate quickly returned to normal. I was less overwhelmed and more often able to enjoy peace in my mind and body.

Meditation and mantras became integral parts of my daily life. In class, I learned that the mantra "Sat Nam" means "I am truth" in the ancient Sikh language Gurmukhi and serves as a foundation in Kundalini yoga. Soon I found myself chanting "Sat Nam" not just in class but throughout the week. As I walked down the street, I silently chanted "Sat Nam" in rhythm with my steps. If I felt anxious, repeating "Sat Nam" calmed me. If I was driving and someone cut me off, "Sat Nam" to them!

Over time, the poses became easier and the mysterious chants became second nature. Soon I was sitting front and center each Wednesday night. I felt myself healing on all levels: emotionally, physically, mentally, and spiritually. I trusted that I'd been led here, guided by a truth that existed inside and outside of me. And I was grateful—grateful I'd let my inner compass lead the way, and grateful to myself for listening. I hadn't let my fear of feeling uncomfortable take over. Instead, I leaned into the discomfort, learned how to work with it, and reaped the rewards.

WRITTEN IN THE STARS

Growing up, my best friend Grace and I had spent far too many weekend nights looking up our crushes' horoscopes in *The Book of Birthdays*, hoping for a glimmer of compatibility. At twenty-six, I found out there was so much more to astrology than little blurbs referring to the day and month you were born.

Through the yoga community I heard about a local community offering a six-week Introduction to Astrology course, and it called to me. Thus, over the next couple months, I learned a new language that taught me how to interpret the stars and planets. I learned that Venus represented femininity, love, and pleasure. I discovered how Mercury related to communication, learning, thinking, and ideas. I created flash cards and memorized the characteristics of the different constellations in the zodiac.

Studying astrology helped me feel less crazy. The more I learned about astrology, the more understanding and compassion I held for myself. For example, all of the fire signs in my chart helped explain my fiery, explosive temper. Since we have free will, I can either let my temper ruin relationships, as it did in college, or I can understand that my anger is an important part of me, learn how to channel it, and harness that power for good. The choice is mine.

Similarly, all the water signs I have in my chart make me more empathic, emotional, and interested in personal transformation and spirituality. Yet they can also make me shut down, icy, and hardened, which is how I survived my childhood. All these aspects of my chart make sense to me, and they wouldn't fit just anyone.

After completing the introductory course, I eagerly signed up for the intermediate and, after that, the advanced program too. Putting together all I had learned, I began to understand how to read an astrology chart, a map of the solar system at the exact moment someone is born; like a fingerprint, everyone's chart is unique—because no two people are born in the same place at precisely the same time, not even twins.

One night, I saw my astrology chart (also known as a birth chart) projected onto the screen at the front of the class. There were about eight of us sitting at tables arranged in a horseshoe shape facing the large screen. Our teacher used the chart to point out various placements and the meanings they represented.

"As you can see here …" the teacher began. Her curly dark hair was swept up, fully revealing her intense facial expression. Her glasses matched her light-blue sweater. "The constellation Scorpio has a lot of different symbols next to it. This one represents how Brinn shows up in the world, how she engages in action, and how she connects with people. But if we go a little deeper and move on to this particular configuration"—she pointed to the twelfth house—"to me, this represents some sort of abuse by a male figure. I see a power differential and abuse in your past."

I froze in my seat as I tried to process the words. All I could hear was the whir of the projector in my ears. Slowly, I nodded in agreement, but she had already moved on to the next student's chart.

How could she possibly know that? She doesn't know anything about me. Part of me wondered if my sister-in-law, an active participant in the same astrology community, had told her about the abuse. But why would she do that? Then another thought crossed my mind: *Maybe it is written in the stars.* There had been so many other accurate revelations in our class. I wasn't the only one whom the teacher had confronted with mind-blowing truths.

I had spent so much time wondering, *Why did he do it? Why was my life the way it was?* But now the symbols gazing back at me from the screen said something different; there was finally an explanation, an answer in the chaos. It was supposed to be this way.

That night, I felt the hole in my heart heal a little. I felt anger release from my body, along with a dash of compassion for myself. What if I looked at my life as if it had happened for a reason? How would that change my perception, my story? How would that perspective contribute to my healing?

It would be another six years before I ventured into another astrology reading. Her name was Lisa, and she lived in Washington state. For some reason, I'd felt a gentle nudge inside me, urging me to get an astrology reading. A coach I'd been working with locally had given me Lisa's information. After a month of trying to coordinate schedules, we finally spoke on the phone together.

At first, Lisa repeated the basics that I'd already known about myself. She spoke about my intense emotions and all of my fire and water energy. She explained that I was someone who had a natural inclination toward teaching and communication. She asked if I had ever considered writing books or public speaking. I chuckled.

"Actually, I've been teaching environmental education for years, and I've had multiple public speaking jobs ever since college. I've also kept journals my whole life and have plans to write a book someday."

"I see you're also very in tune with your emotions."

"Well, I've been in therapy for years—you know, childhood trauma will do that for you," I said, laughing.

I heard her smile over the phone line. Then she grew serious.

"You know, I don't always discuss everything I see in someone's chart. Sometimes the receiver isn't ready to hear what I have to say, but given what you've just shared, there is something else I see."

My knee bounced up and down under the table where I was sitting. I had no idea what she would tell me.

"I am curious, was there any abuse between you and a sibling?" she asked tenderly.

My eyes burned as they filled with tears.

"You can see that?" I whispered. I couldn't believe what I was hearing.

"I can. I see it was sexual in nature too." She paused. "I know this is a lot to take in, but you've obviously done work to heal this trauma. With some of your other placements, I see that you sharing your story is going to help a lot of people."

It was written in the stars.

When I was younger, I rejected the idea that bad things happened for a reason, because that would have indicated God was cruel or the Universe wasn't fair. When I considered the possibility of predestination, it was easy to look at my life and ask, *Why did I get handed such a messed-up situation?*

But now my spiritual journey pointed to another conclusion—one that provided hope, inspiration, and purpose. What if all this was meant to happen so that I could learn how to heal and then support others in their healing?

"From what I can tell in your chart, I'd say that in your most recent past life, you played a subservient role. You were held back in some way. You had not yet fully stepped into your power. But this lifetime is the opposite. You're being asked to step up, and into owning your truth and expressing it."

Owning my truth. I suddenly recognized the challenge I had faced ever since I was eighteen, when I'd first confronted the reality of the abuse. This idea of owning my truth scared Brinn Emily. *It's too much pressure. What if I can't do it? What if nobody cares about me? It's too much to think about helping everyone else.*

My Adult understood and responded back to her. *Of course you're scared. Of course you think those things. Honey, it's not your job to talk about your journey—it's mine.*

My journey learning about astrology has helped me create meaning from my difficult past. It's validated what I've been through and shown me how I've taken these challenges and turned them into gifts. It's helped bring compassion to myself and others.

The same year I started studying astrology, I had a session with a different kind of healer named Willow. Willow was a curvy, slightly excentric-looking woman with short curly hair. She was an intuitive healer, Reiki master, and certified hypnotherapist. My mom had gifted me a session with her for my twenty-seventh birthday, just one month before.

I sat in a soft blue velvet high-back chair in the corner of Willow's home office.

"I sense a big iron gate around the topic of your family," she said, looking at me as she bounced gently on her blue exercise ball across the small room from me.

Willow knew my mother from the equestrian community, but I doubt she knew much about our relationship. In public, my mom had always behaved as if she had a perfect family and close relationships with her kids. But in reality, my mom and I still lived on an emotional roller coaster. I was never quite sure what would set her off.

"I feel like you're trying to hide or protect something about your family. There's a lot of pain and suffering there. But don't worry, we can work on letting it go."

Soothing music played in the background as the scent of lavender and rose wafted through the air. I hadn't known what to expect when I scheduled the appointment, but now, without saying a word, Willow was reading me like a book.

She invited me to lie down, face up, on the massage table. I cautiously slid under a fluffy white blanket and rested my head on a soft pillow. Opening with a prayer, she asked her spirit guides to enter the room and work through her, sending me whatever messages I needed to receive.

"I am only the messenger for the guides. So sometimes I say things that will need a little more context from you to fully understand."

I nodded, still a bit skeptical but open-minded as she began her work. She hovered her hands over my body.

"I can see red around your torso. This area feels very hot, meaning you're holding a lot of anger there. Since this is happening at your core, I imagine it's dictating how you show up in the world."

We both knew she was right. How I showed up in the world was irritated, annoyed, and easily triggered. Lately, I felt unnamed emotions swirling inside me and was often teary-eyed without knowing why. But my anger had been leaking out since I was young. I often couldn't articulate why I was angry, or who I was angry at, but my anger constantly sought a target, either someone else or myself.

When I was in college, my drunken outbursts and sober explosions alike had manifested the rage I held toward my parents for not protecting me, and toward Jake for betraying me, disappointing me, hurting me, and traumatizing me. I was angry that my family had forced me to live a double life, where no one really knew who I was, how I was feeling, or what I was experiencing. But holding my long-standing fury inside only hurt me.

Silently, she performed energetic surgery to release my pent-up anger. I didn't feel anything, but I trusted her process, and I knew releasing the painful energy inside my body would deepen my healing.

Finally, she said, "I keep being told to give you a message. My guides are insistent, although it might sound a little strange." She paused. "I'm not sure why, but they want you to know that it's okay you're not a *boy*."

The weight of these words crushed me. I tried to hold back tears, but deep sorrow welled up from inside me, and I let out a heavy sob. Startled at my own reaction, I apologized for crying.

She handed me a tissue. "Don't apologize. You're actually doing exactly what you're supposed to be doing. You're releasing. Let me give you some advice. You know that moment when you start to cry, but that little voice inside says 'Stop?' That's when you keep crying. That's where the healing is. Otherwise, all these emotions get stuck in your body and come out in mental and physical ways. It's better to just release them naturally when they want to flow."

"Thank you. You're right, I hold myself back from crying all the time. It is probably best to let that energy flow and trust that it's showing up for a reason." I wiped my eyes.

My sorrow showed me that the message her guides had given her about me was true. She had given voice to a thought I had never even consciously held but now knew I had built my life around: I had grown up wanting to be just like my brothers.

As a young girl, I had seen that my parents treated my brothers as if their lives were more valuable than mine; I had wished for such a life, filled with the attention and admiration I didn't receive. My brothers had privileges, freedoms, and acceptance to be themselves, while I found myself confined to a role, stuffed in a box, isolated and alone.

Throughout my life, I'd found it difficult to embrace my femininity and often purposefully reshaped my behavior to detract from my feminine nature. To be feminine was to be weak, overly emotional, dramatic, and attention seeking, I thought back then. From my dad, I received the message never to become an "emotional woman" like my mom. My brothers advised me not to become a high-maintenance "girly girl." Starting in elementary school, my mom encouraged me to become a cool tomboy because "Guys like girls who are their friends." Don't be too much, don't share too much, don't be emotional, don't be dramatic, don't be a *girl*, don't be *you*.

Early memories flashed in my head as I recalled standing over the toilet, wishing I had a penis. I begged my mom to cut my hair short and allow me to dress like my brothers. Starting at eighteen months, I refused to wear dresses or skirts, and as a preteen, I stopped wearing shorts completely. I was afraid of showing the girlish parts of my body. Every time I left the house, I worried that people were staring at me and felt ashamed of what they might see. I preferred baggy, athletic clothes because they helped me feel safer, and less on display.

As a proud young feminist in high school, I refused to shave my legs, and eventually my armpits, not wanting to conform to society's standards of beauty. I rolled my eyes at girls who wore makeup every day and at those who cared about their appearance. Deep down, I was insecure about how I looked, but I felt it was easier to excel at being masculine than fail at being feminine.

To this day, I have received many messages from different healers, but whether I receive it through astrology, tarot cards, or psychic readings, the same message keeps on recurring: embrace your femininity.

As I lay on the massage table and allowed waves of anger and sorrow to flow through me, Willow spoke to me of the divine feminine.

"Remember, the true nature of femininity is strong and powerful. To be a woman is to be a creator of life. To be soft, gentle, and receptive, while also a fierce protector, is to inspire and free not only yourself but others as well. Qualities like comfort and empathy are not only strengths but essential for humankind. Embracing your emotional intelligence and giving grace to yourself and others are just some of the many ways you can tap into your powerful femininity."

I let her words sink in as pride for being a woman filled me up. I felt the socially conditioned confines of being a woman loosening their grip. I still don't quite understand what she did that day, but I am certain it would have taken years of traditional therapy for me to have experienced the same awakening.

Walking away I felt lighter, more myself, and more secure. I began following Willow's advice and allowing myself to cry, giving Brinn Emily even more compassion and empathy. I'd never noticed how much I held myself back from feeling. Reclaiming this vulnerable part of myself allowed me to step into a new way of being. It didn't happen overnight, and it took practice, but each time I approached my authentic self with more grace, that grace healed the feminine me who had been shut down for so long.

TRISTAN

"How's your new giiiirrrrlllllfriend?" I said in a teasing voice to my best guy friend, Tristan. We were on the phone with each other and hadn't talked in about a month.

"What girlfriend?" he responded playfully with his deep, scratchy voice. "I broke up with her."

In my mind, I tried to imagine him in his new home, perhaps sitting in a camping chair on the patio of his tiny house surrounded by tall pine trees, his blue eyes covered with dark sunglasses and his wavy brown hair hanging messily around his ears.

"Oh really? Why'd you break up with her?" I was surprised. He usually dived quickly and deeply into a new relationship.

"Because she wasn't my best friend."

My stomach did a somersault.

Tristan and I had a long history of being "best friends." The moment we'd met, at the beginning of seventh grade, we'd felt an instant connection. We dated for one week, the second week of middle school, though at thirteen years old, when he was only tall enough to reach my chest, I had a hard time looking at him as more than a friend. But every day I'd see him at our adjacent assigned lockers, and we spent many nights talking on the phone. Typically, I'd help him through whatever drama was happening in his love life, earning myself the nickname Dr. Brinn.

But our relationship largely hinged on whatever mood he was in or whether he was getting along with whatever girlfriend he had at the time.

There were days when he'd completely freeze me out for no reason. Or he'd shoot me a sideways look of disgust before storming off after I said something he didn't like. But whenever he was ready, or wasn't getting along with his girlfriend, he'd show up at our lockers, throw his arms around me, and go on and on about how much he missed his best friend. When we were together, it was so much fun and I felt like we were really bonded. I could never stay mad at him long.

In high school, we dated each other's friends but mostly kept our lives separate, especially after I moved to Chicago. To my surprise, though, at the end of senior year, he asked me to walk arm in arm across the graduation stage with him. While I was excited and flattered by the invitation, part of me didn't quite trust his motives. Was it really a gesture of long-standing best friendship, the way he described? Or was I, once again, his fallback plan because his girlfriend was already walking with someone else? Was his excitement and exuberance around graduating with his "best friend since seventh grade" real? Or was it a fantasy he'd created in his mind because it was more fun than acknowledging that we didn't really know each other anymore? Either way, I was just happy to be chosen.

After graduation, we lost touch until my last year of college, when I found him on Facebook and wished him a happy birthday. Our new connection sparked a memory of a promise he had written me in my year book five years prior: a promise to come visit me at college. A few weeks later, after an argument with his then girlfriend, he showed up in my college town. Laying eyes on him for the first time in five years, I could see a lot had changed. This tall, thick, muscular man was nothing like the short, scrawny kid I remembered.

As we explored our new connection, we found parallels in our post–high school lives. While I ran the ultimate Frisbee team, he captained his college disc golf team. He was also majoring in education, aspiring to be a teacher, while I taught environmental education. We seemed to be interested in the same spiritual philosophies, and we bonded over our mutual love of the outdoors and adventures. At the time, we were dating other people, but our chemistry felt palpable.

A few years later, I saw him the night before I left for Asia with Tom. We shared a bottle of wine, and he wished me luck on my travels.

After Asia, Tom and I remained on and off for way longer than we should have; the relationship officially ended right after my twenty-seventh birthday. Now, a few weeks later, I was calling Tristan to catch up.

His comment about his now ex-girlfriend not being his best friend made me feel cautiously optimistic. Tristan had made casual references to having feelings for me, but this time the message was clear. I let out a girlish giggle.

"Well, maybe I should come visit? How about next weekend?" I asked.

His new home in the woods at an environmental education school sounded like a perfect escape from the city. We secured our plans and hung up.

The next week, I drove an hour and half into the foothills, arriving at sunset. Colorful clouds hung just above a sea of evergreen ponderosa pines. It was late autumn, and black oak trees lined the roadways, their colorful leaves now littered on the ground. I could tell this place was special.

As I snaked my way through the campus roads, I noticed small groups of people wearing all white. Tristan met me in the parking lot. I got out of the car and embraced his strong body.

"I can't believe I'm here! This place is amazing!" I said, almost breathless from excitement.

"I know, it's great. I'll give you the tour. Oh, and by the way, there's a yoga group here. On weekends, we host lots of events."

I knew the white clothing looked familiar! About a hundred and fifty Kundalini yogis were gathering for an intensive workshop. I told Tristan about my love for the practice, and he arranged for me to sit in on the classes. That weekend, I spent fourteen hours on my yoga mat one day and eleven hours the next. By the end of the weekend, feeling blissed out from the yoga, I was certain the Universe was showing me I was exactly where I needed to be.

When I wasn't on my yoga mat, Tristan and I laughed together, playing cards and board games while talking openly about our feelings for each other and discussing our goals for partnership. By the time I returned home, we were looking forward to a new life together.

Back in the city, I juggled three jobs while trying to figure out my next career move. Since that conversation with Tom on the Mekong River about becoming a therapist, the idea kept rattling around in my brain. *Me? A therapist?* It seemed like a natural yet terrifying step.

Through diving into my own healing work, I had grown to love analyzing emotions and having deep conversations. Small talk had always made me feel uncomfortable, and I preferred discussing real, felt experiences. But the prospect of becoming a licensed therapist felt daunting. Too much schooling, too much debt, responsibility, and structure. I doubted I could handle it all.

So I signed up to volunteer as a coach for the next ALC and began attending formalized coach practice every six months.

"In addition to our coach practices, you can come to my Friday morning group too," Daniel offered during the next training.

He went on to explain, "Since I'm now a licensed psychologist and supervisor, I teach therapists about the Parts Work model we use at ALC. On Friday mornings, there's a group where my trainees practice using those skills."

"Is it okay that I'm not a therapist? And that I have no formal training?" I asked, aware that both my Inner Critic and my Inner Child felt very uncomfortable with my lack of preparation.

"Yes, absolutely. Since it's a coaching group, it's an open meeting. Anyone is allowed to come, just like anyone is allowed to call themselves a coach," Daniel said.

His words intrigued me. I wanted to learn more about what being a professional coach would entail. It seemed easier than becoming a therapist.

Excited by my first group session, I committed to Fridays like it was a job. After about six months of group practice and coaching a few ALC trainings, I grew from an inexperienced observer into an active, participating coach. My confidence increased, my self-understanding grew, and I felt capable when supporting others.

While I soaked up all the knowledge I could from Daniel like a sponge, I still felt that something was missing. Yes, we explored people's emotions, thoughts, and behaviors, and we helped people shift their inner experience by understanding the different parts of themselves, but what about healing on a physical or spiritual level?

Excited to combine all that I'd learned through yoga and astrology, I decided to combine that knowledge with my coaching experience and start seeing clients individually, taking a whole-person approach to healing that I called the Wholistic Approach.

However, at twenty-seven, I was barely making enough money to pay my rent, let alone make a dent in my college student loans. I longed to create a thriving coaching business but had a hard time drumming up consistent coaching clients. Despite the fact that I had been raised by two entrepreneurs, the concept of running a successful business felt overwhelming and completely foreign.

So reluctantly, I looked for a full-time environmental consulting position with firms downtown. I tailored my resume for corporate life again, put on a suit leftover from my time at the lobbying firm, and walked a few blocks to deliver my resume.

After looking up at a massive building of windows, I rode the elevator to the eleventh floor. The doors opened, spitting me out and into a generic office space. To the right lay an empty conference room with bland walls. I peered into a waiting room void of color and life. The whole place smelled like chemicals. Having been denied access to anyone of rank, I handed my resume to the person working the front desk.

Walking home, I felt not only discouraged but scared about my future. I didn't want to be locked into a corporate job, but I didn't want the stress of my rent and loans to haunt me every day either.

As I walked, I prayed, *Universe, thank you for all the abundance I have in my life. I am open and willing to receive your guidance, and trust I will be in my right place.*

When I got home, I called Tristan and filled him in on my experience at the consulting office.

"Apply to work at the school up here with me!" he said immediately. "With your experience, you'll easily get the job. We could live up here, together, rent-free!"

Living in a forest, teaching kids about the environment, and being with my best friend sounded like a perfect option and an answer to my prayers. I applied and was quickly welcomed into their mountain family.

Before this big move up the hill, Prakti invited me to attend a Kundalini retreat in exchange for offering astrology readings to the class. The retreat center was snuggled deep into the woods, and our group was small, only about ten people. On our last night, we all sat on mats, our legs crossed, our arms stretched out to our sides, our index and middle fingers pointed straight out, our eyes closed and locked on our third eyes. Prakti told us to breathe deeply inwards through our gritted teeth and exhale through our noses. For twenty-three minutes, we held this intense posture, its purpose to release childhood anger.

At first, as I sat on my mat, my arms shook and my mind raced as I focused on the anger I still felt from childhood. Old memories, old beliefs, and old patterns surfaced, flowing through my mind like scenes from a movie. About halfway through, this inner chatter quieted as I focused more deeply inward, using the tools of my breath and the mantra we'd been instructed to repeat.

After the gong rang, indicating that time was up, I exhaled loudly, dropping my arms like sandbags. They ached and burned, and my leg was cramped.

"Now, you will write down whatever anger you want to release from your life. Next, we will walk to the fire and burn our intentions, allowing them to dissolve away," Prakti instructed.

I looked down at my blank piece of paper. I knew exactly what I wanted to release, so I wrote: *I want to release all the resentment I hold toward Jake.*

That night, he appeared in my dream, but it wasn't a nightmare. This time, his energy felt peaceful. He was trying to be my friend. Maybe the meditation and ceremony had worked.

The day after the retreat, I sat in front of my altar in my apartment practicing the meditation again, but for a shorter amount of time. After a few minutes, a quiet inner voice said, *Call Jake.* Confused, I asked, *Are you sure?*

Picking up my phone, I scrolled to Jake's name in my contact list. As I stared at his name on my screen, I checked in with myself. *How do I feel? How does my stomach feel?* That had always been an indication of my nerves. But I felt zero anxiety, so I pushed Call.

Jake and I had had almost no contact with each other since Caleb's wedding two years before. Every so often, I received a random text or email from him that inevitably sent me into an angry panic. One day, while I was working at Patty's house, he sent me a direct message that popped up on my computer screen. Outwardly, I wore my armor and refused to let my emotions disrupt my professional life. Yet on the inside, I was screaming, trembling, unable to concentrate, and filled with rage, fear, and frustration. I left early, taking the long way home and crying the whole way.

But today would be different. I felt empowered. I felt Adult.

Listening to the phone ring, then go to voicemail, I noticed that the sound of Jake's voice didn't destroy me. At the beep I spoke. "Hi Jake, it's Brinn. I just wanted to call and check in. Give me a call when you get a chance, and I'll talk to you later."

Surprisingly, that was it. No rush of feelings in my body, no anxiety, nothing. Almost immediately, he called back.

"Hey, Brinn! It's so great to hear from you. I'm at work, but I just wanted to take a second and give my little sister a call back. What's up? How's life?"

His voice sounded a little forced, his enthusiasm a little fake. Ignoring the fact that he still insisted on referring to me as "my little sister," I quickly caught him up on my recent happenings. I asked if he remembered Tristan from middle school, which he did, so I told him about the advancement of our relationship. I let him know about my recent yoga retreat and about my interest in Kundalini. As a fellow spiritual enthusiast, he was familiar with the practice but hadn't tried it himself.

We only spoke for a short time. At the end, I asked if he knew his birth time so that I could look up his astrology chart. He told me he was already versed in his major signs, and he was curious to see what else I could find out about him.

After we hung up, I typed in his information, pulling up his chart on my computer. I was shocked; his chart was so similar to mine. Despite the fact that we had been born in different months, and years apart, we had similar signs in similar placements. I saw his volatility and intensity displayed right there on the page. I recognized our similarities, along with our differences. Seeing his chart humanized him, illuminated his struggles, his challenges, and his strengths. I felt compassion and understanding in a new way. If my astrology chart was aligned for a specific purpose, then so was Jake's. What if it was all supposed to have played out this way? As I witnessed our lives connecting through the stars, I felt the wound in my heart mend a little more.

HE'S BACK

Over the next couple weeks, the more Jake and I communicated, the more I felt a prickle in his tone. What had started as a few friendly calls catching up soon turned intensely personal.

"Some people say I have demons inside," he admitted on the phone, "so I shut myself off from everyone and immerse myself in my music. Between the depressive and manic mood swings, and the anger I feel toward so many people, I keep myself pretty isolated. It's a lonely life."

My heart hurt for him. At this point, I still felt anger toward him, but I didn't want him to suffer. I felt so much empathy for him that I didn't even notice he wasn't concerned about the feelings I'd been experiencing over the two years since we'd last talked.

Instead of returning his next phone call, I decided to email him because it felt safer. I said I preferred emails and told him about the Kundalini class I'd just taken. I also shared that I had just taught my first communication workshop to a group of students at a school where I was working. I explained that I had a deep fear of speaking my mind and that I hadn't had a lot of power to use my voice when I was younger. I went on about my daily routines and asked him if he had any daily practices that he used for his own self-care.

Sitting in a bustling coffee shop, I saw his reply in my inbox.

"Brinn Emily ..." I read. The words made my skin crawl. How dare he address my Inner Child. I'd spent years trying to heal, comfort, and protect her from him!

His words dripped with condescension. He argued with me about my memories of growing up, even those that didn't involve him, and he invalidated my experiences, even feeling the need to remind me of how much of a brat I was. He was playing out our expired dynamic—he still saw himself as the older, wiser brother and me as the naïve kid sister.

Was he actually arguing with me about my own memories? I sipped my lukewarm coffee as heat filled my chest.

His accusations continued as he hit me with phrases like "victim mentality" and "a rageful, cruel, and very spoiled child." He insisted that if I *really* looked at myself, only then would I be able to drop my victim story and move on with my life. After all, that's what he had done.

Perhaps it was the protection of the screen, the hundreds of miles between us, or the work I had done on myself, but finally, after receiving multiple invalidating emails from him, I spoke my truth.

Jake,

So I fully understand your email, yet I don't think you understood my point. You see, Jake, all those old stories that you've mentioned about me being a spoiled, tantrum-throwing brat, those are old beliefs that I used to hold about myself because, just as you're reminding me now, I used to hear them from Mom all the time.

But what I'm talking about happened a little past the age you described in the above email. It was because of you and Mom calling me a "tantrum-throwing brat" that I learned to adapt. As I grew up, I learned not to throw tantrums as much. I learned to be quiet. I learned not to tell people when I was upset. I learned to bottle my feelings up inside of myself, and take them out on myself in ways like cutting, eating disorders, and substance abuse. I learned to be silent and comply with anything and everything you wanted me to do.

I did this because I wanted nothing more in the world than the approval of my older brothers (and my parents too, of course). But when I was a brat, you hated me. So I learned how to be cool, how to be chill, and how to bite my tongue. Unfortunately for me, I went too far. I never said no to you when you wanted me to suck your dick anytime, anywhere. I never learned to call you out when you stole money from me. I never learned to call you out on all your lies and manipulation. I never told Mom when I found your stash of heroin under the bathroom sink. I never got mad at you, past a certain age, because I wanted you to like me. I was constantly protecting you, and protecting myself from your disapproval. It has only been recently that I've really stopped caring at all what you think. I don't care if you like me. I don't care if you love or hate me, and you want to know why? It's because I am whole, with or without your approval.

When I talk about telling my story, this is not something that I cry victim about. On the contrary, I am a survivor. However, the one victim card I do have is very big. It's so big that I have not yet told that part of my story to anyone other than paid professionals. Our family doesn't even know the extent of it because I don't want to burden them with how real and how often our sexual encounters were.

It's a very big deal to be sexually abused, consistently, by someone in your family whom you look up to and admire, for years. I was essentially your sex slave. You said when and where. It happened at family events, at both of our grandparents' houses, when I had friends over, in the middle of the night, even when I pretended to sleep so you would go away. It happened in Mom's room, Caleb's room, your room, my room, the bathtub, the shower, the hot tub, outside at pools, on the side of the house, and at the school, for YEARS.

You say that people have said you have demons. Well, I think they're right. I've seen it in your eyes for a long time. I don't think you have self-love, I don't think you've forgiven yourself for the things you did to me and to other people. I hear you talk about radical forgiveness, but forgiveness starts with yourself, and it doesn't seem like you've done that yet.

To really live a full life, you need to connect with other people. I don't see you having any connections, Jake, which is a pattern, like you mentioned. True, you were ostracized by friends and family, but for very good reason. All those things you mentioned about not having friends and having people not like you, well that's what happens when you lie, cheat, steal, and abuse. It's not a shock.

It just bears the question, are you going to change those beliefs about being an outcast? Are you going to let go of those old stories you hold about yourself? Are you going to forgive yourself for what you've done to those people? Do you give to friends? Do you give to a community? Do you build a support system? I see you grasping at every form of spiritual practice you can muster, but do you seek community? Do you seek psychological help? Do you open up and become vulnerable? Do you let people in, or just push them away?

I am your sister, but that doesn't mean I am the sister you remember having. You may think I am your coolest sibling (and I very well might be because I am pretty fucking awesome ;)), but being siblings and being friends are two different things. Yes, you are a sibling, but you are by no means a friend—yet. And being siblings is nice and all, but a real relationship is only worth having if there is also a friendship.

~Brinn

I sat back and stared blankly at the screen. The words blurred together. Letting out an aggravated sigh, I hit Send.

A few minutes later, his reply appeared. Carrying a tone of humility, he apologized again for hurting me. He said he still didn't understand why he had done what he did but that he had always been extremely horny. And when we were older, it was all because of our parents' divorce. He also mentioned that sexual relationships between siblings are way more common than society thinks, which while true, felt like an excuse I wasn't interested in entertaining.

He wanted to let things go. He had been through hell on Earth, from living on the streets to narcotics and worse. He wanted to put his anger behind him, and behind us, but after this volatile back-and-forth, he suggested we cease communication.

I rocked back and forth in my seat. Rubbing the palms of my hands against my jeans, I looked around the space. There was a couple at the table next to me, both working on their computers. There was a group of friends in the corner, all chatting loudly and laughing. This intense contrast between my internal and external experiences felt familiar. And so did Jake's inability to *see* me, to understand and really empathize with me regarding how much his actions impacted my life.

Plus, I couldn't begin to comprehend why he wasn't seeing a therapist. I wanted him to know that I recognized the trauma *he* had endured, not only from our parents but also from our relationship. He, too, needed to heal from the shameful, secretive, confusing, abusive relationship he had been a part of. I wanted him to push beyond his surface-level emotions and feel deep grief and sadness for the loss of his sister and his family.

Ignoring his request for space, my mind swirling with anger, I shot back, only to receive another tongue-lashing, urging me to never contact him again. He was a wounded animal who needed to lick his wounds. I, too, needed mending.

Brinn Emily still felt that familiar sense of guilt for being too angry, too much, too emotional. But my Adult wasn't going to put up with the way

Jake talked to me. That part of me finally knew how to express herself and had the courage to say how she felt. So while I knew my temper had gotten the best of me, another part of me was proud that I had spoken up for myself, expressed my anger, and stood in my truth.

BREAKING FREE

A few months after cutting off communication with Jake, I packed up all my things in my Honda Accord and headed up the mountain to join Tristan at the outdoor school. There, we were immersed not only in beautiful scenery but also in a community of like-minded people passionate about the environment and teaching kids.

Our workdays consisted of hiking through the woods, and weekends looked like drinking beer while playing disc golf and laughing at inside jokes, silly songs, movie quotes, and stories about our childhoods. On sleepless nights under the full moon, Tristan and I planned our wedding and dreamed about our life on the other side of outdoor school.

But after a few months of silence, Jake reached out to me again, asking if he could attend our grandmother's ninetieth birthday celebration. I felt gutted when I saw his message. I hated that we had to navigate family events as if we had a custody agreement. I'd feel guilty if I said no, he couldn't attend, and I'd feel trapped if I said he could. I appreciated his sentiment in asking, but at this point, his question felt like a setup. It took me six weeks to respond.

Early in our relationship, I'd told Tristan that Jake had abused me, just as I'd told every one of my partners since Ben. Tristan was understanding but hadn't been to therapy himself, so I imagined it was hard for him to relate to all that I'd been through in my life, both in childhood and throughout my healing journey. As a result, we rarely talked about it.

When I finally wrote back to Jake, I apologized for my previous emails. I hadn't wanted to cause him pain when I had originally reached out, but I understood that I'd hurt him. In retrospect, maybe it would have been best if I'd just left him alone and never contacted him in the first place.

When I responded to his question about the birthday party, I acknowledged that we both still had unsaid words and pent-up emotions. I let him know he was welcome at any family event, but I requested no contact with him if he decided to attend. I didn't want to sweep anything under the rug, and I didn't want either of us to have to pretend we felt okay with the other. I also asked him to stop addressing me with family nicknames because they made me uncomfortable. Then I wished him well.

The next morning was gray and overcast. The students noisily ate their breakfast in the cafeteria as Tristan and I sat outside, finishing a helping of eggs and home fries. Checking my phone, I saw Jake's response.

He told me that I lacked humanity and was filled with malice and indignation. He no longer cared what I asked for; he was going to behave however he wanted. After swearing off all communication, he wrote again minutes later.

Brinn,

I plan to brief Caleb and Dad about what happened between us as kids. They've never heard my side of the story and now they will. I am going to hold you accountable just like Daniel from ALC held you accountable during our therapy session. I am going to expose you as the liar and pure manipulator that you are.

I shot out of my seat, practically throwing my phone from my grip. For the last six months, I had dealt with his bullshit. I'd taken it in stride, using it as an opportunity for my own growth. This time, he had crossed a line.

Having the audacity to call me a liar and a manipulator, while bringing my father and brother into his manipulations, was too much for me to bear.

Tristan grabbed my phone, reading Jake's email.

"Let's get in the truck," he said calmly.

I had barely made it the thirty feet to the safety of the cab when my tears exploded. I half cried, half yelled, gasping for air between sobs.

I had spared our family details of the abuse to protect them, and now Jake was trying to tell them for the purpose of arguing that the abuse was my fault. And to involve Dad! Brinn Emily felt as though someone had tattletaled on her, and now she was about to be caught and punished. But my Adult sensed that Jake's actions were unfair and wrong. I was furious.

Tristan drove around for about fifteen minutes while I tried to calm down. Looking at the clock, I saw that work hadn't started yet, but it would soon. Driving back to campus, Tristan parked and quickly went inside the office, bringing out our boss, who looked at me with concern.

I told him I'd received an upsetting email from someone in my past. "Do you feel safe here?" he asked.

"Yes," I said, "I do." It was true. Jake didn't know where I was, and I didn't think he would come after me.

"Okay. Well, whatever this is, you don't deserve it. I'm here for you in any way you need me to be." He took a deep breath. "Don't worry about teaching today; I'll take care of it."

Feeling supported, and relieved not to have to force a smiling face, I walked down to Tristan's and my little home, sat on the couch, and cried.

What do you need right now, Brinn Emily? my Nurturing Adult asked.

I want to leave, Brinn Emily said.

I grabbed my keys. Long drives had always been my mother's antidote when I was feeling upset.

The road ahead stretched in front me like a winding snake. My hands gripped the steering wheel hard. I wanted to run away, hide, and never come back.

Brinn Emily's here, I thought. *What does she need right now?*

She needs an adult to protect her. I recognized my intuitive voice.

Throughout my childhood, what had happened between me and Jake stayed between me and Jake. Adults felt like enemies; telling them our secrets could get us in trouble. Brinn Emily had to keep everything inside her far from them, which left her to deal with scary, hard things on her own. Breaking the pattern would mean not hiding this time. It would mean telling a safe adult about what I feared.

Suddenly inspired, I turned the car around, driving back down the hill to where I had service. If Jake was going to tell Dad about our dirty little secrets, I might as well have a conversation with him on my own terms.

"Princess-ah!" Dad answered affectionately.

Hearing his voice, I was too choked up to speak. Immediately, he knew something was wrong.

"Brinn, what's going on? Are you okay?"

"I'm okay," I managed to say, wiping away tears.

Finally, I told him about Jake's email.

"Brinn," he said calmly, "I am not interested in talking to Jake about the two of you. He can try and talk to me about whatever he wants, but I am not going to listen."

I nodded silently.

"As far as I am concerned, Jake had one job to do—to protect his little sister. He failed at that job, and he's never acknowledged that to me. So I don't want to hear anything else Jake tries to say about the situation. He can try, but I'll tell him exactly what I just told you."

My breath started to feel normal again. I felt Jake's powerful grip release Brinn Emily. In such a brief phone call, I had broken a pattern of suffering and disempowerment.

Driving back to campus, I felt Adult. Calm. Clear. Steady.

Thank you, Universe. Thank you for the thought to call my dad. I'm so grateful I listened.

Between Tristan, my boss, and Dad, I felt supported, protected, and loved, which, for Brinn Emily, was exactly what she had always needed.

A few weeks later, Tristan and I arrived at my grandmother's small upstairs condo overlooking the San Francisco Bay. There seemed to be enough people filling the small space, so I felt confident I would be able to avoid Jake.

Moments after his arrival, however, he weaseled his way through the crowd toward me and Tristan.

"So how's the new job?" he asked nonchalantly.

"Fine," I responded, walking away.

Too polite to excuse himself, Tristan got caught in the cross fire and talked a little longer with Jake. For the remainder of the party, I made sure to keep a buffer between Jake and me.

With a long drive back to the mountains, Tristan and I said our goodbyes before most people. As I turned to follow Tristan out the front door, Jake appeared right behind me. Squeezed between Jake and the door, with Tristan ahead of me, I heard Jake say, "I'll walk you to your car." It was a statement, not a question.

No words came out of my mouth, my only thoughts, *He's breaking the boundary! He's breaking the boundary!*

None of my family members seemed to notice, and Tristan was following my lead. Walking down the stairs, I shrank with each step.

Stepping into the parking lot, Jake turned to Tristan. "Can you excuse us, please?"

Tristan looked at me, concerned, as if to ask, *Is that okay?* I just shrugged and slightly moved my head up and down. He hesitated a moment before turning and walking toward the car.

Jake's lengthy body stood above me at six foot one inch. His small, narrow eyes felt evil. Silently, I stared him down as a river of rage rushed through my veins, out my eyes, and into his. Every part of me screamed inside, drowning out his words.

After he had finished talking, I walked away so angry I felt calm. I never wanted to feel like Jake held that much power over me ever again. I now recognized that he would never respect my boundaries and that I could not rely on anyone else to keep me safe—that was my responsibility. It was up to me to remove myself from uncomfortable situations. It was up to me to refuse conversations with Jake. I didn't care if he kept on approaching me at family functions—I wasn't going to engage. I was done.

As Tristan drove us home, my phone rang. It was Mom, clearly upset. "I'm worried about Jake—he called me sobbing. He said something about feeling like you hate him."

My tone was flat. "Yeah, that's how I feel. I asked him not to talk to me at the party, and he did anyway. I'm mad at myself for letting it happen." My stiff body felt sore. "It will never happen again."

"I just don't want you to hate him. I wish you would forgive him and move on," she begged.

"I can't talk about this right now," I said, hanging up.

Her incessant encouragement to forgive him left a nasty taste in my mouth. Once again, she wasn't listening. She was trying to mold us into the big happy family of her mind, but that isn't how family works. I do not need to be around someone who blatantly disrespects my wishes, crosses my boundaries, and, as a result, leads me to cross my own.

Her definition of forgiveness required reconciliation to Jake and his will, but to me, forgiveness and reconciliation were two separate concepts. Forgiving Jake would not mean I wanted to interact with him. Real relationships were earned, built on trust by people who valued each other. It was clear to me that my brother did not value me, and I did not trust him.

The next morning, I woke up to another email. This one felt different. Jake explained that for the first time, when we stood in the parking lot together, he *got* it. He realized that I had suffered *more* than he had. He finally felt empathy for me. Standing in front of me the day before, he felt as if he had absorbed my emotions and was shocked by how much pain I was in. This made him want to commit his life to helping me resolve my pain—he told me that his suffering no longer mattered, and yet again, he promised that was going to dedicate his life to my healing.

I rolled my eyes. His words felt bombastic, dramatic, and fleeting. I knew the moment I didn't react the way he wanted, he would turn on me. Not to mention the fact that he was contacting me, again, after both of us had agreed to stop communicating with each other. While part of me felt acknowledged, I still didn't trust him. I didn't trust his words, his actions, or his emotions. It was interesting that he had sensed my anger, even without my words. Words had never reached him, but maybe my energy did. I wasn't exactly sure what I needed, but after the last six months, I knew I needed space.

Over the next year, my life was peaceful, Tristan and I living happily in our mountainside community. Jake and I had stopped communicating, and I was focused on my future.

Tristan had built a youth outdoor program down the hill, and we planned to move back to the city after the coming school year. I'd taken over the teen leadership program at the outdoor school and was busy coordinating community events across multiple counties. We hosted service projects and overnight conferences with workshops on communication, yoga, cooking, and nutrition. I brought guest speakers from ALC to teach teens about the Inner Critic and help them overcome their internal negative self-talk. By the end of the school year, I was the one leading the workshops and, eventually, training staff as well.

Sharing the information I'd learned in my early twenties with young adults was exactly what I'd promised myself I would do way back when I had completed Going Deeper, my second ALC training. It turned out that I loved creating curriculum and teaching others the tools and techniques I'd learned in my own healing journey. Helping young people navigate their inner worlds was the most fulfilling job I had ever had.

Knowing Tristan and I couldn't stay at the outdoor school forever, I'd always suspected my experiences there would serve as a launching pad for whatever might come next in my career. The idea of becoming a therapist was still on my mind, but I was also still afraid of drowning under the pile of student loans that would come with grad school.

Discussing this topic while we were out driving one day, Tristan turned to me and said, "Brinn, stop being scared. Go back to school, take out the loans, and do what you want to do."

Tristan was typically carefree and lighthearted, but this time he was serious. "You're good at this personal growth therapy stuff, and you're passionate about it, so just do it!"

"Okay! I'll do it!" I said triumphantly. Chills spread across my body. "I'm going back to school!"

We grabbed hands, and I leaned over, kissing him on the cheek. Giddiness took over as we danced in our seats. Tears filled my eyes, and I knew—my life was about to change forever.

BREAKING UP

received my admissions email to graduate school for clinical psychology one week after Tristan dumped me. It was October, and we were about a month into the school year. The weekend before the breakup, I'd been standing in the kitchen making lunch when he walked in.

"When I went into town this morning, I bought you something." He handed me a little gift with an envelope and a card.

I opened the box and found a pair of hand-carved earrings that I had admired hanging in a store window months before.

"Oh my gosh! I can't believe you remembered!" I said, throwing my arms around him.

"They were sold out, so I tracked down the artist to make another pair. That's why it took so long."

I could tell he was pleased with himself.

"Aw, I can't believe you did that for me!" I opened the envelope. The card read, "I can't wait to spend another year in the forest with you. This year is going to be the best yet! I love you so much!"

Finally he said, "I also looked at rings today, but the one you want is too expensive."

Taken aback, I felt my body stiffen. The water on the stove began to boil. I had no idea he had been engagement ring shopping. We had talked about rings our entire relationship and had even gone to get my ring finger sized a few months ago, but I hadn't considered that he might be ready to propose this soon. Between his two jobs, this was his first day off in months. I thought he'd gone to town for alone time and to relax. I felt confused.

"Really? I didn't think that's what you were doing today," I said, trying to sound casual. "How much was the ring?"

"Like $1,500."

I balked. *Seriously? That's not that expensive!* While we didn't have a lot of money in the bank, it wouldn't have been that hard for him to scrounge up the money if he'd really wanted to. Not that I needed anything fancy—I would have been happy with anything that meant we were fully committing to each other.

"Oh! I guess that's all I'm worth to you," I fired off without thinking. Turning my back to him, I occupied myself with stirring the macaroni I'd just poured into the pot. That rejection must have stung.

One week and a pointless fight later, we were done. There was no discussion about the engagement ring conversation or about breaking up. He simply informed me that he no longer looked at me romantically and we were over. In one moment, my life had completely changed. Inside my head, someone screamed, *Leave! Now!*

Throwing open the bedroom door, I grabbed clothes off hangers, stuffing them into a bag. I didn't know where I was headed, but I couldn't stay there.

Charging up the hill to my car, a subtle, soothing thought crossed my mind. *This is happening for a reason. It's all part of the bigger plan.*

I held on to that thought as if it were my only source of oxygen. I needed to trust the Universe.

At the end of the weekend, I returned to our tiny home and moved all of my things into a separate dome at the top of the hill. But I still had to see the person who'd crushed my heart every day.

My overflowing boxes and piles of clothes crowded the entryway of my new space and took over the bed, as if they too were afraid to fully move into a new home. Every night, I'd watch episode after episode of *Friends*, hoping to drift off at some point to escape my brain.

Analyzing our two-year relationship was all my mind could do. I dissected sentences, words, and body-language signals, searching for evidence of where I had screwed up. Food made me nauseous, and the only things I wanted to ingest were alcohol and weed.

The words *I guess that's all I'm worth to you* hung in my head constantly. Steeped in regret, I begged Tristan to hear my apology, but he told me that statement hadn't bothered him.

I knew differently. I had a remarkable talent to cut deep with only a few words, aiming right for someone's insecurities. For Tristan, money was a sensitive topic in relationships, just as it was for me. But there was no way we could have a conversation about that.

The comment was a cover-up for many hard conversations we weren't ready to have. We didn't yet have the emotional maturity to create shared financial goals and budgets. Off-work time was spent day drinking, which lead to sloppy nights and hangovers, not real-life conversations. We hadn't yet built the emotional safety with each other and comfortability with ourselves to say what was on our minds about our fears of the future. Although we had wistful conversations about our fairy-tale wedding, we didn't have discussions that could build a lifelong marriage.

I have come to learn that every challenge in our lives pushes us one of two ways: either deeper into denial and distraction or into opportunities to face our fears and acknowledge we need to change. Now I stood at a crossroads, just as I had when I was alone in Asia. I could either sit and think about all of the ways my ex had done me wrong, or I could think about how I could learn from this experience and better myself for my next relationship.

Was I doomed to end up in dysfunctional relationships forever? Or was my trauma rearing its ugly head again?

I prayed it was trauma, because at least then I had a chance of doing something about it. My inner knowing and intuition told me that I still needed to heal my deepest wound: the one my brother had caused within me.

On the surface, part of me had been happy with Tristan, but deep down, I had longed for more. I'd craved more vulnerability, safety, emotional intimacy, communication, and authenticity. In every relationship, I'd always wanted more, and at my core I knew, if I didn't completely work through my brother wound, I would forever feel that lack. I'd never feel whole enough to give all of myself, openly, to anyone else.

I decided that the anger, shame, anxiety, sadness, and loss I carried under the surface every day were burdens I wanted to leave behind—for good. I was rapidly approaching thirty and eager to break free of those shackles of my past. I dreamt of a long-lasting, soul-connecting partnership. And I wanted to attend family events without subjecting myself to the emotional roller coaster that had accompanied them for the past twelve years. My future depended on my actions now.

So I went on a mission: my goal, to forgive Jake by my thirtieth birthday, eleven months away. I had little idea what forgiveness meant to me and had no plan for how to get there. But I felt that even just holding the intention of forgiveness could shift me in the right direction.

One month later, I said goodbye to Tristan and left the mountain, finding myself, once again, back in my hometown with no job and nowhere to live. Luckily, a friend offered me her couch in exchange for watching her dog for a few weeks. After that, Caleb and his wife were going on a four-month trip to Asia and needed someone to watch their two dogs. Every day, I affirmed to myself that I had secure housing waiting for me. I hoped to push out having to pay rent as long as possible to stretch the small amount of savings I had left.

I'm so grateful for the abundance coming to me was the phrase that became my mantra. Signing up for a forty-day Kundalini yoga prosperity challenge, I started meditating with this intention daily.

Within a few weeks, I was back at my old teaching job and was offered a new position at the outdoor school, the one I'd just left. Conveniently, it was an off-site position coordinating school assemblies and teaching students about mental, physical, and nutritional health.

One day, while staying at Caleb's house, I scanned his bookshelf, finding familiar authors' names like Eckhart Tolle, Brené Brown, and Don Miguel Ruiz. But then, up on a higher shelf, I glimpsed a small rectangular box with worn golden corners and a light-blue pattern. I reached up and pulled it off the shelf and read the cover: *Healing with the Angels Oracle Cards.*

Sweet memories floated into my mind: My brothers and I sitting around in pajamas as Mom read us angel stories out loud. Those stories about "good Samaritans" showing up in uncanny ways, stories of impressive coincidences, unexplained events, and prayers being answered in real time. Growing up, my mom had even had a license plate holder that read "I only drive as fast as my angels can fly."

I moved into the living room and settled in, cross-legged on a cushion on the floor, so that my eyes aligned more with the height of the coffee table. Opening the box, I found a well-used booklet containing descriptions of each of the forty-four cards in the deck. Lifting out the cards, I thumbed through them, each one a beautifully illustrated depiction of a central theme: Spiritual Guidance, Power, Emerging, Harmony, et cetera.

I picked up the booklet and read the instructions. They encouraged the reader to ask the angels a question while shuffling the cards. I could ask a specific question or a general question inviting the angels to send whatever message they felt was appropriate at the time.

After reading the various suggestions on how to select and arrange the cards, I settled on pulling three cards, representing the past, present, and future.

Not knowing what question to ask, I simply took a deep breath, closed my eyes, and said, "Angels, thank you for supporting me. Please, let me know whatever message you have for me right now."

I shuffled, liking the feeling of the cool cards in my hand. Over and over again, I took cards from the front and added them to the back, then from the middle and from the back to the front. They were larger than playing cards, so I felt awkward trying to shuffle them together, but I managed. Finally, I stopped, laying out three cards: Divine Timing, which represented the recent past; Focus, which represented the present moment; and Study, which represented the future.

They knowingly stared up at me from the table. Filled with curiosity, I searched the booklet for their descriptions.

> **Divine Timing:** Pay attention to the doors that are opening and shutting for you right now. Learn to walk through doors that open and leave behind doors that have shut.

Whoa. I let the card's message sink in. My mind went back to the intuitive thought I'd had the moment Tristan broke up with me: *This is all happening for a reason.* This card was telling me to keep trusting, keep surrendering to the process, and keep using this challenge as an opportunity to deepen my relationship with God and with myself. Everything is happening in divine timing, but learning to accept that is the lesson here.

> **Focus:** Think about what you want, not what you don't want. Guard your thoughts carefully because they create your experience.

This card represented focusing my mind to create loving, peaceful thoughts and, therefore, experiences. Did the angels know I had just been arguing with Tristan in my head? This card also aligned with my recent fear of never securing a stable place to live or a consistent income. It was a reminder to keep focusing on what I wanted, and not let the anger and fear of my past take over my mind in the present.

> **Study:** You are engaged in learning and study right now. Your angels guide you to take time to read, listen, and grow.

I couldn't believe it. While the book said that study didn't necessarily mean actual school, at this moment, this card representing the future held a literal sign to move forward with continuing my education. I felt more aligned than ever with my goal.

Excited by the three cards I'd just pulled, I was eager to try again. I shuffled, bringing the back cards to the front and the front cards to the back, then cutting the deck into three groups. Putting them all together, I shuffled them like playing cards about three or four times before stopping. I put the stack down and picked from the top of the pile, laying out three cards. Study. Focus. Divine Timing.

I stared in disbelief. Chills ran down my body. Had I really just pulled those three cards again? I'd shuffled so much! The message was clear. In the midst of my broken heart, the Universe was telling me to trust myself and forge ahead. This journey was all a part of my spiritual growth: It was time for me to focus on what I wanted, make my education a priority, and trust God's timing as life continued to unfold.

Combining the cards again, I played with them in my hands. Moving through the deck, I slowly inspected each one. I felt excitement, along with skepticism and faith, as if I had just witnessed an unexplained miracle. The cards had validated and assured me like some wise older sage reminding me that I was a spiritual being having a human experience. As I prepared to put the cards back in their box, one slipped, falling to the ground upside down. I reached to pick it up and read the front. *Focus.*

FORGIVENESS

BACK TO SCHOOL

Before the breakup with Tristan, I'd planned to go to a state university for my graduate degree. That summer, I'd even had an appointment with the dean of the psychology department at a state university to discuss my options about starting school the next year.

"So you want to work with young people, right?" she said after hearing me out.

"Yes, I would love that. I want to give young people the tools and education around mental health that I didn't have," I replied.

After telling me about their three-year program, she said, "Let me connect you with someone who's working in schools. I think he'd be a really good person for you to talk to."

She wrote down a phone number, and I called the next day. The following week, I found myself on the phone with the founder of a school-based therapy nonprofit. He also happened to be a professor of psychology at a private university in town. That university had night classes and an accelerated program, meaning I would finish a year before students at the state university. And since this new program accepted new students every eight weeks, I'd also be able to start right away instead of waiting until the next fall. If I hadn't had made that connection, my transition away from Tristan and the outdoor school would've been that much harder. Once again, I thanked the Universe for placing this program in my lap.

When the first day of school arrived, I was ecstatic! Part of me had thought I would never make it to grad school. It had always seemed too big of a dream to dream. But I no longer felt overwhelmed by the commitment I was making to myself. While I'd never had a plan for my future—ever since graduating college, I felt as if I were shooting in the dark—now I understood. This unseen step had always been right in front of me, but only the Universe could tell me when the timing was right for me to accept my path.

Walking into class, I felt nervous but excited. About fifteen people occupied the tables and chairs. I sat down next to another woman who looked about my age, with shoulder-length dark hair. Scanning the room, I noticed people chatting with one another, most of them older than I was. But I was comfortable being the new person. It was as though I'd been training for this moment for the last seven years as I navigated my own healing journey and had begun supporting others on theirs. I was ready to take this step. Surprisingly, I felt like I belonged.

On the second night of school, one of my professors invited his wife to speak to our class. She was a therapist in her late fifties named Sue Bowen. Sitting in one of the open seats among us, she wore a cream-colored cardigan and tan dress slacks. Her demeanor was calm and quiet, yet she spoke enthusiastically about how much she enjoyed working with psychology students as a therapist. In order to graduate from our program, every student would need to go to therapy, and she was offering her services.

"In my free time, I love to travel in our RV and write. Actually, I published a book about forgiving my father after experiencing childhood sexual abuse."

Suddenly she had my attention. *Did she really just say what I thought she said?* It was as if every cell in my body was listening to her. Opening my laptop, I ordered her book immediately, and when she shared her phone number, I wrote it down.

At Caleb's house, when I heard a knock at the door followed by the rumble of a delivery truck pulling away, I knew the book had arrived. I tore open the package and began devouring Sue's book right at the kitchen table. I absorbed the information as if I were dehydrated and drinking fresh water. As the words moved through my body, I felt keenly aware of their cooling presence. I could have used more of them earlier, but they quickly made up for lost time. I had never read about someone's struggle to heal from sexual abuse before.

The next day, I called her office and was relieved to hear that she not only had availability but could also accommodate a sliding scale of $65 per session. The universe had once again answered my prayers. She was another angel on my path, showing up at the exact time I needed her. She knew what forgiveness entailed and could show me the way. I was surprisingly ambitious for someone who barely had a clue about what that word *forgiveness* meant to me.

I knew ancient texts like the Torah, the Tao Te Ching, the New Testament, and the Quran taught the value of forgiveness; sage figures spoke on it, books encouraged it, but I just couldn't understand it. The concept felt oddly elusive, as if other people got it but I had missed the memo.

The antiquated, toxic message "Forgive and forget" had infiltrated my childhood. But that phrase suggested that we should continue to sweep abuse under the rug. It kept the façade of the picturesque family without acknowledging the pain and suffering that occurred inside. If we don't hold perpetrators accountable, they receive a free pass for their wrongdoing. "Forgive and forget" implies we must reconcile with everyone, even people who have harmed us and may continue to harm us.

I was twenty-two at ALC when someone first told me I could forgive without forgetting. That was the first time I heard the saying "Resentment is like drinking poison and waiting for the other person to die." That message began to shift my understanding of what forgiveness meant.

At the time, though I felt I *should want* to forgive my brother, I didn't actually want to. My mother had begged me for years to do it; she'd told me that his life literally depended on my decision. But to even consider forgiving him felt like betrayal to the parts of me who held the pain of his abuse.

But now, my hatred for my brother was eating me from the inside out. And all the hatred in the world would never change the past. So what was I really holding on to, anyway?

***

"What if total healing could come from this relationship with Jake?" Sue asked me in one of our early sessions.

My eyes tingled with the beginnings of tears. Nobody had ever asked me that question before. Even though I had recently decided that I wanted to forgive him, part of me still didn't believe that *total healing* was possible for me. I wasn't even sure what "total healing" meant. But here was a professional, with lived experience of abuse, suggesting that I had the ability to fully heal.

My mind traveled to a conversation with a friend a few months back. I had been visiting him and his wife for a few days when one night, he beautifully opened up about his childhood.

He shared that he too had been sexually abused as a child, and as a result, he went on to abuse his sister. As he spoke, deep emotions stirred inside me. I felt compassion and empathy but also confusion. *Wait, wasn't I supposed to hate him?*

"But I got help," he said. "I went to therapy and sought out different programs for healing. I learned to forgive my abuser for hurting me. And I forgave myself for hurting my sister. She eventually received support too. Since then, we have reconciled, and we have a healthy relationship now."

What if total healing could come from my relationship with Jake?

I didn't know the answer, but I wanted to try to find out.

Sometimes when I'm not sure of my next step, I use a writing exercise called the Wise Inner Teacher Letter. I learned this journaling prompt at ALC: I ask my Wise Inner Teacher a question, skip a line, and begin writing the thoughts that emerge in response. Magically, this process tends to yield astute advice.

After the session where Sue asked me that question, I did the exercise:

Dear Wise Inner Teacher,

Question: What's my next step with Jake?

Answer: Brinn, baby. The next step looks exactly how you want it to look. You're doing the work, and I honestly think this is just the beginning of a pretty powerful breakthrough. Astrologically, the cycle you're in now isn't complete until December, which means you still have a lot of time for transformation. As long as you keep doing your inner work, which you are, you have so much more opportunity for growth.

Question: Wise Inner Teacher, what am I scared of?

Answer: Brinn baby, you're scared of losing power.

Question: Wise Inner Teacher, what power am I afraid of losing?

Answer: Right now, you have power over Jake. By keeping your distance from him and not letting him into your life, you're keeping him "small," as he kept you small for so long. He so desperately wants to connect with you and the rest of the family, so keeping him at a distance feels like power to you. But it's false power. It's ego, not the type of divine power you are really made of. You might think that letting go of the anger you carry and the story you have associated with your childhood means letting a part of yourself go, or abandoning yourself. But that's not true. The story of your abuse does not define you.

I was shocked. I hadn't even been conscious of keeping Jake at a distance to exert power over him, but now I saw this was true. Long ago, my anger had formed itself into a shield to protect me and to keep him at bay. As long as I stayed angry, I could justify that shield. I feared letting go of that anger because maybe without it, I wouldn't be safe.

But I am so angry!

Anger is like an iceberg. From the outside, we can only see one emotion and the behaviors linked to it. But in most cases, other feelings lurk below the surface, feelings we cannot see clearly until we undertake a submarine investigation. Anger is never the only emotion.

So I wrote down a bulleted list of all the reasons why I resented Jake: He had thrown away his talent and career to drugs; he had abused me and used me without even thinking of my own well-being; he had betrayed me by violating the trust in our once-close relationship; he was an asshole who wasn't doing anything to improve his mental health; he had verbally attacked my mom, brother, and sister over the past few years, both online and in person; he had never taken full responsibility for his actions; he'd never acknowledged how much he'd hurt me or acknowledged the major ripple effect that the abuse had created throughout my life. Plus, he didn't have the guts to look at his own trauma, which pissed me off.

So what's underneath?

I was angry he threw his life away, which meant, on some level, I didn't want him to throw his life away. I actually wanted him to succeed. That's weird. *Why did I want him to succeed?*

Because I love him.

Love is under the anger.

I was angry because I wanted him to get better! I wanted him to keep a stable job, have consistent income, and live in proper housing! Even though he was off heroin, he still lived like an addict, floating from job to job and struggling with housing insecurity. I wanted him to acknowledge how much pain and suffering we had both endured. If he could do that, then he would really see me. And if he really saw me, then maybe we could be brother and sister again.

But why would I want us to be brother and sister again?

Because I missed my brother.

I missed my brother.

Sadness is under the anger.

It had never occurred to me that I felt sad about losing Jake! But it made perfect sense. I was heartbroken. I had always wanted so badly to connect with my brother, my friend. The person who used to encourage and believe in me. The person who used to play games and music with me. The person who'd used his imagination to create alternative worlds we could live in. I wanted to feel special to the person I had felt special to for the first fifteen years of my life. I wanted my brother back.

Unfortunately, that person no longer existed. Years of hard drug use, untreated mental illness, and deep, dark shame had impacted my brother's mind. He was resentful, volatile, unpredictable, narcissistic, and callous. When I was young, he'd not only been the life of the party but confident, secure, and protective. I had held him up as a role model. But now I barely knew him.

My grief was real. It was a deep well of sorrow for the person and the relationship I could never find again. Even though Jake still existed in the world, the person and the relationship I longed for were already dead, and that was worth mourning.

My feelings toward Jake ricocheted like a pinball. I wanted to forgive him, and I grieved the loss of our connection, but I still resented him for how he had treated me in the past and hated how his anger and volatility showed up in the present.

But I was starting to realize that if I could forgive him without reconciliation, then maybe I could forgive him without agreeing with how he acted now. After all, I had always recognized that forgiveness and reconciliation held different meanings. Just as I'd always resisted my mother's pressure to acquiesce to him, I could forgive him for the past and still not want to maintain a relationship with him in the present. I could feel angry with how he was now treating the rest of my family while forgiving him for how he had treated me in the past.

The more I fell into these uncomfortable emotions of sadness, longing, and anger, the more they reminded me of how I was grieving the loss of Tristan. After all, I had just lost a man I had known since I was twelve—a partner with whom I'd shared an especially intense connection, someone I had thought would be with me forever.

Tristan had always reminded me of Jake—a smart, rebellious, charismatic person full of talent, charm, and wit but also with a dark, manipulative, and explosive side. I hadn't seen that side of him in our romantic relationship, but having known him since we were twelve, I was aware that it existed. As Jake and I had, Tristan and I had also shared a world that nobody else seemed to understand. When we dated, he didn't feel like a brother, but he did felt like the long-lost best friend I'd never admitted I missed.

So the underlying buzz of anxiety I'd felt throughout my childhood had become a pattern I repeated in relationships. I searched for people to help me escape my grief, but as a result, we escaped adulthood too. It was as if we were little kids playing house as we partied too much and promised each other a future we had little ability to build.

But where was my Adult? Where was my accountability, my follow-through, my healthy communication? Maybe if I learned to embrace my Adult perspective more often, I would attract a more mature partner.

The struggles I'd experienced in my adult relationships were starting to make sense. I was constantly attracted to people who felt lively and fun. But they never seemed entirely safe either. This conflict reminded me of my childhood, a time when I too had often felt lively and fun, before I hated myself. Before I had acknowledged the reality of the abuse. Before I lost my brother.

FAMILY SCENES

"Therapists are both scientists and artists," Andy Henderson explained in my first semester of grad school. He was my favorite professor, bringing passion and lived experience to his teachings about becoming a therapist.

He went on. "As personal guides, therapists delicately, and thoughtfully, work with complex vulnerabilities, eliciting growth and change through specific methods and interventions while simultaneously keeping themselves composed and grounded. It truly is a dance."

I flipped my pen around in my hand. My Inner Critic was starting in on me, doubting my ability to live up to such poetic expectations. But Andy's way of teaching us was to create vulnerability in the classroom. He wanted us to not only learn valuable concepts for practical use but also open up and feel the exposure that our future clients would endure.

"Your assignment is to create a family scene using your classmates to represent your family members. For example, if Mom and Dad argued frequently, then you might place two people standing back-to-back, arms crossed. Or if there was a close sibling unit, then you could show that by asking two people to stand arm in arm. After you have set the scene, then move people around showing how you would have *preferred* those family dynamics to have been. Any questions?"

My only question was *How much do I tell?* I was so nervous, I didn't know what to say or where to place anyone. Finally, when the moment came and it was my turn, I took a deep breath.

No longer arranged in rows, all of the long tables and chairs had been pushed back against the wall, leaving a wide-open space in the front of the large classroom. My eighteen or so classmates sat among the tables. I stepped forward.

Thinking first of my dad and my sister, I asked two people to stand in opposite corners of the room, showing their detachment from my family unit. Then I took one of the free tables and a chair and placed them against the front wall, in the middle of the room. I seated one of my classmates here to represent my mother, who was often at home working behind her desk—involved in the daily events of her three youngest children, yet separate from our inner lives. Then, without words, I placed "Caleb" about five feet in front of the desk, facing forward.

Taking the hand of my classmate whom I had assigned to be "Jake," I led him to another table, far away from Caleb.

"Stand on the table and put your arms above your head, like you're a bear, ready to attack," I instructed.

Without hesitation, I crawled across the floor, curled up in a ball underneath the table, and shielded my head with my arms. Even beneath the table, I still felt Jake's control looming viscerally over me. We were isolated, far away from the others, and I felt scared and alone. My Adult knew I had to move quickly or risk becoming trapped in those emotions. Rising to my feet, I began steadily rearranging the scene.

I brought my mom and dad together, shoulder to shoulder, arms linked, in the middle of the room. I placed Caleb and Charlotte, also arm in arm, directly behind my parents. Behind the wall of my family was where I placed Jake. Then I walked to the front of the group. Standing in front of my parents, I pressed my back into their arms. Feeling the full support of my family unit behind me, and with separation from Jake, I could breathe again. Finally, I felt safe.

***

"So where is your sister within these family dynamics?" Sue inquired during therapy one day. Her office was minimally decorated. A floor lamp in the corner created a soft light in the room. She sat across from me on a low couch, her clipboard in her hand. I sat in an overstuffed chair with my feet curled underneath me.

"Well, my sister and I have an interesting relationship," I said, unsure of how I felt. "I love her very much, and I know she loves me, but she's thirteen years older than I am. Don't get me wrong, we've never had any bad blood between us—we just live different lives." I felt a little guilty, wondering if I was speaking negatively about her. "When everything came out about Jake, she was already married with a young son, working full-time and running a church with her husband." I sighed.

The truth is, I missed my sister. I remembered how when I was young, she'd helped raise me and my brothers. When we were trying to get Charlotte's attention, we used to call, "Mom, I mean, Sis." She would sing "House at Pooh Corner" by Loggins and Messina as she tucked me in at night. I was only five when she left for college, and when I turned six, she sent me a Winnie the Pooh mug for my birthday. I remembered receiving the package in the mail and running excitedly down the hall to my room to open it in private. When I was nine or ten, I would occasionally spend weekends at her apartment, eating candy and watching movies with her.

But we grew more distant after she and her husband became strict born-again Christians and started their own church. Their lives were consumed by their faith, and we had different beliefs. These changes caused some rifts within our family but never a personal one between Charlotte and me. I don't think it was a conscious decision, but as Charlotte and her husband's church friends became their family, somewhere along the way, our family got pushed aside.

"Have you ever talked to your sister about what happened between you and Jake?" Sue asked.

"No, not really," I said hesitantly.

I had always wanted to bring it up but didn't know how to initiate that conversation. I had so many questions I wanted to ask her

"Actually, there is one story, but I don't know the details." I put my feet down on the floor and sat up in my chair, leaning forward. Slowly rubbing my hands together, I took a long, deep breath. "It's weird, but years ago I heard somewhere, probably from my mom, that when she first talked to Charlotte about Jake and me, before she could say anything, my sister asked, 'Does this have to do with the time I found Jake and Brinn in the shower together?'"

Sue's mouth dropped open, her eyes wide. "Really? That's interesting."

I tossed my arms in the air and let out a chuckle.

"Yeah, I know, it's crazy! I have no recollection of Charlotte ever catching us in the shower or her telling my mom what was going on. I've never heard Jake referring to Charlotte finding out, so I don't think any of us remember except her. But I've never had the courage to ask her what happened." My voice trailed off.

"Would you feel comfortable talking to her about it now?" Sue encouraged me.

"I want to. And I do think it would be helpful to talk to her. She's very levelheaded and logical, and I don't think it would be uncomfortable for me or her."

After therapy, I texted my sister, telling her I had a question about Jake and me. It had been a few months since I'd last talked to her, but she responded immediately.

"Does this have to do with when I caught you two in the shower …? I'll call you in ten minutes," the text read.

I waited, pacing in the parking lot with my phone in my hand. While I was nervous, part of me was relieved to finally talk openly with her. After what felt like an eternity, my phone rang.

"Hey, Brinn Ems," my sister said affectionately.

"Hey, Sis, thanks for calling," None of us kids had ever called my sister by her first name. She had always been Sis or Sissy to us. "Do you remember telling Mom that you caught Jake and me in the shower together?"

"Yes, of course I remember."

"Can you tell me about what happened? I don't remember anything about it."

"You must have been about ten or so, because Kevin and I were dating, but we hadn't gotten married yet. We'd stopped by the house like normal, but you and Jake were in the shower together. Looking back, I don't know why it was okay for a twelve- or thirteen-year-old boy to be showering with his little sister, but that's what was happening. I went into the bathroom to say hi, and I saw you sucking his penis. I yelled, *'Hey!'* and immediately told mom and Kevin what I saw. I figured she would take care of it."

Silently, I took in her words. My sister had known. My mom had known. Even my sister's husband had known. To my knowledge, none of these adults had ever intervened.

As these thoughts came to me, I felt nothing, not even anger.

"Did you ever follow up with Mom after? Did you and Kevin ever talk about it again?" I asked, confused by the idea that so many adults had known about the abuse for years.

"Honestly, I thought Mom would take care of it. And I have to say, I was preoccupied with my life. I'm not proud of that, but it's true. I'm sorry for not being there more for you."

It was difficult to feel angry at Charlotte because she had done the right thing by telling my mom what she'd seen. True, she never followed up, nor had her husband, but there was nothing I could do to change the past. What was the point of getting mad at my family all over again? I was tired of being angry.

But now I knew the truth, and there was no way she was lying. The description she gave was too accurate and vivid to be made-up. Perhaps Jake and I were never aware that my sister had seen us in the shower.

Maybe my mom did say something to us. But either way, my mom, Jake and I have no memory of this happening.

This conversation, though, confirmed that my mother had known about the abuse nearly a decade before I told her at age eighteen and had done nothing to protect me. That reality stung. But I wasn't as angry as I thought I'd be. The truth alone was enough.

"I feel like I've missed my window of opportunity to talk to the family about what happened," I said. "It feels like everyone is sick of hearing about it and just wants us to move on. It's like everyone wanted me to talk when I was eighteen, but I wasn't ready. Plus, nobody ever asked any details about how often or in what way I'd been molested."

"Brinn, I will listen anytime you want to talk," Charlotte said. "I'm here for you, and that's never going to change."

I thanked her and hung up. Feeling moved by her words, I let them swirl around in my head. I appreciated her willingness to stay present with me during this vulnerable conversation but didn't quite feel safe enough to speak more about my childhood.

For years, I'd tried to safeguard my family from the full truth—and protect myself from my own shame about what I had done. But I had also been protecting Jake. As far as I knew, he'd never told any details of what had happened to any family member, despite his threats to do so. *How do I tell my parents what he did to their daughter? How do I tell my siblings what really went on? Will they start imagining scenarios in their minds? Will those images ever leave them?* My humiliation haunted me.

After that conversation, I felt my heart healed a little more. I also made the decision not to confront my mother. Honestly, I saw no point—she would deny ever knowing about the abuse, I would get upset at her denial, and then we'd hit a wall in our relationship with no resolution, no apology, only her denial. I wasn't consciously suppressing my feelings; I simply didn't feel angry enough to bother with another fight about the past. I wanted to move forward.

***

Four years later, I worked with a practitioner named Steph Dodds. She specialized in emotional freedom techniques, also known as tapping. Like acupuncture, this technique helps to release energy that's been trapped in the body, but instead of the therapist using needles, the patient gently taps on specific points of their body.

Steph and I were discussing a recent argument I'd had with my mom. She and I still argued on a semiregular basis, but the more healing work I did, the less my Inner Child got triggered and the less they affected me. I, therefore, was able maintain my composure in my Adult-self. My mom had also become softer as the years went on and wasn't nearly as stressed, so her emotions were less intense too. But she still had a way of getting under my skin.

Suddenly I felt tremendous anger and sadness. Hot, heavy tears poured from my eyes as I realized that these strong feelings didn't arise from our most recent argument—they came from the past. Finally, my feelings about my mom knowing about the abuse were emerging, ready for me to release them.

Even though I had no memory of the day my sister found Jake and me in the shower, intense feelings ignited within me. With Steph's gentle guidance, in my mind's eye, I visualized the scene as Charlotte had described it. Then I visualized myself removing little Brinn Emily from the shower and holding her as she cried. After consoling Brinn Emily, I spoke out loud every word I wanted to say to my mom.

"How could you not protect me? How could you turn a blind eye to what was happening under your own roof!" I sobbed as I tapped on my body. "You, my own mother, betrayed me! How could you not protect me from him? It was because of you that I endured more years of pain and suffering."

For a full hour and a half, I tapped, cried, and journeyed through the past. By the end of the session, I felt drained but relieved. I'd released pent-up emotions on a cellular level and managed to reach a calm and peaceful place. What my mother had done wasn't right, but when I thought about her not protecting me, this painful experience no longer held the overwhelming emotional charge it had earlier. I was free from the pain, and my Inner Child felt safe and loved.

That's what I love about doing somatic work that calms the nervous system and processes our pain. I didn't have to spend weeks or months talking about this situation in therapy. I didn't even talk to my mom about my anger. Instead, I dove deep into my feelings, allowed them to flow without shame or judgment. Then I released them from my body, through the tapping. To me, this is ultimate freedom. Regardless of what others are doing around me, I have the confidence, skills, and tools to feel, soothe, and manage my emotional responses.

If I had felt those strong feelings toward my mom when I was twenty-nine, I would have processed them then, but I didn't feel them. We cannot rush our healing. The layers of the onion don't unravel all at once. When our bodies feel safe enough, and the timing is right, then new revelations can occur. So the moment the emotions did surface, four years later, I didn't judge them or try to logic them away by saying it was too late to be angry. I let them rise so they could be processed and then released.

A few years later, I decided to talk to my mom about that day when my sister found Jake and me in the shower. I was at her ranch, and Jake had come up in conversation. Mentioning his name hadn't bothered me like it used to, and I took a chance to be brave, knowing already how the conversation would likely go.

"I just don't remember that happening," my mom said with a pained look on her face.

"I know you don't, Mom, but I believe Charlotte," I said. "There's no way what she described could be made-up. All the details match what was happening at that time. I just think we all blocked it out."

My mom shook her head slowly and stared off into space.

"I just can't believe I wouldn't have killed him on the spot," she said, letting out a dry half chuckle. "It's so embarrassing. Please don't mention this to anyone. I can't bear the thought of people knowing this. It makes me sick to my stomach."

I sat there, studying her face.

Her pain was real. The shame, the embarrassment, the inner conflict. But I'd already released my anger and feelings of betrayal, so I no longer needed her validation or to accept what I knew to be truth. But a genuine apology, an acknowledgement, or at least not making it all about her, would have been nice. I took a breath in.

"Well, I don't think there's shame in people knowing. It's a fact. It's reality. It's part of my story and yours. Consciously or not, you were told about the abuse." I let out a deep sigh. "But it's in the past. None of us can control our past actions, and I can't control how you feel about it today. All I can do is heal my emotional wounds that have lived inside me and then move forward. And I hope you can do the same."

She looked up and made eye contact. Her face softened, and tears filled her eyes. "You really do walk the walk." She reached for me, and we embraced. She whispered, "I am so proud of you."

RAGE AGAINST MY BROTHERS

After four months away, Caleb and his wife returned home at the beginning of April; they agreed to let me keep on staying at their house until May 1. A few days before I moved out, Caleb approached me.

"Jake's been staying at Mom's this week and reached out about getting together." His tone was matter-of-fact. "So we agreed he'd come to the house on Sunday." He paused. "That being said, it might be easier if you weren't here. That way we could get our time in and you won't have to deal with him."

"Sure," I said. "That makes sense. Just let me know when he's coming, and I'll leave."

I got it. Logically, my Adult understood that Jake was my problem, and if Caleb wanted to spend time with his brother at his house, he had every right to.

Sunday, my last day at the house, arrived on schedule. It was a beautiful spring afternoon, and we had all the windows open as we cranked up the music and collectively cleaned house.

It had been challenging for me and Caleb to live together in small quarters. Living on top of each other made me revert to feeling like an annoying little sister who was in the way all the time. But today felt good. Caleb and I felt like a team as we contributed equally to the chores; our spirits were high.

But earlier that day, Caleb had admitted that Jake was really only coming by to pick up some weed and that he wasn't actually looking forward to seeing Jake. The way Caleb accommodated Jake's demands was starting to frustrate me.

If Caleb doesn't really want to see Jake, then why is he coming to Caleb's house? And why is Caleb choosing Jake over me on my last day here? This was supposed to be my safe space.

But I went along with the original plan I had agreed to, waiting for Caleb to tell me when Jake would arrive.

Suddenly, Caleb shut off the music. "Oh shit. Jake's almost here."

My breath caught in my throat.

"I am sorry, Brinn, I just saw his text, and he's almost here. Can you please leave?" he said with a pained look on his face.

I felt as if Caleb had punched me in the gut, even though I could tell he felt bad for the abruptness of this shift. I stammered, "Can you just, like, go meet him somewhere?" My voice shook. "Like at a coffee shop or something?"

"No, I can't. He'll be here any minute. You just need to leave. I am sorry." His tone was frank.

My head spun as anger rushed through my body. I wanted to leave and never come back. I grabbed some clothes and a jacket, stuffing them into a backpack, and slammed the door behind me.

Enraged, I threw open the car door and crashed my body down on the seat. My hot tears flowed as I started the engine and peeled off down the street. I had no idea where I was driving. My initial thought was to call someone, to vent, to seek distraction. But nobody felt right. I briefly considered calling Tristan, but we hadn't spoken to each other since our breakup. Now was not the time to reach out. *I need to deal with these feelings on my own. I am meant to move through this experience on my own right now,* a quiet inner voice told me.

I was strangely aware of my Adult observing my thoughts, almost as if I were watching my own body. This part of me knew it was healthy to feel my feelings. I felt in control, even if from the outside, my face didn't look like it. My Adult made sure I was cautious while driving, so I avoided freeways and drove along the river road with less traffic.

As I drove, I let the tidal wave of emotions wash over me. I sobbed. I yelled. I screamed. Then I cried some more. I felt twelve years old again and furious at my two older brothers. It was a familiar sensation, one that I hadn't felt in a long time. All those times they had ganged up on me, teased me for being too emotional, and messed with my belongings—now those same feelings surfaced in me again.

I was angry at Jake for coming to town and disrupting my beautiful Sunday afternoon, the final day Caleb and I had together in his house. I was angry Jake was coming to the place where Caleb and I lived. But I was also angry at Caleb.

In my car, I yelled at Caleb—for not standing up for me and for kicking me out of my safe space. I yelled at him for choosing my abuser and his weed over me. I cursed Caleb for not protecting me all these years. My rage wasn't just a response to this incident but to the many, many moments in my life before when I had felt mute. And now I was screaming at my whole family for not saving me from Jake.

Suddenly I wondered, *Why am I not telling anyone how I feel? Both my brothers are down the street, and I could let them know right now.* A second later, I turned the car around and headed back to Caleb's house.

Immediately, I felt calm, but I didn't know more than my next step. All I knew was that years of anger were flooding my body, and it only felt right to finally let it out.

I pulled up to the house, parked the car, and stormed up the front lawn. My brothers were standing in the kitchen, and we could see one another through the front window.

"Oh shit," one of them muttered as I opened the door. *Oh shit* was right. In my most controlled, trying-not-to-yell while trying-not-to-cry voice, I exclaimed, "I am fucking pissed at you"—pointing at Caleb—"and I am fucking pissed at you"—pointing at Jake.

"Brinn," Caleb said, trying to stay calm as he stood beside his wife. "I understand you're mad at Jake, but you're not mad at me. You're just projecting your anger about him onto me."

Caleb's wife turned and walked outside. Jake stood silently in the corner, his head down.

I yelled back at Caleb, "I am pissed at you! You let my abuser into my safe space, into the house that I am living in. You're choosing him and pot over me, just like you did when we were kids!"

I followed him into the living room as he rushed around, closing all the windows, fearful the neighbors would hear.

"Go ahead and close the windows—I'll help you!" I yelled, while closing windows myself. "This is actually really good for me, Caleb! Instead of shutting down my feelings, I am telling you my feelings! This is called integration! I am integrating my feelings as opposed to just thinking about my feelings! And I am pissed at you!"

Having shut the last window, Caleb walked outside, obviously fed up and done with me. In one final gasping breath, I sobbed, "I just needed you to protect me!" as I collapsed into a ball on the living room carpet.

The house was quiet except for the low cries I emitted from my body. I was almost out of tears. Jake stood in the doorway, watching me. Very calmly and from far away, he soothed me.

"Honey, I am so sorry. I had no idea you were living here. If I had known, I never would have come," he said slowly. "It makes sense that you're angry. It makes sense that you'd be mad at him for letting me into your space." He let out a sigh. "Brinn, I wish I could hug you right now, but I'm not going to."

On the floor, with tears and snot covering my face, without looking up, I mumbled, "Can you bring me some tissues, please?"

My heart rate slowed as I began to catch my breath. My observing Adult was still present. Jake sat down on the couch and began to cry.

"I am so sorry, Brinn. For everything. I don't know why I did the things I did. If I had an answer, I would tell you. I don't even care about myself anymore—what I care about most is your healing. I would do anything in the world for you to heal from all this. I want to dedicate my life to your healing."

His words lingered in the air.

Eventually, I felt the urge to sit closer to him, and I found myself scooting across the carpet. It was my turn to comfort him.

Not knowing what to say, or how to act, I did the only thing that came to my mind: repeating an old family inside joke. I nudged his knee, and in my best accent I said, "Vell, dis doesn't mean dat I like you."

"Oh, of course not," he said, visibly recoiling at the idea that I didn't like him.

"No, that's not what I meant," I said with a sigh.

Once I had reminded him about the joke, we shared a laugh. For a moment, I felt better.

Breaking the silence, Jake asked, "So how's grad school?"

I just laughed. "Not now, Jake. We're not going to have small talk now."

"I get that. Well, it's probably time for me to go then. I'll go outside and say goodbye to Caleb."

We hugged. And this time, it didn't feel weird.

"You know, Brinn, you're the coolest one out of all of us," he said as he walked out the door.

"I know," I said with a smirk.

I sat on the couch for a long time after that, replaying the events that had just transpired. It couldn't have been more than fifteen minutes from the time Caleb had told me Jake was coming over to the time Jake had apologized and left.

While I felt less angry at Jake, I was still angry at Caleb. I decided to continue to accept that anger. Part of learning to own my feelings was recognizing that I had a right to feel the way I felt. My emotions were here for a reason. They communicated vital information to help me learn about the world.

As a therapist once told me, "Anger is a messenger, so listen to what it's telling you. It usually means a boundary has been crossed."

Through therapy, I'd begun to understand how my family had invalidated my anger when I was growing up. When I expressed my anger, I often heard that I shouldn't feel the way I did. My family called me a brat, or spoiled, or punished me for causing a scene, or, heaven forbid, acting like an "emotional woman."

Yet during a recent session with the healer Willow, she told me, "Brinn, you need to fully integrate your feelings. Right now, you feel emotions in your heart and think about feelings in your head, but you don't express them with your voice."

I was still learning how to validate and communicate my feelings. Confidently expressing my anger to my brothers felt new but empowering.

Now, as I sat on Caleb's couch and reflected on this day, I knew that my prayer had been answered. One month before, I had asked the Universe for the right opportunity to share my feelings directly with Jake. Little did I know I would receive a two-for-one and express myself to Caleb at the same time.

Caleb walked in, testing the waters.

"How you doin'?" he asked, sitting down on the love seat across the room.

"I'm okay. I'm still upset, but overall, I'm doing all right."

"Brinn, I have to say, I did not appreciate you coming into my home yelling at me. I understand you're angry, but you're angry at Jake, not me."

I cut him off.

"No, Caleb, I am angry with you," I repeated. "I'm angry that you allowed Jake, my abuser, into the house where I am staying."

"Brinn, that's hard for me because this is my house. And we had an agreement, but you didn't stick to your end. Also, you storming in here was very triggering for me. It felt like our childhood all over again, with Mom coming out of nowhere and flying off the handle."

"Caleb," I said sweetly, "I get that that was triggering for you. I do. And I apologize for how things went down. But I want to let you know, I was entirely in control of myself. I didn't call you names, I wasn't verbally attacking you, I wasn't flying off the handle, and I knew exactly what I was doing the whole time." All thanks to my Adult.

He responded with an exasperated sigh.

"You know, honestly, I'm just tired. I'm tired of living with all of this drama in our family. I am tired of you being upset at Jake and our family being divided. I don't want to keep accommodating you guys. I just want us to feel like a normal family."

I felt the plea of my brother. I completely understood his perspective. I was sick of the conflict in our family too! I wanted to let go of my anger, sadness, shame, and guilt once and for all! But that didn't mean I liked hearing one of my biggest supporters tell me he was tired of me expressing my feelings about Jake. His words only seemed to confirm my fear that my family didn't want to hear any more of my story. Unfortunately, this was a time when I wanted to share more of myself with them.

I wanted Caleb to understand just how much the abuse had impacted me. If only he understood what I'd experienced, then he would keep Jake away from me. He would understand why I had stormed into the house yelling. If only he knew, then he would really see me.

And yet, I felt something shifting inside me. A letting go.

"Caleb, believe me, nothing like this will ever happen again. There's nothing left to say. I got it all out." I meant it. It wouldn't happen again—because we had reached the climax. I had drawn the final curtain, and my brothers and I had reached closure.

Before this day, the three of us had never acknowledged the abuse together. We had never been able to have that discussion among us because we had separated ourselves from one another, through our literal distance and our emotional masks. I couldn't even remember the last time I had felt angry at Caleb! I'd always held him in such high regard; he could do no wrong. I felt guilty that he had to step up at only twenty-two years old and take care of me when our family exploded. I never dared voice any negativity toward him. How could I? He had done so much for me throughout my life.

But I'd finally released the emotion beneath my mask. I admitted I was angry at him because he couldn't protect me when I was young. Until this afternoon, I hadn't even been consciously aware of feeling that way toward him. But my Inner Child was angry at everyone for not protecting her.

That anger was already fading, though. That little girl did not need protecting anymore. By listening to my anger, and expressing myself when others crossed my boundaries, I could protect myself. I no longer needed Caleb to be my knight in shining armor. He could finally just be my brother.

The Universe was systematically walking me through opportunities to express my true feelings to my family. Looking back, I'm grateful I had the courage to take those opportunities and speak my truth. I had opened up to my dad a few years earlier, and then I'd reconnected with my sister in our phone conversation, and now I had expressed my authentic emotions to my two brothers. These experiences, and many other individual moments, were slowly mending my family wounds.

The journey felt perfectly imperfect, just what we all needed, without actually knowing we needed it. That's what authenticity does. By truly expressing myself and following my intuition, healing occurred in ways none of us could have never predicted.

After the incident with Caleb and Jake, I felt both exhausted and elated. I knew I was uncovering my long-buried emotions and communicating more honestly with my family, but I still had not felt any euphoric moment of *forgiving* Jake.

On the one hand, I appreciated his response at Caleb's house. On the other hand, I still needed time. I felt reluctant to reach out to him because I didn't trust the calm, collected, remorseful person who claimed he wanted to "dedicate his life to my healing."

That said, at Caleb's house, I'd felt as if my brothers had momentarily switched places. When I'd expressed my anger, Caleb had yelled back at me and stormed out. Meanwhile, Jake had actually comforted me.

So when the text messages started, I didn't know how to handle them. The first contact Jake made was to send me a picture of an inside joke from childhood: a license plate that said "DUB-DUB," our nickname for each other when we were kids, one of the words in our made-up language. When I saw the picture, my face fell. My whole body tensed, and I felt a knot in my stomach. Anger bubbled up as I more-than-tossed my phone onto the couch.

Every time he playfully referred to our connection as children, I felt repulsed. *How dare you? Do you not know what you did to me back then?* It felt as if Jake was trying to use the moment of peace between us as an opportunity to rekindle the close relationship of our childhood without navigating the challenges of building a relationship as adults.

I wanted a levelheaded conversation about moving forward, not memories of a life once lived. I didn't want to gloss over our conflicts, leading inevitably to another explosive ending. We had been there, done that.

He didn't know about my mission to forgive him. Nobody knew besides my therapist. I wasn't ready to give up my power to keep Jake away from me, so I held my cards close to my chest. I ignored his text messages, never responding, hoping he would eventually take the hint and stop. Instead of confronting him, I released my frustrations through journaling and writing letters to him I would never send. These actions felt helpful, cathartic, clarifying, and empowering.

I felt my walls growing higher and stronger than before as his repeated attempts to casually contact me destroyed whatever moment we had shared together. I wanted to ignore him forever, to push him away as I had done for years. It felt impossible to set boundaries with him—he never listened. I struggled between feeling as though I should set a boundary with Jake and feeling that I wasn't powerful enough to enforce a boundary once he inevitably crossed it. Since I didn't know what to do, I didn't do anything at all.

LOVE AND BOUNDARIES

Throughout my life, whenever anyone asked about my relationship with my mom, I typically responded with "When we're good, we're really good, and when we're bad, we're really bad."

Growing up, I was either loved and doted upon or we were spitting venom at each other. It didn't help that after every argument, my mother and I swept our feelings under the rug into one giant mountain of unresolved hurt and pain. And we never apologized—until I was twenty-three.

We were sitting in her truck outside my college apartment. It was just before graduation, and recently there had been some relative peace between us.

Blinking back tears, she admitted, "I am sorry for the way I handled everything when I found out Jake molested you." Her words were slow and deliberate. "I didn't know what to do. I wish I had handled it all differently."

I was shocked and uncomfortable. I'd never had an adult genuinely apologize to me before. I didn't know how to respond, so I just sat there quietly.

"Do you remember when you went to that one session with Krista? Right after it all came out?" she asked.

"Yeah, I remember."

"You told me that day that you didn't want to do hypnotherapy because you were afraid that you would see where the molestation had been your fault. At that time, I knew that you were feeling ashamed. So I decided to act like it was no big deal, so you wouldn't feel guilty for what had happened. I know it sounds stupid to say it now, but looking back on it, I was trying to protect you."

I didn't know how to react to her sincerity, so I simply nodded and mumbled, "Thank you."

A hairline fracture of warm light zigzagged its way through my hardened heart. That moment formed the first step of our long road of healing together.

**

Now, having left Caleb's house, I started house-sitting for a friend of a friend, Kari. Early one morning, I tossed and turned in bed, unable to sleep. Many spiritual philosophers refer to the early hours of the day as a mystical time. Around 3:00 or 4:00 a.m. is when the curtain between the physical and spiritual realm is most thin. I often wake up at this time, and on days when I convince myself to, I meditate or write.

Listening to my intuition, I sat up in bed and took out my journal. Along the journey of pen on paper, I realized I was writing a love letter to my mom. A letter filled with overwhelming gratitude for a childhood that was unique—one imbued with amazing experiences, lots of privileges, and love.

But empathy and grief also flowed from me. How much did she blame herself for the person Jake turned out to be? How much did she blame herself for what happened to me? How much guilt did she carry for choosing him over me when I needed her the most? For the first time, I felt how much she felt. Tears streaked my face and stained the paper as I held her pain, her guilt, and her shame.

A week later, on Mother's Day, I drove to her ranch. We walked far into the pasture among freshly blooming wildflowers and wispy white clouds. As we sat in the shade of an old eucalyptus tree, I pulled out the letter and read it out loud to her.

My empathy for her flooded through me as I cried tears for both of us. I wanted her to know how much I appreciated all she had given to me, all she had taught me. Her spirit touched every part of my soul and life. She was the one who had encouraged and made possible my love of camp, sports, spirituality, horses, singing, and theater. She was the one who rescued me from school when I hated it, often brought me lunch just so I could see her, took me skiing on school days, and cared for me on sick days. She was the one who advised me on all of my relationship problems and friendships. I thanked her for all the drives we had taken, all the hours we had talked, all the snuggles we had shared, and for all of her love. I saw now that she had always loved me.

As I read, we healed, and we forgave. I forgave her because she had been the best mother she could be to me with the tools she had at the time. Like all of us, she was far from perfect, and still, she gave her best in raising four children. By the time I was thirteen, she was practically a single mom to three teenagers. She became a mother at twenty-one, and she was fifty-three by the time her youngest left the house. At fifty-five, she chased her dreams, purchasing an eight-acre ranch with a big red barn that matched the picture she'd kept on her computer screen for years. She began another life after children, rescuing animals, hosting B&B guests, teaching horseback-riding lessons, and gardening.

After that afternoon when I read my mom my letter, I felt another internal shift. My inner angsty teenager no longer wanted to rebel, argue, or fight. I saw my mom in a new light. She was an imperfect human, having a perfect spiritual experience, just like the rest of us. Of course I would have wanted some things to be different, but there's no changing the past. Acceptance is the only road that leads to peace.

I no longer needed her to protect me, just as I no longer needed Caleb to. Letting go of my unrealistic image of her, those expectations for the mother I had wanted her to be, allowed me to enjoy and appreciate all she did bring to my life. And now I knew that if I didn't like some aspect of her behavior, I didn't have to engage with it. I recognized that I could establish boundaries with her. I had choice, and where there's choice, there's freedom.

* * *

The next month, I was excited for my family and me to attend my nephew's high school graduation—until I found out Jake would be there too. I spent the next two days in a strange haze. I felt depressed, lying in bed flip-flopping between crying and binge-watching TV. I wasn't sure if I could make myself go to the event.

"He won't sit next to you," my sister assured me. "He'll sit with Caleb, and you can sit with us. You don't even have to talk to him. He'll be away from you the whole time."

Even with this information, I couldn't shake my anxiety.

Halfway through that day of uncontrollable crying, and only an hour before the ceremony, I decided to take action. My body had been sounding the alarm, and I needed to listen. This was my first test. I had released the need for my family to protect me; now I was an adult, and it was my turn to protect myself.

So I texted him.

"Hey Jake, I know you're going to be at the graduation, so I wanted to ask you not to talk with or interact with me. I won't be talking with or interacting with you. Hope you understand. Thank you." Simple, plain, basic. Not too much to ask.

Feeling slightly better and a little stronger, I was finally learning how to set boundaries with the person who had taught me to disregard them. I felt empowered as I got dressed and headed to the graduation.

Purposely arriving right on time to avoid mingling, I sat with my sister and her family while Jake and Caleb sat a few rows behind us. Everything was going as planned.

After the ceremony, I did a wonderful job of avoiding all physical and eye contact with Jake. I felt him respecting my boundaries; we were civil without actually interacting. After saying goodbye to everyone, and still avoiding him, I set off, following my sister through the crowd. Weaving in and out of different groups, we crossed a sea of people until we finally reached the door on the other side of the great hall.

And that's when I felt it. Someone put their arm around my shoulder. In a low voice I knew all too well, I heard "I really wanted to say hi and bye to you." Then he was gone. And I was livid.

How dare he! How could he? Why did he come all the way across the crowded hall just to say that to me? Who does he think he is? How could he possibly think it was all right for him to touch me after I had clearly avoided all contact with him?

Here I was, in public, surrounded by people, and still, on the inside, I was screaming for someone to notice. No one but me had any clue what Jake had just done. Not a single soul around me could tell that this seemingly innocent interaction was, in reality, another form of passive-aggressive control. I felt him violate my personhood all over again.

Still, just as before, I stayed silent. I didn't respond to him. I didn't even remove the smile from my face. I compartmentalized my anger and moved on. There was nothing I could do in that moment to change his behavior. All I could do was move forward and congratulate my nephew.

Leaving the reception, I received a text from Jake.

"I didn't see your text before I went to the ceremony because I left my phone in the car."

Sure, it was probably true, but now my question was *Why would he follow me when I was obviously avoiding him?* Clearly, he had felt my ignoring him and made a feeble attempt to assert power over me. He had tried to show me he could still do whatever he wanted, no matter how many signals I gave him to stay away.

The next day I received a voicemail from him.

"I just wanted to tell you how inappropriate it was for you to send me that text message. It was unnecessary and very hurtful. Please do not ever tell me how to interact with you during family events. I am open to talking to you but not through text or email. Truthfully, I felt very disrespected by that text, and I'm only interested in mutual respect moving forward."

Rage exploded in my chest. I was not only furious but shocked by the way he had simultaneously denied my boundary and asserted his own.

My body buzzed with electricity. I could hardly contain my frustration. I went for a run, I called my support people, and I wrote. When I eventually played the voicemail for my therapist, she commented on how much anger she heard in his superficially calm affect. But I had reached a point where I needed to take action. I wrote him an email stating how I felt, in almost all capital letters and using multiple expletives.

I explained that mutual respect meant respecting *my* boundaries at family functions. I pointed out that my text had been necessary because he talked to me and touched me without my permission. And if he had really "dedicated his life to my healing," as he'd said, then he should honor my space, especially when I didn't respond to his texts. He should respect me enough not to push himself on me or force communication. I explained that I was blocking his number and that if I heard from him again, I would go to the police to report his harassment.

Sending that email was liberating! I found I was no longer afraid of his reaction. I no longer felt like a little girl trying to fight a big, scary monster alone. I was an adult, using adult tactics. Blocking phone calls and texts and threatening to involve the police were adult actions that helped keep people safe.

I had always viewed my relationship with Jake through the lens of a frightened child, so the idea of using those resources had never occurred to me. I had spent decades without any power in this relationship, but now my power was growing. That thought came to me naturally, which meant I was embodying my Adult, not just performatively thinking about how to act like one. When I blocked his number for the first time in my life, it felt fucking therapeutic!

I finally felt prepared to follow through on holding boundaries. Never before had I felt committed to the second part of setting a boundary: enforcing the consequences if the boundary is crossed.

Boundaries are our lines of protection. They are for us to uphold, not the other person. If the person we've informed about the boundary doesn't respect that boundary, we are the ones who need to be prepared to carry out whatever consequences we've set up. That may be walking away from a conversation for fifteen minutes or hanging up the phone. It might mean terminating the relationship, or it might mean taking some space for a while. Either way, the person who sets the boundary is responsible for upholding it.

I was aware that I had never told Jake not to contact me before because I'd been afraid. I feared retaliation. I feared I would not be heard. I feared I would not be able to say the words or even write them. But my biggest fear was that I wouldn't know what to do once he crossed the boundary, as I knew he inevitably would. I'd doubted my ability to follow through, because children don't follow through on boundaries, adults do.

But almost any interaction between us resulted in the same pattern of feelings for me: extreme anxiety, dread, and depression. I would avoid him until he forced himself into my space and pretended everything was fine, and he always left me deeply triggered and upset for days.

But today was different. I was fed up and feeling powerful. I had communicated how I felt. I was ready to break the patterns of the past. No more second-guessing myself. I had set a boundary and trusted myself to follow through on the commitment I'd made to myself.

FORGIVENESS

An anonymous wise person said, "Anger is an acid that can do more harm to the vessel in which it is stored than to anything on which it is poured."[1] I was a living example.

The resentment I held for Jake was eating me from the inside out. It kept me from enjoying my time with my family and seeped out in my romantic relationships. Messages from him nauseated me, seeing him tightened my muscles, hearing his voice boiled my blood. Like a puppet master, he acted and I reacted.

What would life look like if I weren't under Jake's control?

Shortly after seeing Jake at my nephew's graduation, I moved on from Kari's house and began house-sitting for my business mentor, Patty. Her kids were on summer break, and they were traveling for almost eight weeks. Her house was about forty minutes away from the distractions of my hometown and provided a roof over my head, money in my pocket, and time and space for me to untangle my mind. I gave gratitude to the Universe for yet another offering of abundance.

Still in my first year of grad school, I enrolled in a class on childhood abuse and development. Our assignment was to research a topic related to child abuse, and without hesitation, I knew my path. I was finally ready to explore the taboo subject of sibling sexual abuse from a theoretical and research standpoint.

---

1 Garson O'Toole, "Quote Origin: Anger Is an Acid That Can Do More Harm to the Vessel in Which It's Stored Than to Anything on Which It's Poured," Quote Investigator, July 12, 2023, https://quoteinvestigator.com/2023/07/12/anger-vessel/.

As I scoured the internet, I came across little research but felt shocked by what I did find: Statistically, sibling sexual abuse is the most common form of intrafamily sexual abuse, and siblings are the most likely to perpetrate any form of intrafamily abuse.[2] All these years, I'd had no idea; nobody had ever told me how common my experience was!

Relief, validation, heartbreak, confusion, sorrow.

My body released countless tears thinking about the thousands and thousands of boys and girls living through their own versions of hell. I knew that every statistic had a unique story behind it, and still, the impact on all of us must have been similar. I envisioned children, teenagers, and adults—both victims and perpetrators of abuse—trying to make it through life feeling so much shame, guilt, embarrassment, grief, anger, and betrayal, and carrying so many secrets. There was so much healing to be done.

I came across only one step-by-step method of treatment, one outline for seeking healing and forgiveness. My computer screen turned into a lifeline as I held my breath. The process began in family therapy. Every member of the family, individually, crawled on their knees in front of the victim, acknowledging and apologizing for their role in the abuse. For not paying more attention, for not listening, for not protecting.

Protection.

That's all I had ever wanted. That's why I'd enacted that family scene in psychology class. That's what I was seeking from my dad the day Jake emailed me. That's what I wanted from Caleb and my mom. That's what I didn't receive after my sister saw Jake and me in the shower.

Protection.

After the first round of apologies, the offender, on their knees, apologizes to every family member for the violation of their sister, brother, son, or daughter. Finally, still on their knees, they genuinely apologize to the victim.

---

2 Naomi A. Adler and Joseph Schutz, "Sibling incest offenders," *Child Abuse & Neglect* 19, no. 7 (1995): 811–19.

Tingles danced up and down my spine as I imagined this scene in my head. Caleb on his knees, Charlotte on her knees, my dad and my mom both on their knees. And finally, Jake bowing to me, signifying honor, respect, dignity, and humility. Each person would acknowledge their own personal responsibility for the abuse and own what they could have done to keep me safe. It was too much to ask for in real life but a powerful image to hold within me.

At the core of this treatment plan was compassion—compassion for the victim, compassion for the struggles of their family members, and compassion for the offender. This person, typically a teen or a child themselves, needed to be treated with care and concern. These psychologists viewed the offenders as covictims as opposed to an evil, vicious person or a pedophile. Acts of sibling sexual abuse usually occur between minors, and typically, a young perpetrator does not grow up to keep offending; as far as I know, this is true for Jake.

Furthermore, just like my friend who had abused his sister, many young perpetrators are victims of abuse themselves, meaning they have their own trauma to heal in addition to the trauma they caused to themselves when they offended. I wasn't surprised to read that the perpetrator's secretive, guilt-ridden, and shame-filled life often resulted in toxic self-loathing, substance abuse, and even suicide. When the researchers emphasized the possibility of recovery and forgiveness for all members of the family, I finally exhaled.

Knowing other perpetrators had healed simultaneously opened and broke my heart. My understanding of Jake grew, along with my empathy for him. He had been *just a kid*. He had been a rebellious, impulsive, thrill-seeking kid who fed off adrenaline and pushing limits, who suffered from physical and emotional abuse from our parents and, potentially, sexual abuse from who knows who. None of my insights excused Jake's behavior toward me, but they did help my armor soften. He'd expressed to me in Daniel's office how much he hated who he had been back then.

Now I realized that Jake's suffering must have run deeper than any pain I had ever experienced.

The article was clear that while this step-by-step process could promote healing and forgiveness, it did not guarantee, or even encourage, reconciliation. The researchers explained that forgiveness is under your control, but reconciliation involves another person. More confirmation to release the old adage "Forgive and forget" and just work on forgiveness.

Reading these words validated my long-held intuition that forgiveness is how we feel about a situation, while reconciliation is a choice to engage in a relationship. Forgiveness is about letting go of anger and resentment, and releasing the grip we feel other people have on our choices; reconciliation means we want those people in our lives. But our choice to forgive is an independent action; that choice has nothing to do with others' wishes. In choosing to set boundaries with Jake, I had accepted that I could not control him, only assert and enforce my own limits. Now I knew that even if I forgave Jake, I couldn't control his actions. Similarly, even if I didn't forgive him, he was still welcome to find peace on his own and forgive himself for abusing me.

Interestingly, the research found that outside sources should not push for reconciliation. Survivors should only pursue reconciliation if that's what they want.

Vindication!

I finally felt justified in all the years I had swatted away my mother's pleas. I understood her desires, but in the process of pressuring me to forgive Jake, she'd been invalidating my desire to stay away from him and my need to make whatever choices were best for me. The researchers concluded by explaining that reconciliation was not always possible nor could we expect reconciliation at a given time. About 50 percent of families reached reconciliation after proceeding through this process of treatment, but there was no consistency in how many years it took.

It had now been a little over twelve years since I had lifted the veil of my double life. Reading this article affirmed my need for space away from

Jake and my frustration at my mother's pushy behavior. And learning that sibling abuse was so common helped me feel less alone.

Afterward, in my journal, I wrote page after page after page about my pain in missing my brother, about my rage at my broken boundaries and lost dreams of him getting better, about the salve of my healing, my desire to forgive, and my disinterest in reconciliation. The more I thought, wrote, and prayed, the more I prepared to lay down my sword.

I held the *intention* to forgive, to release the weight of Jake's power struggles with me and my power struggles with him. I *wanted* to feel okay, not just in my everyday life but around him too. All summer, I repeated my mantra: "Thank you for helping me through this process of forgiveness. Thank you for my healing."

I wanted to stand strong in my own power—my real power, not the false weapon I had been hiding behind. For so many years, my anger had been both my shield and my sword; I'd used my anger both to protect myself and to wound others. My anger justified my hatred of Jake. If I let that anger go, then I would have nothing left to help me keep him at bay. I would be standing there, on the battlefield, alone, terrified of being trampled on again and again.

But that was simply fear. And as my Christian Science upbringing reminded me, FEAR was False Evidence Appearing Real. The truth was I could never lose my power. Deep down, I knew power was a feeling and a choice. I could choose to feel powerful, and I could choose actions that made me feel powerful. So I could release my rage *and* feel powerful enough to protect myself. I could let go of my resentment of Jake *and* still assert my boundaries with him. I could surrender to peace *and* not keep Jake in my life.

That summer, as I deepened my intention to forgive Jake, I also deepened my understanding of our divine connection. I remembered a quote about forgiveness I'd heard a few years ago in a women's group: "Forgiveness is knowing everything happened for a reason." Then there was a reason why I'd experienced hellish turmoil for years: so I could learn, and heal, and grow with greater understanding and compassion. I'd seen my childhood written in the stars during my astrology reading, and each step I took on this path of healing was making me a stronger, more resilient, and more empathetic person.

On the precipice of becoming a therapist, I was gaining even more clarity about my life purpose: to help other people heal in the same way that I had healed, through Inner Child and Parts Work, meditation, nutrition, yoga, breath work, astrology, writing, reading, communication, boundaries, spiritual understanding, compassion, identifying feelings, rewiring negative core beliefs, and more. I wanted *all* the healing methods to heal *all* the people—because we need healing. The world needs healing. Our world needed healing. It was time for me to add forgiveness to that list of healing gifts.

I had seen the divine connection between Jake and me in my astrology chat, in our intense friendship in childhood, and in my certainty that everything happened for a reason. Before we entered this lifetime, we must have created a contract between our souls, an agreement on the relationship we would hold. But now that contract was up. The dynamics between us had met their expiration date. We could both move forward freely.

On one of the last warm summer nights at Patty's house, I sat outside on a cushioned patio chair and reflected on the past few months. I'd journaled, prayed, meditated, researched, and studied. I'd found compassion and forgiveness for my mom, written Jake an email using adult tactics and boundaries, and gained closure with Caleb by expressing my whole self to him and validating my own feelings toward him. I had also spoken to my sister about Jake, and I now felt comfortable talking with her just as openly in the future.

I never could have choreographed these events, and I knew the Universe had divinely supported my path. I saw how every step along my way, even if it hadn't seemed like it at the time, turned out to be exactly what I needed in order to heal. All my messy conversations, emotions, boundaries, and experiences were all bringing me closer to finding forgiveness by my thirtieth birthday.

I thumbed through my nearly full composition notebook. This journal had been a significant gift over the past nine months. It held pages of anger, sadness, grief, excitement, and joy. Since I was a child, I had collected stacks of notebooks and journals. My habit was to open to a random page and scribble down my thoughts, omitting dates, and never finishing a notebook before starting a new one. But this year was different. I had written in chronological order, time-stamping pages, and my journal was almost finished. Like a book, drawing to a close.

I picked up my pen, and words began to flow—easily and without thought. I didn't know what I was writing until I reached the end.

> I want forgiveness for Jake. I feel forgiveness for Jake. I am clear that everything happened exactly as it should because that's the way it happened. It couldn't have happened any other way because it didn't. And, the fact that I've been able to learn lessons, heal, and in turn, help others, is a beautiful bonus.
>
> I am enough and I finally feel like I am living up to my potential. I fully believe I am connected to Spirit because I am Spirit—there is no separation and there never has been. Just forgetting and remembering over and over again.
>
> I am putting down the victim story. I am figuring out my purpose in life: to help others heal. Am I healed? Have I decided I have had enough? Have I crossed that line in the sand? Have I released all I need to release?
>
> When it comes to Jake, yes.
>
> He is hurting. I've been hurting and now I am done. I am laying down my sword. I am sick of fighting and struggling for power. I am Power, I have Power and I don't need to prove it to anyone.
>
> The facts are still the facts. I was molested by my brother from ages four to fifteen. It did impact me. I also have to admit that there is an underlying "victim card" that I have been playing my whole life. A special card that only I own saying, "My pain needs to be validated by others in order for me to

really be seen," Like, my accomplishes are only great if you know where I've come from.

But we all face challenges. We all have trauma. We all have a "Jake." I am who I am today because of everything I have lived through, the good and the bad. Before now, I've been wearing my secret as a badge of honor, as if all my accomplishments mean more than other people's do because I have had hard times. That's just Ego.

For a long time, part of me has been whispering to myself, *If only someone really knew what I've been through, then they would know how hard I've worked. Only then would they really respect me. Only then would they actually love me. And only then would they protect me. If you only knew how dark my world has been, then you would see how amazing it is that I am standing here today.*

But that's just my Inner Child still wanting someone to see her, and save her. My Adult knows that I am amazing, and powerful, with or without anyone else's validation. I am worthy of love, with or without my trauma. I am loved with or without my trauma. I am love, with or without Jake.

That was it. A warm breeze surrounded me, and the stars sparkled above. Simple, silent tears trickled down my cheeks. It was over, and now I could rest. I had forgiven my abuser.

While I completely understood what I had written, it was still a surprise to read. Confessing that I had been living with a "victim mentality" felt confusing because I didn't identify with any poor-me sob story. I had built myself from the ground up and taken action throughout my life. How could I be a victim?

On one hand, I had been a victim of abuse, and admitting that reality was one of the first steps I took on my journey to heal myself. It was vital for me to recognize that the abuse wasn't my fault, that I'd been only a kid;

I'd been a victim. But now, I felt like holding on to that identity was hurting me. I came to understand that perpetuating that identity was keeping me small and holding me back. At this point, the abuse had stopped fifteen years ago, and the truth was, I was no longer a victim. And the more I kept stoking my rage, the longer the effects of the abuse would impact me.

Throughout my twenties, I'd felt such anger in all my conflicts with Jake and with my mom because I'd wanted their *acknowledgment.* I wanted someone to say, "I see you. I see your pain. I see everything you've been through. And wow, you've done an incredible job making yourself into a great person after all that."

But the reality was I needed to acknowledge that truth myself. I needed to recognize that I was amazing, with or without the pain and abuse I'd endured. As I neared thirty, my childhood was now a story of the past, just one of my many life experiences, and one that I had worked hard to overcome. Just as I no longer needed others to protect me, I no longer needed others to validate that what I had survived was horrific or to validate my own worth.

And so I gave myself everything I ever needed. I finally saw myself and all that I was. I saw the scared little girl whose family had abused, misunderstood, and incredibly loved her. I saw the escape-artist teenager and the exhausted, perfection-driven college athlete. I saw the young adult throwing herself into love, all the while seeking insight into herself and craving her own growth. I saw the professional, showing up every day on time to work and school, who ran a small business, juggled multiple jobs, and wanted to help everyone. And finally, I saw myself. All the glorious, wonderful, imperfectly perfect versions of myself. And none of them would have existed if it weren't for all of my experiences.

I once heard spiritual teacher Wayne Dyer describe his understanding of his abusive father by stating, "I am grateful for my father because he taught me how to forgive." As I reflected on these powerful words that kept popping up in my head, for the first time, I felt grateful for Jake. Because if it weren't for him, I wouldn't be exactly who I am today, and I am fucking fantastic.

FINDING CLOSURE

let a couple months pass by while I integrated these new feelings of forgiveness and self-acceptance. I didn't tell anyone except for my therapist about the awakening I'd experienced. It was a personal process, and I wanted to keep it that way a little longer.

A few weeks before my thirtieth birthday, I began thinking about calling Jake so that I could read him a letter I'd written. In order to prepare for the call, I unblocked his number from my phone. As I scrolled through the contacts and found his name, I checked in with my body to notice how I was feeling. I felt calm and grounded, without stomach pain or butterflies, so I proceeded. I tapped his name and selected Unblock This Caller. Just like that, I lowered a boundary that I had set. I wasn't planning on actually calling him that day, I just wanted to mentally prepare myself, and my phone, for when the call actually happened.

The next day, I had one thing on my to-do list: call Jake. I went for a walk, typically how I do my best communicating, and mentally prepared myself to speak with him. I still felt calm, and now I felt empowered too, ready to rip the bandage off my final wound and move forward in peace. There was no answer, so I left a message stating my request to set up a time to talk.

When we finally did connect, Jake sounded a little apprehensive. Granted, the last time we had spoken, I had threatened to call the police if he ever contacted me again, so I understood his worries. I told him that I wanted to talk and that I had written him a letter that I wanted to read to him. I told him it wasn't anything terrible, just that I had some things I wanted to get off my chest and explain to him. He was willing to hear me out. We arranged a time for a phone call the next day, when we would sit down and I would read him the letter. At 4:00 p.m. on October 23, 2017, Jake and I sat down, four hundred miles apart, and I read him these words.

"'Jake,'" I began. For the first time, I felt determined to be honest and authentically myself with him, without caring at all how he reacted.

"'Before now, every time I interacted with you, I'd get triggered, and all the negative emotions I'd ever felt about you would come flooding back into me. That was because I hadn't fully healed, so my emotions arose from my deepest wounds.'"

I took a deep breath.

"'However, this past year, I've been on a mission to forgive you, and now I'm finally at a place where I can say that I have. I feel free of all the anger and resentment and pain that you have evoked in me. That being said, I do have some things I need to say, for myself, in order to feel final closure.'"

My heart beat faster, but I felt steady.

"'I need you to know that for the last twelve years, I needed to exclude you from my life because I wasn't ready to accept and release all of the emotions I've felt. I wasn't ready to hold my rage, sadness, grief, and my longing for my long-lost-brother, all at once. In grad school, I learned about a concept called "splitting," where we either idealize or demonize someone because we don't have the emotional capacity to see the gray area that encompasses their full humanity. It is easier to fully unconditionally love or fully hate someone, but it is harder to acknowledge that someone who hurt and abused us is also someone we miss. Is also someone we wish we could talk to again. Is also someone we love dearly.'"

I went on to explain that I hadn't been ready to accept him as a covictim in my story. I had not yet been ready to acknowledge that he too had been abandoned by his family in his darkest hour. I hadn't been willing to see that the burden he carried was so heavy, it continued to weigh him down as he tried to walk through life. I told him I couldn't imagine what his life must have been like, all the self-hatred, the pain, the sadness, the loneliness, the drugs, the white-knuckle sobriety, the isolation, and the perseverance.

I described how, for years, I had told myself that he didn't understand the deep harm he'd done to me throughout my life. He didn't understand how his series of vicious emails made all of his apologies fruitless. I felt as if he had never acknowledged the fact that I'd been his sex slave, that he'd used me solely for his own pleasure, without any regard for my mental or physical health. He seemed not to recognize that I had spent years hating who I was and what I had done, that I'd always thought the whole world could see the red stamp on my forehead that read "I suck dick." He didn't understand the constant fear he'd created in me when we were growing up, the anxiety I'd felt around older males, or the way I'd felt dependent on attention from guys my own age.

I told him that I knew my part in all of it. I'd accepted and released my shame about my behavior. I knew I'd craved a connection with him when we were kids, but I had never wanted it *like that*. I recounted my memories of trying to avoid him, pretending to be asleep. But I also knew I'd wanted his attention, to feel special and have an experience nobody else was having. But I was unaware of the price it came with. Of feeling terrified that I was pregnant long before I even knew how anyone got pregnant. Of constant stomachaches, migraines, tantrums, and outbursts. And then, all the self-harm I engaged in—cutting, not eating, throwing up, and wanting to end my life. The substances and unhealthy relationship dynamics. And finally, the gnawing feeling that I was so different from everyone else while I had no idea why.

I told him that I used to wonder if other siblings were like us. And while now I knew that sibling sexual abuse was fairly common, and that one in three families experienced some form of sexual abuse, I still didn't think the "bad years," as I called them, were times many people experienced. That was hell. It was all the time, in different places, and when we were both much older than kids.

I told him how much he, as my brother, had impacted me. How I'd only ever wanted to be cool like him and Caleb, and how I'd tried so hard to be chill as they taught me. But also how he, Jake, had taught me to stay silent, suppress my emotions, and never say no—if I wanted to be accepted. I told him that I had struggled from deep codependency in my relationships, stemming largely from the way he had treated me, and that I was proud to be working through those issues, slowly but surely.

Furthermore, I said I was ready to let go of those old stories and allow in a more fully healing understanding of our lives, including both of our pain. And I was also well aware of the trauma that perpetrators experience. I told him that anyone who's abused another person has also endured trauma, even if they don't fully realize it; that trauma affects how they view themselves, which ultimately impacts everything in their life.

I continued by explaining how I had found forgiveness. First off, I told him that I believed we had a cosmic connection, and that we had just happened to be brother and sister in this lifetime. Second, more recently, I had been able to view him as a victim of abuse as well. I felt compassion for him, for his pain that was perhaps lifetimes deep, for his experiences in this life, and for all that he had endured, for I believe he'd suffered more than I had.

"'I'm not really sure where to go from here,'" I said as I drew near the end of my letter. "'We don't really know each other anymore, and we have a lot more work to do in order to reach a place where I would want us to create a closer relationship with each other. Up until now, the more you contacted me, the more it pushed me away because the story I'd told myself was that you weren't respecting my healing process, and you were thinking only of yourself.'"

I ended by telling him that I now felt complete in explaining all I needed to explain. I'd forgiven him completely, and his past actions no longer destabilized me. I hoped he'd be able to find his own healing and forgiveness, in his own way, in his own time. I told him that I truly believed that everything happened for a reason, and I thanked him for being the most important example of that lesson in my entire life.

Finishing the letter, my whole body was vibrating with energy. I sat back in the chair, catching my breath, prepared to listen.

I heard Jake take a deep inhale. In a tense tone of voice, he explained, "Brinn, first off, I just want to say that I am *not a victim*. The victim identity is one I dropped a long time ago, and it has served me well to not go back there. I highly hope you are able to do the same, as it is liberating when you do."

Hearing these words, right after I had told him that I had forgiven him and that I understood that everything had happened for a reason, felt like yet another punch in the gut. This time, however, the blow felt more distant, as if its intensity were removed.

Finally he said, "I need some time to process this letter before responding. Can you please send me a copy?" I agreed to this request and emailed him a copy, although I never heard anything from him about it again. But his reactions no longer bothered me. I was already free.

Now that I had forgiven Jake, I felt elated, exhausted, relieved, and light. I immediately knew I wanted to share this experience with the world. Words flowed out of me as I typed out a social media post highlighting the power of forgiveness.

> Today I sat across from my abuser and I told him I forgave him. I forgave him for the 12 years of sexual abuse he inflicted on me. I forgave him for my many years of self-doubt, silence, anger, and hatred. I forgave him for my years of constant questioning, PTSD, and taking things out on other people. I've struggled through holidays and family get-togethers, have endured uncomfortable conversations, hurtful exchanges, belittling, and invalidation of my own experiences. And today I chose forgiveness.

Why, you might ask? Why would I forgive someone who did so much harm to me? Well, what I have realized is, while he might have had power to physically do things to me when I was young, he has absolutely no power over how I feel, how I react, how I feel about myself, and how I treat other people today. But, because I had not forgiven him and truly healed, he still did have that power over me.

Forgiveness is something that took me a long time to understand. I thought that it meant we had to forget and become friends. I thought it was this nebulous thing, out there, that other people had. I wanted the pill I could take that would cure me of my anger and replace it with forgiveness. But like many pills, that would only mask the symptoms, rather than healing the root of the problem.

I recognized that every time I felt furious with my abuser or utterly defeated by him, I was really letting the abuse continue. I was allowing myself to be further controlled by actions that occurred over half my lifetime ago. I am turning 30 next week, and my only goal for this past year was to find forgiveness.

Reaching this goal took work. It took therapy. It took prayer. It took listening to the Universe and acknowledging the signs all around me. And when it all came down to it, it took me being sick and tired of being a victim. I am sick of thinking that a story of victimhood is what created who I am. It's not. Things happened to me, but that does not define me or my future. And it doesn't give me a free pass in this world to hate another human being and discredit the amount of hurt that they feel. I am sick of being a victim, so I am choosing to no longer be one, by letting go of my pain.

I truly think this action, this active participation I am taking in my life and in my own forgiveness, will open me up to healthier relationships, to healthier communication, and to healthier boundaries. I also think it will help me help others who have experienced trauma, on both sides of abuse.

In a society where 1 in 4 women, 1 in 6 men have been affected by sexual abuse, and 1 in 3 families have been affected by intrafamily sexual abuse, there is such a need for deep healing and forgiveness. We live in [a] world where people walk around with the trauma of inflicting abuse and then continue to perpetuate that abuse in other forms, in other ways, to themselves and to others. Abuse hurts both people involved. Both people are hurting. For someone to be so twisted as to inflict control and pain on someone else, they must be hurting more than their victim.

We need the healing, we need forgiveness, and we need to put an end to all this pain. You can start with yourself, right now, by praying for those who are hurting, and include yourself. Pray for those who need extra love, and those are often the people who hurt others. See white healing light circling them. Pray for help with forgiveness, and watch how slowly, but surely, things start to shift and change. They will. I promise. Because I have lived it. I honestly don't know how I could have done it without the support of the Divine Universe around me and the emotional support of family and friends. I am so beyond grateful for that, and grateful for the opportunities and time I have had to dedicate myself to healing and growth. Namaste and Sat Nam.

My phone rang almost immediately. It was my sister. "I just saw your post. Are you okay? What happened?" she asked gently.

We spoke for a while, and I told her everything about my conversation with Jake. I told her how I felt lighter and more at ease. I felt as though I had truly accepted my past, what I had done, who Jake was, and everything in between us. Her calling me meant the world to me because she was the only family member who did.

My dad told me that he saw my post and immediately deleted his social media account. My mom read it and then, without talking to me, called Jake and told him about it. She also told me that she didn't want to discuss my post with me because she did not want to impose her views on me.

"You did what you needed to by writing the post, and for that I'm happy for you, but I'm not comfortable with it."

I didn't need her to be comfortable. I didn't even need her support. I had written those words for me, and that was all that mattered. Caleb simply gave his support in the post's comments.

After seeing my post, numerous people reached out to me personally and thanked me for my strength and vulnerability. Among them were extended family members who had known me my whole life, people who'd never had any idea what I had been dealing with and healing from, and fellow survivors who shared their stories with me too. I felt empowered. I was finally owning my truth, and my words and experiences were making a difference in others' lives too.

Reflecting on these new connections, I walked aimlessly around the house and eventually settled on my bed. Stretching my body out in all directions, I rested my head on the soft pillow as I stared up at the ceiling. Recalling the glow-in-the-dark stars of my childhood room, I closed my eyes. Slowly inhaling, I felt oxygen filling up my lungs like balloons. Exhaling through my mouth, I let out a loud sigh as my body sank deeper into the support of the bed underneath me.

Then, there she was. I saw her chin-length brown hair and the frilly pink bow on top of her head. She was waiting for me over by the door. As soon as I met her eyes, she ran and jumped onto the bed. Smiling, I opened my arms as she crawled toward me, burrowing herself in the nook of my right arm. Her warmth, her joy, her excitement, and her relief filled my body.

Nuzzling deeper, she wiggled her small frame, searching for the perfect position. Once she stopped still, I unclipped the bow from her head and tossed it on the floor. She'd never liked those bows. Lightly running my fingers up and down her back, I leaned my head into hers, smelling the sweetness of her hair. I gently kissed the top of her head.

"Brinn Emily, we did it!" I whispered, squeezing her closer to me.

"Yes, we all did it," said a different, familiar voice. This voice was older and deeper. I tilted my head up and saw my Critic sitting to my left. He was turned toward us, legs tucked under him, leaning back against the headboard, one arm draped around my shoulders. His demeanor felt calm, assured, and protective.

Resting on the bed, I felt grounded, safe, strong, and soft. I felt excited, curious, silly, and wise all at the same time. This was all of me. Lying between these two, I felt proud to be Brinn Emily, my Critic, and now, especially, my Adult. All these parts, and others, were sewn into the fabric of the person I'd become.

I felt integrated. Whole. Complete. Now I had—and still have—inherent trust that everything will be all right, and even if it isn't in every moment, I will make it through. I am the one who knows that there is nothing wrong with me—there never was—and everything has always made perfect sense.

EPILOGUE

Around 12:30 a.m. on January 1, 2020, my friend Olivia and I sat on her couch enjoying one last glass of champagne before turning in for the night. Olivia, the same friend I'd met for coffee years ago to ask questions about her career as a therapist, was now listening to my story about my childhood.

At this point, I held a master's degree in psychology and was already seeing clients as a therapist, although still one year away from full licensure. After being friends for over five years, this intimate discussion flowed easily, but I had no idea how much it would change my world.

After I shared the condensed version of my life experiences before age eighteen, she said, "I get it. I see a lot of clients who've dealt with this type of trauma. For some reason, over the years, it's actually become a specialty of mine." My jaw fell open. "It's so tragic. It ruins families, people's lives, and it affects so many." I had no clue my friend was an expert in sibling sexual abuse.

We talked for hours that night, and after a quick nap on her couch, I drove home, head spinning with ideas. As the sun rose on the first day of the new year, I opened my laptop and began writing my story.

Six months later, I called my sister and asked her to edit a very rough first draft of my manuscript. Equipped with an English major and a professional editing background, she happily agreed and quickly created a work schedule for us. Every week, she'd read and edit ten pages, and every Thursday I'd come over for dinner to discuss the progress.

Those evenings spent poring over pages describing my life were the first time she saw into my world. It was her chance to be a part of my childhood in a way I didn't know was possible. She witnessed me, encouraged me, and never discounted my pain or my experience. In fact, she'd often added in her own perspective as a mother and shared her disapproval about the ways I'd been left to fend for myself.

She acknowledged her absence in my life and apologized for not being there when I needed her the most. The time spent sitting around her dining room table together meant so much to me, and I am forever grateful for her time, energy, and insights that went into making this book what it is today.

As far as the other members of the family go, their support of the writing process has been an evolution. At first, the idea of putting my story out into the world scared, and even angered, other family members. While I was encouraged to write, ideally it would only be for catharsis's sake, not for anyone else to read.

But I've always known I would write a book about my life, ever since I was a little girl. I knew what I was going through wasn't normal, and I wanted my secrets to be heard. As an adult, the goal became less about being heard and more about helping others. It's about letting people know that they're not crazy, broken, or too much. It's about spreading the word that healing is possible and that forgiveness is your right.

Forgiving Jake was the most liberating experience of my life to date. While he and I don't have much of a relationship, there's no animosity there. He doesn't have much of a relationship with anyone in the family, aside from the sporadic occasions where he connects with our mom or shows up to a Thanksgiving dinner once every ten years. While I do worry about him and wish he would get support, I have to accept his life choices and make peace with not having him in my life.

I now think about my life as two different phases: before forgiveness and after forgiveness. After forgiveness all my relationships—be it romantic, platonic, or familial—have improved drastically, and my nervous system feels more calm and regulated. I don't abuse substances the way I used to and have established a healthy relationship with my body. Forgiveness gave me a sense of power and control over my life which made me feel safe in my own skin.

That being said, my life is far from perfect. I still seek out help and support and get in my own way. But that's because I'm human. I still have lessons to learn, and there will always be room for growth. But now the growth can be focused on expanding my capacity to love, serve, and help as opposed to surviving.

The closer I got to putting this work out into the world, the more I began to explore different communities and groups related to intrafamily sexual abuse, and that's when I met Jane. In 2022, Jane Epstein, a sibling sexual abuse survivor and mother of two from northern California, gave the first ever TEDx talk on sibling sexual abuse. As of today, it's been viewed over six hundred thousand times. She, along with four other women, created 5WAVES, the first nonprofit and comprehensive website to be solely dedicated to the topic.

From there, I was welcomed into a community of advocates, educators, survivors, parents, and supportive loved ones from all over the world who are doing the work to shift the narrative and perspective on this taboo topic through books, conferences, podcasts, support groups, and various online and in-person events. I feel honored to be walking alongside others who are bringing awareness, prevention, education, and healing to those in need.

The more I focus my own life on helping others, be it through therapy, coaching, speaking, writing, or other ways of advocating, the more everyone in my family has gotten on board with the book and my mission. I feel grateful to now have the full support of my entire family behind me for this project, and we look forward to seeing the positive impact it can make in the world.

RESOURCES

- **Authentic Leadership Center (authenticleadershipcenter.com)**. This center provided a few of the trainings that Brinn went through, including Leading From the Center and Going Deeper.
- **brinnlangdale.com** This website includes information about how to work directly with Brinn as a therapist, speaker, and trainer. You'll also find years of blog posts and the podcast Wholistic Approach to Healing.
- **5WAVES (5waves.org)**. WAVES stands for Worldwide Awareness, Voice, Education and Support. This nonprofit, founded by Jane Epstein and four other women who have also been personally impacted by sibling sexual abuse, is devoted to confronting and healing sibling sexual trauma.
- **Incest AWARE (incestaware.org)**. An alliance of survivors, supporters, and organizations on a mission to keep children safe from incest through prevention, intervention, recovery, and justice.
- **Jane Epstein's TEDx Talk "Giving Voice to Sibling Sexual Abuse"** (www.ted.com/talks/jane_epstein_giving_voice_to_sibling_sexual_abuse). As a survivor of sibling sexual abuse (SSA), Jane Epstein spent years thinking she was alone. However, recent studies show that SSA is the most common form of child sexual abuse, an epidemic enabled by silence. In this talk, Jane explains why we need to help survivors share their stories in order to build a community of people who can inspire new research, solutions, awareness, prevention, and support. She shares

her story to help other survivors gain the courage to speak out, knowing they are not alone.

- **1in6 (1in6.org).** At least one in six men have been sexually abused or assaulted. This website exists to support men on their path to a happier, healthier future.
- **Parts Work University (www.partsworkuniversity.com).** Parts Work University is founded by Brinn Langdale and provides courses, meditations, and other resources related to befriending your Inner Critic, soothing your Inner Child, and strengthening your Adult-self.
- **The Saprea Retreat (saprea.org).** A free, clinically informed four-day experience followed by a self-guided online course for adult women who were sexually abused at or before age eighteen.
- **Sibling Sexual Trauma (siblingsexualtrauma.com).** This was the first website solely dedicated to bringing awareness and resources to anyone who has been impacted by sibling sexual abuse. It has great information for survivors, family members, and loved ones.
- **#SiblingsToo (siblingstoo.com).** This website and the podcast by the same name were created "in order to raise awareness of sibling sexual abuse and its impacts on individuals, families, and society as a whole."

IMPACTFUL BOOKS

- *Autobiography of a Yogi* by Paramahansa Yogananda
- *Awakening Intuition: Using Your Mind-Body Network for Insight and Healing* by Mona Lisa Schulz, MD, PhD
- *Breaking the Habit of Being Yourself* by Dr. Joe Dispenza
- *Codependent No More* by Melody Beattie
- *Everyone Was Silent* by Diane Tarantini
- *The Courage to Heal* by Ellen Bass and Laura Davis
- *The Four Agreements: A Practical Guide to Personal Freedom* by Don Miguel Ruiz
- *How Not to Cry: A Guide to Emotional Freedom for Sensitive People* by Steph Dodds
- *I Feel Real Guilty* by Jane Epstein
- *The Invisible Key: Unlocking the Mystery of My Chronic Pain* by Maria Socolof
- *Outrageous Openness: Letting the Divine Take the Lead* by Tosha Silver
- *Resolve: A Story of Courage, Healthy Inquiry and Recovery from Sibling Sexual Abuse* by Alice Perle
- *Sibling Sexual Abuse: A Guide for Confronting America's Silent Epidemic* by Brad Watts
- *You Can Heal Your Life* by Louise Hay

ACKNOWLEDGMENTS

I, first and foremost, want to thank my family. Without all of you, there wouldn't be me, and there wouldn't be this book. We've been through so much together, and through all of that, there's always been love. Sis, thank you for those Thursday nights poring over my first draft. For witnessing me, hearing me, and validating my life experiences. Homie, thank you for all your unwavering protection, care, and friendship throughout the years and for trusting me with this project.

Dad, that day in the hospital when I finally shared my vision of this book with you is one of my most special memories. Once you saw what this book could do for others, you made it clear you were behind me one hundred percent.

Mom, we've come so far. A true testament of love, courage, and continuing to show up as better versions of ourselves. Thank you for being my first spiritual teacher and for all the endless conversations, support, and love.

Thank you to my Van Man; I really don't know where I'd be without your love, support, and hugs throughout this whole process.

Janna Maron at More to the Story, you were an answered prayer, and I'm so grateful you took my raw, vulnerable words and helped me craft them into an actual book that actual people will actually read.

To my team at Warren Publishing—Mindy Kuhn, Amy Ashby, and Lacey Cope—thank you so much for helping my dream come true. To my editors, Amy Klein and Susan Wenger, I can't thank you enough for caring for my work and gently pushing me to keep going.

To my whole crew at ALC, I absolutely would not be the person I am today without each and every one of you. You are the reason why everything makes perfect sense.

My friends are the real unsung heroes of my life's journey and you know who you are. To those who've encouraged me, tapped with me, listened to me, laughed, cried, and believed in me, thank you, thank you, thank you.

Thank you to all the brave souls who have come before me in the Sibling Sexual Abuse and Incest Aware advocacy communities. To those who have shared their stories of overcoming hardship and showed me that the courage to use my voice is absolutely worth it. Your relentless dedication to educating the public and helping survivors and families is inspiring.

Finally, I'd like to thank source energy (aka God/the Universe/whatever you want to call it) for guiding, inspiring, and providing for me, not only throughout my life, but as I step forward into the world, sharing my truth. Thank you.

ABOUT THE AUTHOR

Brinn Langdale is a licensed therapist, coach, speaker, and founder of Parts Work University. If you would like to explore options of working together or collaborating with Brinn, please contact her through her website, **www.brinnlangdale.com**. Also, if you are connected to any podcasts or other media outlets that could help spread the word about the important topics addressed in this book, please reach out.

If you would like to begin connecting with your own Inner Critic, Inner Child and Adult parts of yourself, you're invited to download a free Parts Work Meditation Bundle at **www.brinnlangdale.com/meditations**.

Follow Brinn:
- **Instagram:** @brinn_langdale
- **TikTok:** @brinnlangdale.therapist

www.ingramcontent.com/pod-product-compliance
Lightning Source LLC
Chambersburg PA
CBHW032052090426
42744CB00005B/183